MARY BERRY'S
Baking Bible

MARY BERRY'S
Baking Bible

OVER 250 CLASSIC RECIPES

BBC
BOOKS

20 19 18 17 16

Published in 2009 by BBC Books, an imprint of
Ebury Publishing. A Random House Group Company

The Random House Group Limited Reg. No. 954009

Addresses for companies within the Random House
Group can be found at www.randomhouse.co.uk

A CIP catalogue record for this book is available
from the British Library.

ISBN 978 1 846 07785 2

The Random House Group Limited supports The Forest Stewardship Council
(FSC®), the leading international forest certification organisation. Our books
carrying the FSC label are printed on FSC® certified paper. FSC is the only
forest certification scheme endorsed by the leading environmental
organisations, including Greenpeace. Our paper procurement policy can be
found at www.randomhouse.co.uk/environment.

Commissioning editor: Muna Reyal
Project editor: Laura Higginson
Photographer: Dan Jones
Home economist: Annie Rigg
Design and illustration: Smith & Gilmour, London
Production: Antony Heller

Colour origination by AltaImage, London
Printed and bound by Firmengruppe APPL, aprinta druck, Wemding, Germany

Contents

Conversion Tables

Conversions are approximate and have been rounded up or down.
Follow one set of measurements only – do not mix metric and Imperial.

Weights			Measurements	
METRIC	IMPERIAL		METRIC	IMPERIAL
15 g	½ oz		5 mm	¼ in
25 g	1 oz		1 cm	½ in
40 g	1½ oz		2.5 cm	1 in
50 g	2 oz		5 cm	2 in
75 g	3 oz		7.5 cm	3 in
100 g	4 oz		10 cm	4 in
150 g	5 oz		12.5 cm	5 in
175 g	6 oz		15 cm	6 in
200 g	7 oz		18 cm	7 in
225 g	8 oz		20 cm	8 in
250 g	9 oz		23 cm	9 in
275 g	10 oz		25 cm	10 in
350 g	12 oz		30 cm	12 in
375 g	13 oz			
400 g	14 oz			
425 g	15 oz			
450 g	1 lb			
550 g	1¼ lb			
675 g	1½ lb			
750 g	1¾ lb			
900 g	2 lb			
1.5 kg	3 lb			
1.75 kg	4 lb			
2.25 kg	5 lb			

Volume

METRIC	IMPERIAL
25 ml	1 fl oz
50 ml	2 fl oz
85 ml	3 fl oz
100 ml	3½ fl oz
150 ml	5 fl oz (¼ pint)
200 ml	7 fl oz
300 ml	10 fl oz (½ pint)
450 ml	15 fl oz (¾ pint)
600 ml	1 pint
700 ml	1¼ pints
900 ml	1½ pints
1 litre	1¾ pints
1.2 litres	2 pints
1.25 litres	2¼ pints
1.5 litres	2½ pints
1.6 litres	2¾ pints
1.75 litres	3 pints
1.8 litres	3¼ pints
2 litres	3½ pints
2.1 litres	3¾ pints
2.25 litres	4 pints
2.75 litres	5 pints
3.4 litres	6 pints
3.9 litres	7 pints
5 litres	8 pints (1 gallon)

Oven Temperatures

140°C	Fan 120°C	275°F	Gas 1
150°C	Fan 130°C	300°F	Gas 2
160°C	Fan 140°C	325°F	Gas 3
180°C	Fan 160°C	350°F	Gas 4
190°C	Fan 170°C	375°F	Gas 5
200°C	Fan 180°C	400°F	Gas 6
220°C	Fan 200°C	425°F	Gas 7
230°C	Fan 210°C	450°F	Gas 8
240°C	Fan 220°C	475°F	Gas 9

Introduction
and Techniques

Introduction

When I published my first major baking book, *Ultimate Cake Book,* in 1994, it was with the hope that it would encourage more people to take up homebaking, and show inexperienced cooks that cake making isn't as complicated as it might first appear. The success of that book has been tremendous and I have been touched by how many people still rely on it even now, nearly fifteen years later!

In 2003, as I wrote the introduction for the revised edition, I remember marvelling at the continuing demand for cake-making instruction. Now, it seems, people are turning to homebaking even more than before whether it be to save money as basic baking ingredients are so inexpensive, with greater awareness about their food and a desire to know that what they feed their families is natural and free from unwanted extras, or simply for the enjoyment of baking because baking is fun!

In light of this increased interest in homebaking, I felt it was time to create a new 'ultimate' cake book, and here it is – my Baking Bible. I hope this book will inspire a new generation of cooks as well as prove useful to seasoned bakers.

The aim was to produce an easy-to-use baking collection to satisfy all your baking needs. For the first time, I have included a bread section, containing my new bread recipes. There are some unusual cakes to try, like Courgette Loaf, and recipes for the latest craze, Cupcakes. But as this is a 'baking bible' I have tried to include as many classic recipes as possible. There are lots of traditional celebration cakes for occasions such as Easter, Christmas and christenings, birthdays and weddings, and some well-known favourites like Victoria Sponge and Chocolate-Chip Cookies.

I've included lots of simple recipes for children to make (with supervision), and some more challenging recipes that require careful timing, and more skill, including patisserie-style desserts, such as Gâteau Saint Honoré. Cooks of all levels of experience should find something to make and to challenge them here.

Since I first started writing recipes, the equipment available has evolved and improved enormously. Now we have reliable ovens with fan assistance, food processors and electric whisks, non-stick tins and trays, and bread makers. With the help of these aids, baking has become quick, easy and stress-free. All you need is to carefully measure your ingredients and follow the tested step-by-step instructions.

I have tried to include recipes for all occasions and I hope you will find plenty of bakes to suit your tastes, but most of all, I hope that this new collection of my favourite and trusted recipes will help you enjoy homebaking. Cakes are made to be shared so, once you have mastered a recipe, invite your friends and family to enjoy the fruits of your labour with a good pot of tea – happy baking!

Mary Berry

MARY BERRY 2009

Baking Equipment

Some people may be put off from baking because they think it requires lots of expensive utensils, but this really isn't the case. Although electric-powered equipment saves time and effort, it's not essential and many of the recipes in this book, such as the traybakes, Victoria sponges, cookies and biscuits, require little more than a set of scales, a wooden spoon to beat the ingredients, a mixing bowl and a cake tin or baking tray.

A lot of the equipment you will probably have already, and some you can improvise. If you are buying new equipment, do buy the best you can afford; good-quality baking equipment will last a long time so it will be a worthwhile investment.

Scales
One piece of equipment that is critical to achieving the perfect bake is a good set of scales. Some people prefer old-fashioned balance scales with weights, but there are now a number of very reliable electric and battery-operated digital scales that can measure weights and volumes in metric, Imperial and liquids. Test the scales for accuracy by putting something on them that has the weight printed on it, such as an unopened bag of flour or sugar.

Measures
You will need a set of measuring spoons including a teaspoon, ½ teaspoon, ¼ teaspoon, tablespoon and dessert spoon. All the amounts given in the recipes are for level spoonfuls unless otherwise stated. To measure liquids, use a transparent heatproof jug that shows both metric and Imperial measures.

Spoons
A wooden spoon is vital, but it should have a rounded edge to get into all the bends of the bowl. A large metal spoon for mixing egg whites into a mixture is useful, as its sharper edges flatten the egg foam much less than a wooden spoon does. Use a bendy, rubber or silicone (also heatproof) spatula to get all the cake mixture off the sides of the bowl.

Whisks

Use a balloon whisk or a hand-held electric whisk. It's useful to have two sizes of balloon whisk: a large one for whisking eggs and a small spiral one for small amounts of mixture.

Mixing Bowls

I have a range of different sized bowls that fit inside each other for easy storage. If you are baking for the first time, invest in one large and one small, preferably Pyrex, mixing bowl with a rounded base so you can get to every bit of mixture with your whisk, spoon or spatula. For all-in-one cakes you will need only one bowl, but it's useful to have at least two as some recipes require you, for example, to whisk egg white separately, then add it to the rest of the mixed cake ingredients.

Food Mixers

A free-standing mixer is not essential but saves time and effort! Choose one that comes with a range of attachments so you can use it to beat and cream cake mixture, knead bread dough, whisk egg white and whip cream. Free-standing table mixers are good for large cakes and are easy to clean but do take up a lot of room. Alternatively, you can use a hand-held electric mixer. I find that I only use the beating and whisking attachments.

Food Processors

These useful time-saving machines can easily overmix a mixture so take care – if you don't keep a careful eye on them, they can chop nuts and fruit to nothing. It is best to fold in such ingredients by hand. Processors don't get air into the mixture in the same way as food mixers do as they combine ingredients rather than beat them, thus are not suitable for making meringues and fatless sponges.

Tins

Good-quality, solid cake tins will last you a lifetime. Cheap cake tins can be very thin, may warp with use and do not conduct heat evenly.

Choosing the right-sized tin for the recipe is crucial to successful baking and particularly critical in sponge making; if the tin is too shallow the cake will spill over the top of the tin as it rises, whereas a tin that is too large will produce a pale, flat-looking cake. If you don't have the right cake tin for a recipe, it is better to use a slightly larger tin and test the cake 5–10 minutes early, as it will cook more quickly.

I've included a list of all the tins used in this book (right). If you are a first-time baker, don't be put off by the long list! Start off by buying two 18 cm (7 in) or 20 cm (8 in) loose-bottomed sandwich tins to make a variety of round cakes; a 30 x 23 cm (12 x 9 in) traybake tin (if your roasting tin is not the right size); a 900 g (2 lb) loaf tin; and a 12-hole muffin tin. As you bake more frequently, add the other tins listed to your collection.

Non-stick tins are easier to clean, but it is safer to follow the greasing and lining instructions in the recipes and not to rely solely on their non-stick properties. Choose black-lined tins as they conduct heat more effectively.

Avoid tins with thick, insulated bases. They're designed to prevent cakes from burning on the bottom, but they prevent the cake from cooking evenly in most modern ovens.

Baking Trays

Ideally have at least three baking trays. They should be flat, rigid and heavy. Check that they fit inside your oven!

Cake tins for keen bakers

deep (4 cm/1½ in) round cake tins: 15 cm (6 in), 18 cm (7 in), 20 cm (8 in), 23 cm (9 in), 30 cm (12 in)

deep (4 cm/1½ in) loose-bottomed or springform sandwich tins: 18 cm (7 in), 20 cm (8 in), 23 cm (9 in), 25 cm (10 in)

deep (4 cm/1½ in) square cake tin: 18 cm (7 in)

deep (4 cm/1½ in) traybake or roasting tin: 30 x 23 cm (12 x 9 in)

square cake tin: 18 cm (7 in)

square ovenproof baking dish: 28 cm (11 in)

swiss roll tin: 33 x 23 cm (13 x 9 in)

loaf tins: 450 g (1 lb), 900 g (2 lb)

deep (5 cm/2 in) loose-bottomed fluted flan tins: 18 cm (7 in), 20 cm (8 in), 23 cm (9 in), 25 cm (10 in)

deep (5 cm/2 in) ovenproof dish: 18 x 23 cm (7 x 9 in), 18 x 27 cm (7 x 10½ in)

12-hole muffin tin

12-hole bun tin

12-hole mini muffin tin

ring mould: 1.75 litres (3 pints)

1 French madeleine tray

10 dariol moulds

12 mini brioche tins

shallow pie dish: 900 ml (1½ pints)

shallow ovenproof dish: 900 ml (1½ pints), 1.5 litre (2½ pints)

4 pudding basins: 175 ml (6 fl oz)

4 individual soufflé dishes or 1 large soufflé dish: 225 ml (8 fl oz) or 1.2 litres (2 pints)

Baking Parchment

A useful cake-making aid that has evolved over time. Baking parchment is also sometimes called non-stick baking paper. The baking parchment used in this book is non-stick silicone paper, which doesn't require greasing. It comes in a variety of sizes and shapes to make lining tins and trays easy.

Silicone baking parchment and greaseproof paper are available in rolls. If you're using greaseproof paper you must grease the tin and then the paper (after you've lined the tin). Also available is Bake-O-Glide. It's a reusable, tough surface that comes in a variety of tin sizes. It lifts off easily and just needs to be washed, dried and kept flat when stored.

Most recipes only require the base of the tin to be lined with baking paper, some the sides and base, so I included here instructions for lining the most frequently used tin shapes in this cookbook.

To line the base of a round cake tin, using baking parchment from a roll, place the base of the tin on the baking parchment, draw around it in pencil and then cut out just inside the pencil line.

To line the sides of a round cake tin, cut a strip (or two strips if necessary) of baking parchment to reach around the tin and a little extra to overlap the ends. The strip(s) should be about 5 cm (2 in) wider than the depth of the tin. Fold the bottom

❶
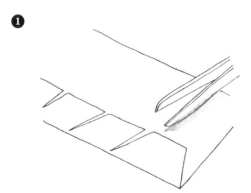

❷

edge of the strip up by about 2.5 cm (1 in), creasing it firmly. Open out the fold and cut slanting lines into the folded paper at about 2.5 cm (1 in) intervals (see figure 1). Fit the strip(s) around the greased tin (greasing the tin helps to make the lining stick to it). The snipped edge will help the parchment fit snuggly around the base of any shaped tin. Fit the base parchment over the cut, part of the side strips then grease well with a pastry brush (see figures 2 and 3).

To line a swiss roll tin, place the tin on the baking parchment and cut a rectangle about 5 cm (2 in) bigger than the tin. Snip each corner then press the parchment on to the greased tin, folding

up the edges to create a paper basket. Hold the corners together with metal paperclips. Do not use plastic coated clips as they will melt (see figure 4).

To line a loaf tin, cut a piece of baking parchment to fit the widest sides and over the base of the tin with about 5 cm (2 in) overhang. Press the paper into the greased tin. You do not need to line the ends of the tin, just loosen the cake with a palette knife before turning out.

To line a traybake or roasting tin, follow the method for lining a swiss roll tin, or mould aluminium foil into the tin and grease well.

Griddle

Used in this book to make drop scones and Singin' Hinny. If you don't have a griddle pan, use a heavy-based, non-stick frying pan instead.

Wire Rack

To cool cakes once they have been baked; they allow air to pass under the cakes or cookies as they cool. If you don't have a wire rack, you can use the rack from a grill pan.

Knives

A palette knife has a flexible blade with a rounded end, making it the best tool for spreading and smoothing cake mixture into tins or icing on to cakes. Use them to lift biscuits off baking trays or loosen a cake from the sides of the tin before turning it out on to the wire rack. A fish slice is also good for lifting out traybakes and lifting biscuits off baking trays. For recipes in which the cake is cut into layers, use a long, sharp serrated knife for the cleanest finish.

Sieve

For sifting flour and icing sugar, and pressing through jam glazes to remove the seeds and solid fruit. Strong stainless steel sieves are good as they come in a variety of sizes and can be put in the dishwasher (wire sieves can become misshapen).

Cake Skewer

A long, thin metal skewer is indispensable for testing cooked cakes. Insert it into the centre of the cake, where the mixture is at its most dense. If it comes out clean, the cake is ready. Use a skewer that has flat sides.

Icing Sugar Shaker

A canister that has either a fine mesh sieve lid or a lid with tiny holes in. A shaker is ideal for finishing the top of a sponge or tart with a dusting of icing sugar.

Rolling Pin

For making pastry I find a long wooden rolling pin with no handles is best.

Pastry Brush

Use a pastry brush for greasing tins and glazing tarts with jam or uncooked scones with milk.

Baking Beans

Use ceramic or metal baking beans when a recipe calls for pastry to be baked blind (see page 20 for definition). You can also use uncooked dried pasta or pulses.

Cutters

For biscuits, cookies and scones. Keep a set of plain and fluted round cutters in a range of sizes, and some fun-shaped cutters to make novelty biscuits such as gingerbread men. The most useful sizes of round cutters are 5 cm (2 in) and 7.5 cm (3 in). Metal cutters are best but make sure they are thoroughly dry before storing them. If you don't have cutters, use the rim of an appropriately-sized glass.

Icing Nozzles

I have a box of metal icing nozzles of all sizes, but for the recipes in this book you only need 5 mm (¼ in) and 1 cm (½ in) plain nozzles and a large and medium star nozzle. Nozzles can be plastic or metal, and are fitted to a piping bag.

Piping Bag

Used for decorating cakes with icing and whipped cream. A nylon piping bag is good as it is easily washable. You can make your own piping bag by slotting one small plastic food bag inside another, then snipping off the corners at one point. You can also buy disposable piping bags from cook shops.

Baking Terminology

Cooking techniques can be confusing as the invention of new technology means that old baking techniques like creaming and beating can be done in more than one way. You will find the following terminology in the book, so I include some short explanations of what they mean.

All-in-one Method

The easiest cake-making method, suitable for most cakes and traybakes. Measure all the ingredients into a mixing bowl, making sure the butter is soft, and beat with a free-standing or hand-held mixer or food processor. If using a baking spread from a tub, make sure that it is over 59 per cent fat and use it straight from the fridge.

Baking Blind

A method of cooking pastry before the filling is added, it results in the pastry being really crisp. To bake blind, pre-heat the oven to 200°C/Fan 180°C/Gas 6. Line the flan tin with the pastry, cover with baking parchment and fill with ceramic or metal baking beans (or old dried pasta or pulses). Bake for 10–15 minutes. Remove the paper and beans and bake for a further 5 minutes to dry the pastry completely. Remove from the oven and add the chosen filling.

Beat

In cake making, this can be done either with a wooden spoon or with a free-standing or hand-held food mixer. Beat cake ingredients until they are well blended, but be careful not to over-beat in a machine. It should take a couple of minutes to beat cake mixture until smooth. Beat an egg with a metal fork, breaking up the yolk and blending it into the egg white.

Combine (or Mix)

Mixing ingredients that don't require as much air to be added, such as biscuits. Use a wooden spoon or food processor to do this.

Cream

The beating of butter and sugar together until the mixture turns light and creamy. Cream with either a wooden spoon or food mixer until the colour of the butter and sugar lightens and the texture is fluffy. This is not needed for cakes that can be made with the all-in-one method.

Crimp

Used in pastry and pie making, it means to press the pastry edges together to seal. You can do this with a finger, the handle of a knife or a fork.

Dust

To sprinkle a fine coating of icing sugar, cocoa powder or flour over a cake or bread using a sieve.

Fold

A technique used to keep plenty of air in a cake mixture when adding ingredients such as sifted flour or whisked egg whites. Use a metal spoon or spatula to carefully mix the ingredients, folding the mixture at the edges over into the centre of the bowl and cutting through the middle.

Grease

Using kitchen paper or baking parchment, cover the insides of the cake tin with a layer of butter, margarine or white vegetable fat to prevent the cake mixture from sticking as it cooks. You don't need to grease and line a tin if you are baking pastry as there is enough fat in the dough to prevent it from sticking.

Knead

Essential in bread making, this can be done by hand or with a food mixer fitted with a dough hook. It is the act of mixing together the ingredients to form a smooth elastic dough. It warms and stretches the dough so that, as the bread bakes, it retains air pockets. If the dough is not kneaded enough, the bread will be dense and heavy.

Knock Back (or Punch Down)

Similar to kneading, this is done after proving to get rid of any large air pockets in the dough before it is baked.

Line

Lining a cake tin with baking parchment to prevent the cake from sticking and ease its removal from the tin after baking. Some cakes require both the base and sides of the tin to be lined, others just the base. Due to the high-fat and low-sugar content in pastry, it does not require the tin to be lined (see note on baking parchment on pages 16–17 for instructions on lining tins).

Melting

Usually golden syrup or black treacle is melted with sugar and fat in a pan, then the other ingredients are added and combined. The mixture is then poured into the tin.

Prove

After bread dough has been kneaded, it is covered in oiled clingfilm and left in a warm place to allow the yeast to convert the glucose and other carbohydrates into carbon dioxide, causing the dough to rise. It also creates alcohol, giving the dough its flavour. The dough should double in size.

Rubbing in

I use this method for scones and pastry. Dice the fat and then rub into the flour with your fingertips, or with an electric mixer or food processor, until the mixture resembles fine breadcrumbs.

Whisk (or Whip)

This can be done by hand with a balloon whisk, with a hand-held electric whisk or with a food processor. Most often used to describe the whipping of double cream or egg whites to a stiff consistency.

Key Ingredients

The ingredients listed here are those used most frequently in the book. I think it's useful to know what role each has in the baking process, to help you choose the right type of ingredients for the recipe you are following.

Butter and Baking Spread

In previous baking books, I have used margarine in my recipes. However, these days margarine (80 per cent fat) is rarely available in the shops and to some people it seems out-dated.

For the majority of recipes in this book, I have used butter. I tend to use salted or lightly salted butter, but you can use whichever you prefer – unsalted works just as well. It's important for the butter to be at the right temperature and consistency before adding it to the mixture.

In cake making, butter needs to be softened but not melted before using in the creaming method. If you have time, leave the butter at room temperature for at least 30 minutes before using. Even then it is better to cream the butter on its own to soften it before adding the sugar. Use softened butter for all-in-one cake methods too. If rubbing into pastry, cut cold butter into pieces or grate it into the flour.

My own trick to bring refrigerated butter to the right temperature is to cut it into cubes and put them into a bowl of cool/lukewarm tap water (approx. 28°C). Leave for 10 minutes or until a butter cube can be easily compressed.

It is not always necessary to use butter in baking, unless you specifically require a buttery flavour. Baking spreads have replaced margarines on the domestic market and are more economical than butter. You can use them in any of the recipes here if you prefer, however, I would advise that recipes without heavy flavourings, such as **Fork Biscuits** (page 195) and **Very Best Shortbread** (page 231) should be made with butter as the buttery flavour is important. You can buy hard or block baking spread which is best used in melting or rubbed-in methods and, again, should be used when the flavour of the fat isn't important, such as in **Cappuccino Cake** (page 53) or **Classic Sticky Gingerbread** (page 82).

Be careful that you do buy baking spreads with a minimum of **59 per cent fat** and ideally **75 per cent fat**. A lot of spreads available to buy are not suitable for baking and contain a lower fat content, which will dramatically affect your bake – particularly cakes and pastries.

As well as checking the fat content, do check that the spread specifies that it is suitable for baking. Low-fat spreads are not suitable for baking because of their high water content. Check the manufacturer's instructions to see if the brand of baking spread you have needs to be used at room temperature or if it can be used straight from the fridge.

Some recipes call for lard, white vegetable fat or oil. Cakes made with oil are very easy to make, and tend to be very moist, but they do need a little extra raising agent in the form of either baking powder or whisked egg whites to prevent heaviness. Choose an oil with as little flavour as possible, like sunflower or groundnut oil.

Flours and Raising Agents

There are a variety of different flours with different properties for baking. The main distinction is the amount of gluten each contains, and some also have an added raising agent. It's important to use the type of flour stated in the recipe, as the wrong flour will affect drastically the texture and appearance of the cake, pastry or bread. Keep an eye on the use-by date on flours, they do deteriorate over time.

In theory, you should always sift flour when baking, particularly cakes, to lighten the flour by incorporating air. Although, I have to admit that I rarely sift flour! The only time I do is when I am folding it into a whisked, fat-less sponge, when the sifting helps to combine the flour evenly into the mix.

PLAIN AND SELF-RAISING FLOUR

For making cakes, you need to use flour with a low gluten content. It is more starchy and so absorbs the fat well, giving a lighter texture. As the name suggests, self-raising flour contains an added raising agent and so is the most frequently used flour in cake making.

For recipes that do not require the bake to rise (usually biscuits and pastries), plain flour is used. You can also buy wholemeal plain and self-raising flour, which I have used in fruit recipes like **Jane's Fruit Cake** (page 66) and my **Apricot Sandwich Bars** (page 237).

Wholemeal flour has not had the bran and germ extracted, which gives it a coarser texture that complements dense fruit like currants and raisins, and cooked stone fruits, like apples, plums and apricots, very well.

BREAD FLOURS

When making bread, it is important to use the correct flour. The two main bread flours used in this book are strong white flour and strong wholemeal flour. These are plain flours that have a higher proportion of the protein that forms gluten when mixed with water. This then creates air pockets that cause the bread to rise.

I have also used a granary flour to make **Quick Granary Rolls** (page 284). The name of these flours does vary between brands and they are not always clearly labelled as bread-making flours, so double-check that you are buying the right flour!

OTHER FLOURS

I have used other types of flour, including semolina, cornflour and rice flour. These give a crunchier texture that works well in shortbread recipes. I have also used potato flour and buckwheat flour, which has a stronger flavour that is delicious in my **Courgette Loaves** (page 313).

BAKING POWDER

This raising agent is the most commonly added to cake mixture. It consists of an acid (usually cream of tartar) and an alkali (bicarbonate of soda) mixed with a dried starch or flour. When liquid is added the chemicals react, producing carbon dioxide that expands during baking, making the cake rise. Beware, if you add too much baking powder the cake will rise at first and then collapse!

Baking powders these days are slow-acting, which means it is not a disaster if you make a cake but can't put it in the oven straightaway.

BICARBONATE OF SODA

Also known as baking soda, this raising agent has a bitter flavour so is best used in recipes with strong flavours, such as gingerbread. It is most effective in recipes where there are natural acids present in the ingredients such as black treacle, lemon juice or buttermilk.

CREAM OF TARTAR

Cream of Tartar is not used as a raising agent on its own, but it can be mixed with bicarbonate of soda as the acid ingredient in baking powder.

YEAST

The raising agent used in bread making. I use fast-action yeast, which is a dried yeast that comes in helpful 7 g sachets.

It's easy to use – simply mix it with the flour and then add the liquid. If you use ordinary dried yeast instead, follow the manufacturer's instructions when adding liquid. It will require a more lengthy process.

READY-MADE PASTRY

Don't feel guilty about using bought pastry, if you're short of time. There are a number of very good, butter-based pastries to buy now. They can be found in either the refrigerated or frozen sections in the supermarket.

Sugars

In my cakes, I prefer to use unrefined sugars, such as golden caster and granulated sugar as they have more flavour, but do experiment with the wide range of sugars and sweeteners now available. The only time I would use white caster sugar is for meringues as it makes them really white.

CASTER SUGAR

Most commonly used in cake making, especially for whisked sponges, creamed mixtures and meringues, as its small, regular grains ensure that it blends smoothly, giving an even texture. You can make vanilla sugar by adding two or three vanilla pods to a jar of caster sugar. Leave for two weeks to allow the vanilla to infuse. You can refill the jar as you use the sugar.

GRANULATED SUGAR

This has a coarser texture than caster sugar and is best used in melting and rubbed-in methods. If used in a creamed mixture it will give a slightly gritty texture and speckled appearance, and will reduce the volume of the cake.

ICING SUGAR

Not generally used in cake mixtures as it will create a hard crust and reduce the volume of the cake, but it is essential in making Meringue Cuite. It's most frequently used to make glacé icing and dust cooked bakes before serving.

MUSCOVADO SUGAR

Made from raw cane sugar, the colour and flavour vary with the molasses content. Light muscovado sugar can be used to make many cakes as it creams well. Use it for brown sugar meringues, using half light muscovado and half caster sugar. Dark muscovado sugar can be overpowering but works well in gingerbreads and rich fruit cakes. To prevent muscovado sugar going damp, put a sheet of kitchen paper in the bag or jar and seal.

DEMERARA SUGAR

This is traditionally unrefined, but it has a lower molasses content than muscovado sugar. It is best suited to cakes made with the melting method to dissolve its large crystals, and to being sprinkled on top of cakes or added to cheesecake bases for extra crunch.

NIBBED SUGAR

'Nibbed' is an old-fashioned term meaning coarsely chopped. Nibs are the rough-shaped 'shavings' formed when sugar cubes are cut. I use it to top cakes before baking, but you can use crushed sugar cubes instead as nibbed sugar is difficult to get hold of.

GOLDEN SYRUP, BLACK TREACLE AND HONEY

Light, sweet golden syrup and darker, strong black treacle, which has added molasses, are both made from crystallized refined sugar. Nature's equivalent, honey, is the oldest sweetener in the world. Use clear or runny honey in recipes as it dissolves more quickly.

MALT EXTRACT

Made from powdered malt that has been reduced into a syrup, this is added to breads to add a sweet flavour and to aid the action of carbon dioxide.

CONDENSED MILK

Milk that has had half the water content removed and sugar added, sold in cans. I have used it as a sweetener in some recipes to give a fudgey flavour. When heated with butter and muscovado sugar it turns to a thick caramel, used in **Millionaires' Shortbread** (page 235).

Milk, Cream and Cheese

MILK

Recipes use semi-skimmed milk, unless otherwise stated. Full-fat milk will obviously add a richness to baking, but skimmed milk works just as well, if you prefer it.

CREAM

I use whipping cream for filling cakes as it is healthier and cheaper than double cream, but you can use either. Double cream is best for piping because it holds its shape for longer than whipping cream. Use whipped double cream if you are adding other flavourings, like brandy. Cream is best whipped from cold.

As a more economical and healthier filling for a cake, I often use a mix of half whipped cream and half low-fat yoghurt. Remember that yoghurt is wetter than cream, so use a full-fat natural yoghurt if you want a firmer filling.

CHEESE

For cheesecakes, use low-fat or full-fat soft cheese. You can use fromage frais as a lighter substitute for low-fat soft cheese, if you prefer. Curd cheese is useful too, and has a slightly tart flavour, or you can use ricotta instead. This book does use hard cheese too, mainly Cheddar and Parmesan, in savoury scones and biscuits, including **Cheese Straws** (page 211) and **Dorchester Biscuits** (page 203).

Eggs

I use large eggs throughout, unless otherwise stated, and preferably free-range or organic. Allow eggs to come to room temperature before using. Store leftover egg whites in the fridge in a container covered in clingfilm. Spoon a little cold water over leftover yolks to prevent a skin from forming, then cover with clingfilm. Keep for up to one week.

Chocolate

PLAIN CHOCOLATE

There are a number of brands of plain chocolate that contain a high proportion of cocoa solids. Although they are delicious to eat, their high percentage of cocoa solids does not make them ideal for baking as the flavour can be too bitter. The finest-quality block chocolate always contains a high proportion of cocoa butter. The more cocoa butter the chocolate contains, the softer and creamier it will be. Some cheaper brands replace cocoa butter with palm or vegetable oils.

The cocoa-solids and cocoa-butter content will affect the consistency of your cake or icing. The cake might not rise properly, the icing might separate or not set, or heavier ingredients such as chocolate chips might sink to the bottom if there is not enough fat to hold them in place as the cake cooks. The cocoa flavour might also be too overpowering.

I recommend using a plain chocolate that contains **39 per cent cocoa solids**. This will ensure a ratio of cocoa solids to cocoa butter that will produce a cake or icing with the correct consistency and flavour. There is no need to buy an expensive brand for baking unless the recipe specifies.

MILK CHOCOLATE

This has the addition of full-cream milk and sugar, so is much sweeter and has a milder cocoa flavour. Milk chocolate is only ideal for decorating as the chocolate flavour is lost in baking.

WHITE CHOCOLATE

Contains cocoa butter but not the dark cocoa solids. The amounts of cocoa butter used varies between brands, and some cheaper ones replace the cocoa butter with vegetable oil.

When buying milk and white chocolate for cooking, choose Belgian chocolate and check that it does not contain vegetable oil.

COCOA POWDER

This is a very good and inexpensive ingredient in baking, but always sift it with the dry ingredients or mix with a little hot water before using. Don't use drinking chocolate instead as the added sugar gives it a mild, sweet flavour not suitable for baking.

MELTING, CHOPPING AND GRATING

When melting chocolate, it is essential that you do not let it overheat. Break the chocolate into small pieces in a heatproof bowl that fits snugly over a pan of hot, but not boiling, water. If the water boils, the chocolate can be become solid and lose its shine. Heat liquids with the melting chocolate, do not add them to the chocolate once it has melted as this may cause the chocolate to 'seize'. White chocolate is more likely to separate on heating so keep the heat low. You can melt chocolate in the microwave, but again heat gently on a defrost or low setting to avoid burning.

If a recipe calls for chopped or grated chocolate, put the bar in the fridge to chill first and make sure the grater or knife are cold and completely dry. You can chop chocolate in a food processor but be careful not to overwork it, as the chocolate might melt or stick together.

Baking Tips

All the recipes in the book include individual cake-making instructions and for certain recipes I have given specific tips that are useful to know. However, there is some general advice that can be applied.

🧁 Always read the recipe carefully, checking that you have enough time and all the ingredients to make the cake before you begin.

🧁 Weigh ingredients using accurate measures and scales and follow the order of the recipe making sure nothing is missed out – ticking off ingredients and instructions as you complete them helps prevent you from missing anything.

🧁 Mix ingredients by hand or in the food processor or mixer until the mixture is the specified colour and texture. Make sure you follow a recipe using the right utensils when it instructs you to beat, whisk or fold ingredients; these are different techniques and have specific effects on the cake mixture consistency – the success of the cake depends on this!

🧁 Always pre-heat the oven before starting to make a cake. It must be at the correct temperature by the time the cake is ready to go in. Make sure the oven shelves are in the right position beforehand – unless specified otherwise, cook cakes in the centre of the oven.

🧁 Be patient and don't open the oven door or move the cake in the first stages of baking, as this can cause the cake to sink in the middle.

🧁 Don't overload your oven with trays of biscuits as they will cook unevenly – biscuits on a high shelf or at the edges of a tray can brown too quickly, while the others are still uncooked. There needs to be a good circulation of air as they bake. If you put more than one cake in the oven at a time, they will take a little longer to cook.

🧁 Most cakes are cooked when they begin to shrink away from the sides of the cake tin, and when the centre of the cake springs back after being pressed lightly with a finger.

🧁 Check the recipe to see what colour the cooked cake or biscuits should be. Test fruit cakes by inserting a skewer into the centre of the cake; it should come out clean. If there is any cake mixture stuck to the skewer, it needs a little longer in the oven. Biscuits and scones are cooked when they are lightly and evenly coloured on top; underneath, biscuits should be lightly coloured and scones golden.

🧁 Cover cakes with foil if they are browning too quickly, and perhaps turn the oven temperature down a little. Oven temperatures do vary.

🧁 Follow each recipe for individual cooling instructions. Generally, sponge cakes should be left to cool for a few minutes before turning out on to a wire rack. The sides of the cake will shrink away from the tin, making them easier to remove. For sponge cakes, turn the cake the right side up on the wire rack and then cover with the cake tin. This prevents the moisture evaporating while the cake cools, but doesn't make it soggy. Leave fruit cakes to cool completely in their tins.

🧁 Don't leave biscuits and cookies on their trays to cool completely, as they can stick. Remove them with a palette knife or fish slice while still warm.

🧁 To turn cakes out of a loose-bottomed or springform cake tin, stand the base on something like a large can so that the sides can slip down, leaving the cake still standing on the tin base.

🧁 Make sure a cake, bake or biscuit is completely cold before decorating, unless the recipe specifies otherwise. Fill when you are ready to serve. I like to keep the decoration simple, but there are so many decoration options available now that you can get creative and experiment with lots of different toppings.

🧁 If you have time, brush the cake with an apricot glaze before icing. Make the glaze by pushing warmed apricot jam through a sieve. The glaze will prevent crumbs getting into the icing, and the icing will remain glossy as the cake won't absorb its moisture. Apricot glaze is also useful when covering a cake with almond paste: when spread over the cake before the paste is applied it acts as 'glue'.

🧁 Most cakes should be eaten soon after making but they can be kept fresh for a short time in an airtight container, or wrapped in foil or clingfilm. Sponges that have a low fat content or no fat (such

as swiss roll) do not keep well and should be eaten on the day or wrapped well and then filled and eaten the following day. Bakes with a fresh cream filling or icing should be kept in the fridge. Biscuits, flapjacks and bars made with the melting method do keep well but should be stored in an airtight container to prevent them going soggy.

🧁 Don't store cakes and biscuits in the same tin as the moisture from the cake will make the biscuits soggy. If biscuits do go soggy, refresh them in a moderate oven for 5–10 minutes, then cool and eat.

🧁 Freeze undecorated cakes and biscuits wrapped tightly in foil, clingfilm or freezer-proof bags, as soon as they are cold, to preserve their freshness. Keep them frozen for no longer than 3 months.

🧁 Open-freeze (freeze unwrapped) iced or delicate cakes until hard, then wrap well. Refresh small cakes such as scones by warming them through in a moderate oven after thawing.

🧁 If cakes crack on top during baking, it means that the oven was too hot or the cake was placed on too high a shelf.

🧁 If fruit sinks to the bottom of the cake, it means that either the mixture was too runny to support the fruit, the fruit was too wet or the wrong fat was used (see page 24 for information on baking fats). If not enough fat was added the cake may be dry.

🧁 A cake may sink if too much baking powder was used, the cake was taken out of the oven before it was cooked or the oven door was opened before the cake mixture had time to set. It may also not rise properly if the mixture was overbeaten (so that the air was beaten out), or if not enough raising agent was added.

🧁 Make pastry either by hand in a mixing bowl or in a food processor, but be careful not to over-whizz otherwise the dough will be tough.

🧁 Once the pastry case is lined the dough freezes very well, making it perfect to have in the freezer ready for a special occasion.

🧁 When proving and rising bread, do not prove in too hot a place otherwise the yeast will be killed and the rising process will stop.

CHAPTER ONE

Classic Cakes

The cakes in this chapter are not fancy cakes, but trusted staples for teatimes, morning coffee breaks and lunch boxes. The majority have been familiar favourites for many years and most are traditional to Britain, with a number dating from Victorian times.

The **Large All-in-one Victoria Sandwich** (page 40) is my speedy version of a much-loved sponge said to have been popularized by Queen Victoria. Victoria sponges can be made with cream and jam, but I prefer the simple filling of good-quality raspberry or strawberry jam and a sprinkling of caster sugar on top.

In the nineteenth century, cakes were often eaten with a sweet wine such as Madeira, hence the creation of the **Madeira Cake** (opposite), and **Battenburg Cake** (page 54) is said to have been created to honour the wedding of Queen Victoria's granddaughter to Prince Louis of Battenburg.

One cake in this chapter that is not so obviously British is the **Swiss Roll** (page 45). It is said that, at the turn of the twentieth century, British enthusiasts of the new sport, skiing, persuaded a St Moritz patissier to part with the recipe, and thus it became a stalwart of the British tea tradition!

The all-in-one method makes the preparation of large cakes quick and easy. Mixing all the ingredients together means that there is no danger of the mixture curdling. The use of self-raising flour and baking powder together also means that the threat of the cake not rising due to insufficient mixing is overcome. Place all the main ingredients into a bowl and beat with either a wooden spoon or, even easier, an electric free-standing or hand-held food mixer until smooth. This should only take a few minutes, so be careful not to over-beat the mixture.

Madeira Cake

This is a rich, densely textured sponge cake. It is essential that the butter is a creamy spreading consistency before mixing the ingredients together.

175 g (6 oz) softened butter
175 g (6 oz) caster sugar
225 g (8 oz) self-raising flour
50 g (2 oz) ground almonds
3 large eggs
finely grated rind of 1 lemon
a thin slice of citron peel

1 Pre-heat the oven to 180°C/Fan 160°C/Gas 4. Grease an 18cm (7 in) deep round cake tin and line the base with baking parchment.

2 Measure the butter, sugar, flour, ground almonds, eggs and grated lemon into a large bowl. Beat for 1 minute to mix thoroughly. Turn into the prepared tin and level the surface.

3 Bake in the pre-heated oven for 30 minutes. Place the slice of citron peel on top of the cake and continue cooking for a further 30–45 minutes or until a skewer inserted into the centre comes out clean. Leave to cool in the tin for 10 minutes then turn out, peel off the parchment and finish cooling on a wire rack.

TIP
If a fruit or Madeira cake has a slight dip in the centre when it comes out of the oven, turn on to baking parchment on a cooling rack *upside down*. The action of gravity and the weight of the cake will level the top while it cools.

Large All-in-one Victoria Sandwich

This must be the best known and loved of all family cakes. The all-in-one method takes away the hassle of creaming, and ensures success every time. Baking spreads give an excellent result, but the cake won't keep as long.

225 g (8 oz) softened butter
225 g (8 oz) caster sugar
4 large eggs
225 g (8 oz) self-raising flour
2 level teaspoons baking
    powder

**FOR THE FILLING
    AND TOPPING**
4 tablespoons strawberry
    or raspberry jam
a little caster sugar,
    for sprinkling

1 Pre-heat the oven to 180°C/Fan 160°C/Gas 4. Grease two 20 cm (8 in) sandwich tins then line the base of each tin with baking parchment.

2 Measure the butter, sugar, eggs, flour and baking powder into a large bowl and beat until thoroughly blended. Divide the mixture evenly between the tins and level out.

3 Bake in the pre-heated oven for about 25 minutes or until well risen and the tops of the cakes spring back when lightly pressed with a finger. Leave to cool in the tins for a few minutes then turn out, peel off the parchment and finish cooling on a wire rack.

4 When completely cold, sandwich the cakes together with the jam. Sprinkle with caster sugar to serve.

TIP
Here are the ingredients and baking times for smaller cakes so that you don't have to calculate the quantities. Follow the instructions for the Large All-in-one Victoria Sandwich and fill with 4 tablespoons of strawberry or raspberry jam, or a little less, if you like.

For an 18 cm (7 in) Victoria Sandwich, use 3 large eggs, 175 g (6 oz) of softened butter, 175 g (6 oz) of caster sugar, 175 g (6 oz) of self-raising flour and 1½ teaspoons of baking powder. Bake in two 18 cm (7 in) greased and lined sandwich tins for about 25 minutes.

For a 15 cm (6 in) Victoria Sandwich, use 2 large eggs, 100 g (4 oz) of softened butter, 100 g (4 oz) of caster sugar, 100 g (4 oz) of self-raising flour and 1 teaspoon of baking powder. Bake in two 15 cm (6 in) greased and lined sandwich tins for about 20 minutes.

Coffee Victoria Sandwich

This is a simple but delicious alternative to the classic Victoria Sandwich that's perfect for coffee time.

4 large eggs
2 heaped teaspoons instant coffee granules
225 g (8 oz) softened butter
225 g (8 oz) caster sugar
225 g (8 oz) self-raising flour
2 level teaspoons baking powder

FOR THE FILLING AND TOPPING
50 g (2 oz) softened butter
175g (6 oz) sifted icing sugar
1 tablespoon coffee essence
1 tablespoon milk

1 Pre-heat the oven to 180°C/Fan 160°C/Gas 4. Grease two 20 cm (8 in) sandwich tins then line the base of each tin with baking parchment.

2 Break the eggs into a large bowl, beat with a fork then stir in the instant coffee until dissolved. Add the remaining ingredients and beat until thoroughly blended. Divide the mixture evenly between the tins and level out.

3 Bake in the pre-heated oven for about 25 minutes or until well risen and the tops of the cakes spring back when lightly pressed with a finger. Leave to cool in the tins for a few minutesthen turn out, peel off the parchment and finish cooling on a wire rack.

4 To make the butter cream filling and topping, blend together the butter, icing sugar and coffee essence until smooth, adding the milk if necessary. When the cakes are completely cold, use half the butter cream to sandwich the cakes together. Spread the remaining butter cream on top.

TIP
Instead of the coffee essence in the icing, you can use 1 heaped teaspoon of instant coffee granules dissolved in 1 tablespoon of hot water.

Chocolate Victoria Sandwich

This light chocolate cake is sandwiched together with a white butter cream and looks as good as it tastes.

2 tablespoons cocoa powder
3 tablespoons boiling water
225 g (8 oz) softened butter
225 g (8 oz) caster sugar
4 large eggs
225 g (8 oz) self-raising flour
2 level teaspoons baking
    powder

**FOR THE FILLING
AND TOPPING**
50 g (2 oz) softened butter
175 g (6 oz) sifted icing sugar
1 tablespoon milk
coarsely grated plain
    chocolate, to decorate

1 Pre-heat the oven to 180°C/Fan 160°C/Gas 4. Grease two 20 cm (8 in) sandwich tins then line the base of each tin with baking parchment.

2 Blend the cocoa and water in a mixing bowl then leave to cool slightly. Measure all the remaining ingredients into the bowl and beat until thoroughly blended. Divide the mixture evenly between the tins and level out.

3 Bake in the pre-heated oven for about 25 minutes or until well risen and the tops of the cakes spring back when lightly pressed with a finger. Leave to cool in the tins for a few minutes then turn out, peel off the parchment and finish cooling on a wire rack.

4 To make the butter cream filling and topping, blend together the butter, icing sugar and milk until smooth. When the cake is completely cold, use half the butter cream to sandwich the cakes together, then spread the remaining butter cream on top and decorate with the grated chocolate.

To make an Orange or Lemon Victoria Sandwich, follow the recipe for a Large All-in-one Victoria Sandwich (page 40), adding the grated rind of an orange or lemon to the cake mixture. Sandwich the cooked cakes together with either orange marmalade or lemon curd and sprinkle the top with a little caster sugar.

Swiss Roll

This fatless sponge is a nice alternative to a round cake at teatime. The filling can be easily jazzed-up to serve the Swiss Roll as a dessert.

4 large eggs
100 g (4 oz) caster sugar
100 g (4 oz) self-raising flour

FOR THE FILLING
4 tablespoons strawberry
    or raspberry jam

1 Pre-heat the oven to 220°C/Fan 200°C/Gas 7. Grease a 33 x 23 cm (13 x 9 in) swiss roll tin and line with baking parchment.

2 Whisk the eggs and sugar together in a large bowl until the mixture is light and frothy and the whisk leaves a trail when lifted out. Sift the flour into the mixture, carefully folding it in at the same time. Turn the mixture into the prepared tin and give it a gentle shake so that the mixture finds its own level, making sure that it spreads evenly into the corners.

3 Bake in the pre-heated oven for about 10 minutes or until the sponge is golden brown and begins to shrink from the edges of the tin. While the cake is cooking, place a piece of baking parchment a little bigger than the size of the tin on to a work surface and sprinkle it with caster sugar.

4 Invert the cake on to the sugared parchment. Quickly loosen the parchment on the bottom of the cake and peel it off. Trim the edges of the sponge with a sharp knife and make a score mark 2.5 cm (1 in) in from one shorter edge, being careful not to cut right through.

5 Leave to cool slightly, then spread with the jam. If the cake is too hot the jam will soak straight into the sponge. Roll up the cake firmly from the cut end.

To make a smaller Swiss Roll, use 3 large eggs and 75 g (3 oz) each of sugar and flour. Bake in a greased and lined 28 x 18 cm (11 x 7 in) swiss roll tin.

To make a Coffee Swiss Roll, fill the basic Swiss Roll with coffee butter cream made with 75 g (3 oz) softened butter, 225 g (8 oz) sifted icing sugar, 2 teaspoons milk and 2 teaspoons coffee essence.

To make a Raspberry or Strawberry Swiss Roll, fill the basic Swiss Roll with 300 ml (½ pint) whipped cream and sliced strawberries or whole raspberries, or both!

Lemon Swiss Roll

This recipe is delicious flavoured with orange too. Substitute an orange for the lemon and orange marmalade for the lemon curd.

4 large eggs
100 g (4 oz) caster sugar
finely grated rind of 1 lemon
100 g (4 oz) self-raising flour

FOR THE FILLING
4 tablespoons lemon curd

1 Pre-heat the oven to 220°C/Fan 200°C/Gas 7. Grease a 33 x 23 cm (13 x 9 in) swiss roll tin and line with baking parchment.

2 Whisk the eggs, sugar and lemon in a large bowl until the mixture is light and frothy and the whisk leaves a trail when lifted out. Sift the flour into the mixture, carefully folding it in at the same time. Turn the mixture into the prepared tin and give it a gentle shake so that the mixture finds its own level, making sure that it spreads evenly into the corners.

3 Bake in the pre-heated oven for about 10 minutes or until the sponge is golden brown and begins to shrink from the edges of the tin. While the cake is cooking, place a piece of baking parchment a little bigger than the size of the tin on to a work surface and sprinkle it with caster sugar.

4 Invert the cake on to the sugared parchment. Quickly loosen the parchment on the bottom of the cake and peel it off. Trim the edges of the sponge with a sharp knife and make a score mark 2.5 cm (1 in) in from one shorter edge, being careful not to cut right through.

5 Leave to cool slightly, then spread with the lemon curd. If the cake is too hot the lemon curd will soak straight into the sponge. Roll up the cake firmly from the cut end.

Chocolate Swiss Roll

A family classic. You could decorate this roll with butter icing and use it for a Christmas log.

4 large eggs
100 g (4 oz) caster sugar
65 g (2½ oz) self-raising flour
40 g (1½ oz) cocoa powder

FOR THE FILLING
3 tablespoons blackberry jam
300 ml (10 fl oz) whipping or
    double cream, whipped

1 Pre-heat the oven to 220°C/Fan 200°C/Gas 7. Grease a 33 x 23 cm (13 x 9 in) swiss roll tin and line with baking parchment.

2 Whisk the eggs and sugar in a large bowl until the mixture is light and frothy and the whisk leaves a trail when lifted out. Sift the flour and cocoa into the mixture, carefully folding them in at the same time. Turn the mixture into the prepared tin and give it a gentle shake so that the mixture finds its own level, making sure that it spreads evenly into the corners.

3 Bake in the pre-heated oven for about 10 minutes or until the sponge begins to shrink from the edges of the tin. While the cake is cooking, place a piece of baking parchment a little bigger than the size of the tin on to a work surface and sprinkle it with caster sugar.

4 Invert the cake on to the sugared parchment. Quickly loosen the parchment on the bottom of the cake and peel it off. Trim the edges of the sponge with a sharp knife and make a score mark 2.5 cm (1 in) in from one shorter edge, being careful not to cut right through. Roll up the cake firmly from the cut end, with the parchment inside, and leave to cool.

5 Warm the jam gently in a small pan until it is of a consistency that is easy to spread. If it is too warm it will soak straight into the sponge. Carefully unroll the cooled cake. Remove the parchment, spread with jam and whipped cream and re-roll.

Maple Syrup Cake

**This Canadian-inspired cake is a real treat for a special gathering.
Fill and cover ahead of time, so that the cake keeps moist.**

225 g (8 oz) softened butter
225 g (8 oz) light muscovado
    sugar
grated rind of 1 orange
4 large eggs
100 ml (3½ fl oz) maple syrup
350 g (12 oz) self-raising flour
2 level teaspoons baking
    powder
½ level teaspoon ground
    ginger
50 g (2 oz) chopped pecan nuts

**FOR THE FILLING
AND TOPPING**
450 ml (¾ pint) double cream
2 tablespoons maple syrup
shredded rind of 1 orange,
    to decorate

1 Pre-heat the oven to 160°C/Fan 140°C/Gas 3. Grease a 20 cm (8 in) deep round cake tin and line the base with baking parchment.

2 Measure all the ingredients for the cake except the pecan nuts into a large bowl and beat until evenly blended. Stir in the chopped pecan nuts.

3 Spoon the mixture into the prepared cake tin and level the surface. Bake for 1–1½ hours, until well risen, golden and springy to the touch. Leave to cool in the tin for a few minutes then turn out, peel off the parchment and finish cooling on a wire rack.

4 To make the filling and topping, whip the cream until it just holds its shape and then fold in the maple syrup.

5 With a long sharp knife, split the cake horizontally into three and fill and cover with the cream, smoothing it evenly over the top and sides. Decorate the top with the shredded orange rind. Keep chilled in the fridge.

American Apple and Apricot Cake

This is a version of a cake that has been a favourite with my family for many years. It can be served with coffee or as a dessert and is best eaten warm.

250 g (9 oz) self-raising flour
1 teaspoon baking powder
225 g (8 oz) caster sugar
2 large eggs
½ teaspoon almond extract
150 g (5 oz) butter, melted
225 g (8 oz) cooking apples, peeled, cored and thickly sliced
100 g (4 oz) ready-to-eat dried apricots, snipped into pieces
25 g (1 oz) flaked almonds

1 Pre-heat the oven to 160°C/Fan 140°C/Gas 3. Grease a 20 cm (8 in) loose-bottomed deep, round cake tin and line the base with baking parchment.

2 Measure the flour, baking powder, sugar, eggs, almond extract and melted butter into a large bowl. Mix well to combine, then beat well for 1 minute. Add the apples and apricots to the bowl and gently mix them in with a spoon.

3 Spoon the mixture into the prepared tin, gently level the surface and sprinkle with the flaked almonds. Bake for 1–1½ hours, until the cake is golden, firm to the touch and beginning to shrink away from the side of the tin. Leave to cool in the tin for a few minutes then turn out, peel off the parchment and put on to a plate to serve.

Coffee and Walnut Sponge Cake

The walnuts in this cake really complement the coffee flavour and provide extra bite to contrast the moist cake and the smooth butter cream.

100 g (4 oz) softened butter
100 g (4 oz) caster sugar
2 large eggs
100 g (4 oz) self-raising flour
1 level teaspoon baking
    powder
50 g (2 oz) chopped walnuts
1 tablespoon coffee essence

**FOR THE FILLING
AND TOPPING**
75 g (3 oz) softened butter
225 g (8 oz) sifted icing sugar
2 teaspoons milk
2 teaspoons coffee essence
8 walnut halves, to decorate

1 Pre-heat the oven to 160°C/Fan 140°C/Gas 3. Grease two 18 cm (7 in) sandwich tins and line the base of each tin with baking parchment.

2 Measure all the cake ingredients into a bowl and beat until thoroughly blended and smooth.

3 Divide the mixture between the sandwich tins and level the surface. Bake for about 35–40 minutes or until well risen and the top of the cake springs back when lightly pressed with a finger. Leave to cool in the tins for a few minutes then turn out, peel off the parchment and finish cooling on a wire rack.

4 To make the filling and topping, beat together the butter, sifted icing sugar, milk and coffee essence in a bowl until smooth. When the cakes are completely cold sandwich together with half of the filling and use the rest for the top of the cake. Decorate with the walnut halves.

TIP
If you don't have any coffee essence in the cupboard use 2 teaspoons instant coffee granules mixed with 1 tablespoon hot water. Use a little more in the cake mixture than in the icing.

Cappuccino Cake

Make sure you use deep sandwich tins for this recipe, as the shallower tins tend to overflow. This cake is best eaten fresh, store it in the fridge if necessary.

50 g (2 oz) cocoa powder
6 tablespoons boiling water
3 large eggs
50 ml (2 fl oz) milk
175 g (6 oz) self-raising flour
1 rounded teaspoon baking
    powder
100 g (4 oz) softened butter
275 g (10 oz) caster sugar

**FOR THE FILLING
AND TOPPING**
300 ml (½ pint) double cream
1 teaspoon instant coffee,
    dissolved in 2 teaspoons
    hot water
a little cocoa powder or
    drinking chocolate,
    for dusting

1 Pre-heat the oven to 180°C/Fan 160°C/Gas 4. Grease two 20 cm (8 in) loose-bottomed deep sandwich tins and line the base of each tin with baking parchment.

2 Measure the cocoa powder into a large mixing bowl, add the boiling water and mix well until it has a paste-like consistency. Add all the remaining ingredients to the bowl and beat until just combined. The mixture will be a fairly thick batter (be careful not to over-beat).

3 Divide the cake mixture between the prepared tins and gently level the surface. Bake for 25–30 minutes, until the cakes are well risen and beginning to shrink away from the side of the tin. Leave to cool in the tins for a few minutes then turn out, peel off the parchment and finish cooling on a wire rack.

4 To finish the cake, whip the double cream until it just holds its shape and then stir in the dissolved coffee. Use half the cream to fill the cake and spread the remainder over the top. Gently smooth the surface with a palette knife and dust with sifted cocoa powder or drinking chocolate.

Battenburg Cake

You can use either homemade or bought almond paste, or marzipan for this famous chequerboard cake.

100 g (4 oz) softened butter
100 g (4 oz) caster sugar
2 large eggs
50 g (2 oz) ground rice
100 g (4 oz) self-raising flour
½ level teaspoon baking
    powder
a few drops of almond extract
red food colouring

TO FINISH
about 3–4 tablespoons
    apricot jam
225 g (8 oz) almond paste
    or marzipan (see page 388
    for almond paste recipe)

1 Pre-heat the oven to 160°C/Fan 140°C/Gas 3. Grease an 18 cm (7 in) shallow square cake tin and line the base with baking parchment.

2 Measure the butter, sugar, eggs, ground rice, flour, baking powder and almond extract into a large bowl and beat for about 2 minutes until smooth.

3 Spoon half the mixture into the right half of the prepared tin as neatly as possible. Add a few drops of red food colouring to the remaining mixture to turn it a deep pink colour, then spoon this into the left half of the tin. Try to get the join between the 2 mixtures as neat as possible. Smooth the surface of each half.

4 Bake in the pre-heated oven for about 35–40 minutes or until the cake is well risen, springy to the touch and has shrunk slightly from the sides of the tin. Leave to cool in the tin for a few minutes then turn out, peel off the parchment and finish cooling on a wire rack.

5 Trim the edges of the cake and then cut into 4 equal strips – you need 2 pink and 2 plain strips of equal size. Gently heat the apricot jam in a small pan. Use the warmed jam to stick the 4 strips of cake together to make a chequerboard effect. Brush the top of the assembled cake with apricot jam.

6 Roll out the almond paste or marzipan into an oblong the length of the cake and sufficiently wide to wrap around the cake. Invert the cake on to the almond paste or marzipan, then brush the remaining 3 sides with apricot jam. Press the almond paste or marzipan neatly around the cake, arranging the join in one corner. Score the top of the cake with a criss-cross pattern and crimp the edges with your fingers to decorate.

Lemon Yoghurt Cake

This is a lovely moist cake. Keep in the fridge and eat it within a week.

300 g (11 oz) caster sugar
50 g (2 oz) softened butter
3 large eggs, separated
225 g (8 oz) Greek yoghurt
grated rind of 1 lemon
175 g (6 oz) self-raising flour

FOR THE ICING
100g (4 oz) sifted icing sugar
about 1½ tablespoons lemon
   juice

1 Pre-heat the oven to 180°C/Fan 160°C/Gas 4. Grease a 20 cm (8 in) deep round cake tin and line the base with baking parchment.

2 Beat together the sugar, butter and egg yolks in a bowl. Add the yoghurt and lemon and beat until smooth. Gently fold in the flour. Whisk the egg whites to a soft peak and carefully fold into the mixture. Turn into the prepared tin.

3 Bake in the pre-heated oven for 1–1¼ hours or until the cake is well risen and firm to the touch. Leave to cool in the tin for a few minutes then turn out, peel off the parchment and finish cooling on a wire rack.

4 For the icing, mix together the sifted icing sugar and the lemon juice and pour over the cold cake. Smooth over with a palette knife and leave to set.

Old-fashioned Seed Cake

You either love or loathe seed cake – this one has a lovely buttery flavour.

225 g (8 oz) self-raising flour
1 level teaspoon baking
   powder
150 g (5 oz) softened butter
150 g (5 oz) caster sugar
2 large eggs
2 tablespoons milk
50 g (2 oz) chopped candied
   peel
2 level teaspoons caraway
   seeds

1 Pre-heat the oven to 180°C/Fan 160°C/Gas 4. Grease a 18 cm (7 in) deep round cake tin and line the base with baking parchment.

2 Measure all the ingredients except the candied peel and caraway seeds into a large bowl. Beat for about 1 minute until thoroughly blended. Carefully fold in the candied peel and caraway seeds, reserving a few seeds to sprinkle over the cake.

3 Turn the mixture into the prepared tin and sprinkle over the reserved seeds. Bake for about 1 hour, or until well-risen and golden brown and a skewer inserted into the centre comes out clean.

4 Leave to cool in the tin for 10 minutes then turn out, peel off the parchment and finish cooling on a wire rack.

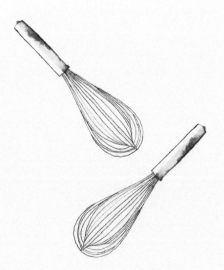

Carrot Cake

This cake is always popular and a great idea for school fêtes or charity events. I'm afraid, though, that it sounds much healthier than it really is!

225 g (8 oz) self-raising flour
2 level teaspoons baking
    powder
150 g (5 oz) light muscovado
    sugar
50 g (2 oz) chopped walnuts
100 g (4 oz) grated carrots
2 ripe bananas, mashed
2 large eggs
150 ml (5 fl oz) sunflower oil

FOR THE TOPPING
175 g (6 oz) full-fat soft cheese
50 g (2 oz) softened butter
100 g (4 oz) sifted icing sugar
a few drops of vanilla extract
walnut halves, to decorate

1 Pre-heat the oven to 180°C/Fan 160°C /Gas 4. Grease a 20 cm (8 in) deep round cake tin and line the base with baking parchment.

2 Measure all the ingredients for the cake into a large bowl and beat well until thoroughly blended and smooth. Turn into the prepared tin and level the surface.

3 Bake in the pre-heated oven for about 50–60 minutes until the cake is well risen and shrinking away from the sides of the tin. Leave to cool in the tin for a few minutes then turn out, peel off the parchment and finish cooling on a wire rack.

4 For the topping, measure all the ingredients, except the walnuts, into a bowl or into a food processor, and blitz until smooth. Spread over the top of the cake, swirling the top with a spatula for a decorative effect. Decorate the top with the walnut halves. Chill a little before serving, and store in the fridge as the topping is soft.

CHAPTER TWO

Fruit and Nut Cakes

Fruit and nut cakes made with fresh or dried fruits and nuts, such as glacé cherries, sultanas, currants, walnuts and almonds, have long been favourites at teatimes. While cakes are unfortunately never going to be truly healthy, they can at least be more wholesome when baked with wholemeal flour and full of nuts and juicy fruit – even vegetables, as with **Carrot Cake** (page 58) or **Courgette Loaves** (page 313).

This chapter includes a wide range of fruit and nut cakes; some recipes are more unusual, like the **Frosted Walnut Layer Cake** (page 71), topped with marshmallowy icing, and some are classic recipes like **English Cherry Cake** (page 77), **Marmalade Cake** (page 74) and **Pound Cake** (page 69). These are economical sponges that are perfect for lunch boxes and relaxed teatimes.

A lot of the fruit used in this book is dried. Most are dried by artificial heat rather than the sun, and some are spread with mineral oils to give them a glossy appearance and to prevent them from sticking together. Look for dried fruit that have been treated with vegetable oils, and check for small pieces of stalk before adding the fruit to your cake mixture. Store opened bags of dried fruit in an airtight container or sealed food bag to help keep its flavour and colour.

Nuts come in a range of shapes and sizes – ground, flaked, shredded or whole – and can be expensive. Some have a short shelf-life, but all nuts will go rancid if left in a warm kitchen. Store unused nuts in the freezer or keep small quantities in an airtight container in the fridge. Whole shelled nuts keep in the freezer for up to 5 years; flaked and ground nuts for 1 year.

Cranberry and Apricot Fruit Cake

This cake is robust enough to pack for a picnic and also makes a good alternative Christmas cake. Instead of dried cranberries, you can use the same weight of red or natural quartered glacé cherries, but wash and dry them thoroughly.

227 g (8 oz) can pineapple in natural juice
350 g (12 oz) ready-to-eat dried apricots
100 g (4 oz) whole blanched almonds
350 g (12 oz) dried cranberries
75 g (3 oz) ground almonds
350 g (12 oz) sultanas
finely grated rind of 2 lemons
250 g (9 oz) self-raising flour
250 g (9 oz) caster sugar
250 g (9 oz) softened butter
5 large eggs

TO DECORATE
50 g (2 oz) blanched almonds

1 Pre-heat the oven to 150°C/Fan 130°C/Gas 2. Grease a 23 cm (9 in) deep round cake tin then line the base and sides with baking parchment.

2 Drain the pineapple, discarding the juice. Coarsely chop then dry thoroughly on kitchen paper. Snip the apricots into pieces and coarsely chop the almonds. Combine all the fruits, nuts (chopped and ground) and lemon rind in a large bowl and mix together well.

3 Measure the remaining ingredients into a large mixing bowl and beat until smooth. Fold in the fruit and nuts, then spoon the mixture into the prepared tin. Level the top with the back of a spoon and decorate with concentric circles of regularly spaced blanched almonds.

4 Bake in the pre-heated oven for about 2½ hours or until the cake is nicely browned. If it shows signs of becoming too browned before it is cooked, cover the top loosely with foil. When cooked, the cake should show signs of shrinking away from the side of the tin and a skewer inserted into the centre of the cake should come out clean. Leave to cool in the tin for about 30 minutes then turn out, leaving the parchment in place, and finish cooling on a wire rack.

TIPS
Like most fruit cakes, they improve on storing and can be made up to 1 week ahead. Leave the baking parchment in place, wrap the cake closely in clingfilm and store in an airtight container.

To freeze the cake, wrap closely in clingfilm as above, seal inside a plastic bag (this takes up less space than a plastic freezer box), then label and freeze for up to 3 months. To defrost, put the cake, fully wrapped, in the fridge overnight or remove from the plastic bag and thaw for 8 hours at room temperature.

Rich Fruit Cake

I use this for Christmas, birthdays and all special occasions – it's a winner. Start preparing the cake the night before you want to bake it, as the dried fruits need to be soaked in brandy so that they become plump.

175 g (6 oz) red or natural glacé cherries
350 g (12 oz) currants
225 g (8 oz) sultanas
225 g (8 oz) raisins
175 g (6 oz) chopped ready-to-eat dried apricots
75 g (3 oz) finely chopped candied peel
4 tablespoons brandy, plus extra to feed the cake
275 g (10 oz) plain flour
½ level teaspoon grated nutmeg
½ level teaspoon ground mixed spice
400 g (14 oz) softened butter
400 g (14 oz) dark muscovado sugar
5 large eggs
65 g (2½ oz) chopped almonds
1 tablespoon black treacle
grated rind of 1 lemon
grated rind of 1 orange

TO DECORATE
blanched almonds
red or natural glacé cherries, rinsed, dried and halved

1 Cut the cherries into quarters, put in a sieve and rinse under running water. Drain well then dry thoroughly on kitchen paper. Put the cherries, currants, sultanas, raisins, apricots and chopped candied peel into a large bowl. Stir in the brandy, cover the bowl and leave in a cool place overnight.

2 The next day, pre-heat the oven to 140°C/Fan 120°C/Gas 1. Grease a 23 cm (9 in) deep round cake tin then line the base and sides with a double layer of baking parchment.

3 Measure the flour, grated nutmeg, mixed spice, butter, sugar, eggs, chopped almonds, black treacle and grated lemon and orange rind into a large bowl and beat to mix thoroughly. Fold in the soaked fruits, then spoon the mixture into the prepared cake tin and spread out evenly with the back of the spoon. Decorate the top with the whole blanched almonds and halved glacé cherries, pushing them lightly into the top of the cake mixture.

4 Cover the top of the cake loosely with a double layer of baking parchment and bake in the pre-heated oven for 4–4½ hours, until the cake feels firm to the touch and a skewer inserted into the centre comes out clean. Leave to cool in the tin then, when the cake is almost cold, turn out, peel off the parchment and finish cooling on a wire rack.

5 Pierce the base at intervals with a fine skewer and feed with a little brandy. Once the cake is completely cold, wrap it in a double layer of parchment and then in foil. Store in a cool place for up to 3 months, feeding at intervals with more brandy.

TIP
You can vary the fruit if you like but make the total weight the same as in the recipe.

Quick Boiled Fruit Cake

I'm often asked for the boiled fruit cake with condensed milk that Granny used to make – here it is. Although, I add fat to make it even tastier!

397 g (14 oz) can
    condensed milk
150 g (5 oz) butter
225 g (8 oz) raisins
225 g (8 oz) sultanas
175 g (6 oz) currants
175 g (6 oz) roughly chopped
    red or natural glacé
    cherries
225 g (8 oz) self-raising flour
2 level teaspoons ground
    mixed spice
1 level teaspoon ground
    cinnamon
2 large eggs

1 Pre-heat the oven to 150°C/Fan 130°C/Gas 2. Grease an 18 cm (7 in) deep round cake tin then line the base and sides with baking parchment.

2 Pour the condensed milk into a heavy-based pan and add the butter, fruit and glacé cherries. Place over a low heat until the butter has melted into the condensed milk. Stir well, then simmer gently for 5 minutes. Remove from the heat and set aside to cool for about 10 minutes, stirring occasionally.

3 Measure the flour and spices into a large bowl and make a well in the centre. Add the eggs and the cooled fruit mixture and quickly mix together until well blended. Turn into the prepared tin.

4 Bake in the pre-heated oven for about 1¾–2 hours or until the cake is well risen, golden brown and the top feels firm. A skewer inserted into the centre should come out clean. Leave to cool in the tin for 10 minutes then turn out, peel off the parchment and finish cooling on a wire rack.

Jane's Fruit Cake

This is a good family cake. It goes quite dark when baked because of the wholemeal flour.

200 g (7 oz) softened butter
350 g (12 oz) light muscovado sugar
3 large eggs
450 g (1 lb) wholemeal self-raising flour
150 ml (¼ pint) buttermilk
350 g (12 oz) sultanas
350 g (12 oz) currants
50 g (2 oz) flaked almonds, for sprinkling

1 Pre-heat the oven to 140°C/Fan 120°C/Gas 1. Grease a 23 cm (9 in) deep round cake tin and line the base and sides with a double layer of baking parchment.

2 Measure all the cake ingredients, except the flaked almonds, into a large bowl and mix thoroughly. Beat the mixture for 2–3 minutes until smooth and glossy. Spoon into the prepared tin and level the surface. Sprinkle with the flaked almonds.

3 Bake in the pre-heated oven for about 3–3½ hours or until a skewer inserted into the centre comes out clean. Leave to cool in the tin then turn out, but leave the parchment on as this helps to keep the cake moist.

4 To store, wrap the cake in more baking parchment and then some foil, and keep in a cool place.

'Boozy' Fruit Cake

Excellent if you are short of time, this cake is quick to make and needs no maturing.

100 g (4 oz) dried stoned dates
150 g (5 oz) softened butter
175 g (6 oz) golden syrup
175 ml (6 fl oz) milk
150 g (5 oz) sultanas
150 g (5 oz) raisins
50 g (2 oz) currants
50 g (2 oz) chopped
   candied peel
100 g (4 oz) chopped walnuts
225 g (8 oz) plain flour
2 level teaspoons ground
   mixed spice
½ level teaspoon
   bicarbonate of soda
2 large eggs
4 tablespoons brandy, rum or
   sherry, to feed the cake

1 Pre-heat the oven to 150°C/Fan 130°C/Gas 2. Grease a 20 cm (8 in) deep round cake tin then line the base and sides with a double layer of baking parchment.

2 Roughly chop the dates. Measure the butter, syrup, milk, fruit, including the chopped dates, candied peel and nuts into a pan and gently heat, stirring occasionally, until the butter has melted. Simmer very gently for 5 minutes. Allow to cool slightly.

3 Sift the flour, spice and bicarbonate of soda into a bowl, add the syrup mixture and the eggs, and beat until thoroughly combined. Pour into the prepared tin and bake in the pre-heated oven for 1½–1¾ hours or until firm to the touch and a skewer inserted into the centre comes out clean. Allow the cake to cool in the tin for 10 minutes.

4 Remove the cake from the tin, peel off the parchment and pierce the top of the cake in several places with a skewer. Spoon in a little brandy, rum or sherry. Replace the parchment paper on the bottom of the cake, as this helps to keep the cake moist. Wrap in more baking parchment and then some foil, and store in a cool place.

5 Feed the cake at intervals with the alcohol, alternating feeding the top and then the bottom of the cake. To give as a gift, wrap in cellophane with a generous bow on top.

Pound Cake

In Victorian times, cakes were made larger than they are now, and so one-pound quantities – hence the name – would have been used. In this version of the recipe, the ingredients are in half-pound quantities.

100 g (4 oz) red or natural
glacé cherries
225g (8 oz) softened butter
225g (8 oz) light muscovado
sugar
4 large eggs
225g (8 oz) self-raising flour
225g (8 oz) raisins
225g (8 oz) sultanas
1 level teaspoon ground
mixed spice
1 tablespoon brandy

1 Pre-heat the oven to 150°C/Fan 130°C/Gas 2. Grease a 20 cm (8 in) deep round cake tin then line the base with baking parchment.

2 Cut the cherries into quarters, put in a sieve and rinse under running water. Drain well then dry thoroughly on kitchen paper. Measure all the ingredients into a large bowl and beat together until thoroughly combined. Turn the mixture into the prepared tin and level the surface.

3 Bake in the pre-heated oven for about 2–2¼ hours, covering the top with parchment after an hour to prevent the cake becoming too brown. When cooked the cake should be firm to the touch, and a skewer inserted into the centre will come out clean. Leave to cool in the tin for 30 minutes then turn out, peel off the parchment and finish cooling on a wire rack.

Frosted Walnut Layer Cake

This is a truly old-fashioned cake iced with a simple 'American frosting'.

225 g (8 oz) softened butter
225 g (8 oz) caster sugar
4 large eggs
225 g (8 oz) self-raising flour
2 level teaspoons baking
    powder
100 g (4 oz) finely chopped
    walnuts

FOR THE FROSTING
2 large egg whites
350 g (12 oz) caster sugar
4 tablespoons water
¼ level teaspoon cream
    of tartar

TO DECORATE
walnut halves

1 Pre-heat the oven to 160°C/Fan 140°C/Gas 3. Grease three 20 cm (8 in) sandwich tins then line the base of each tin with baking parchment.

2 Measure all the ingredients for the cake into a large bowl and beat until thoroughly blended. Divide the mixture equally between the tins and level the surfaces.

3 Bake in the pre-heated oven for about 25–30 minutes until the cakes are golden and springy to the touch. Leave to cool in the tin for a few minutes then turn out, peel off the parchment and finish cooling on a wire rack.

4 For the frosting, measure all the ingredients into a bowl over a pan of hot water and whisk for 10–12 minutes until thick. Sandwich the cake layers together with a little of the frosting, then use the remainder to cover the top and sides of the cake, swirling the icing to form softened peaks. Work quickly as the icing sets rapidly. Leave to set in a cool place, but not in the fridge. Decorate with the walnut halves.

If you have a sugar thermometer, try the alternative American frosting recipe on page 393.

TIP
Don't be tempted to use more baking powder than specified or the cake will rise up and then sink back again. In this all-in-one method, self-raising flour and baking powder are used together to give the cake the necessary lift. The quickness of the method means that less air is whisked into the mixture than if making the cake the traditional way.

Crunchy Top Lemon Cake

The same crunchy topping can be used on traybakes and teabreads. The secret is to pour the crunchy topping over the cake while it is still warm so that the lemon soaks in and the sugar stays on top.

100 g (4 oz) softened butter
175 g (6 oz) caster sugar
175 g (6 oz) self-raising flour
1 level teaspoon baking
    powder
2 large eggs, beaten
4 tablespoons milk
finely grated rind of 1 lemon

FOR THE TOPPING
juice of 1 lemon
100 g (4 oz) caster or
    granulated sugar

1 Pre-heat the oven to 180°C/Fan 160°C/Gas 4. Grease an 18 cm (7 in) deep round cake tin then line the base with baking parchment.

2 Measure all the ingredients for the cake into a large bowl and beat for about 2 minutes until smooth and well blended. Turn the mixture into the prepared tin and level the surface.

3 Bake in the pre-heated oven for about 35–40 minutes or until the cake has shrunk slightly from the sides of the tin and springs back when lightly pressed with a finger.

4 While the cake is baking, make the crunchy topping. Measure the lemon juice and sugar into a bowl and stir until blended. When the cake comes out of the oven, spread the lemon paste over the top while the cake is still hot. Leave to cool completely in the tin, then turn out and peel off the parchment.

TIP
If a softened cake has sunk disastrously in the middle, cut this out, fill with softened fruits and whipped cream, and serve as a dessert.

Double Orange Cake

A lovely light sponge cake, this is always popular and is especially good on the day it's made.

175 g (6 oz) softened butter
175 g (6 oz) caster sugar
3 large eggs, beaten
175 g (6 oz) self-raising flour
1½ level teaspoons baking powder
grated rind and juice of 1 large orange

TO FINISH
about 2 tablespoons apricot jam
100 g (4 oz) icing sugar
finely shredded rind and juice of ½ orange

1 Pre-heat the oven to 180°C/Fan 160°C/Gas 4. Grease a 20 cm (8 in) deep round cake tin then line the base with baking parchment.

2 Measure all the ingredients for the cake into a large bowl and beat until thoroughly blended. Turn into the prepared cake tin and level the surface.

3 Bake in the pre-heated oven for about 35 minutes until well risen and springy to the touch. Leave to cool in the tin for a few minutes then turn out, peel off the parchment and finish cooling on a wire rack.

4 Measure the apricot jam into a small pan and gently warm through. Brush over the top of the cake. Sift the icing sugar into a bowl and mix in the orange juice to a coating consistency. Pour over the top of the cake and gently spread out with a small palette or round bladed knife. Leave to set and then decorate with the shredded orange rind.

Marmalade Cake

Don't overdo the marmalade or the fruit will sink to the bottom of the cake. Too much marmalade alters the sugar proportion of the recipe, slackening the mixture, which causes the fruit to drop.

40 g (1½ oz) red or natural
    glacé cherries
100 g (4 oz) softened butter
100 g (4 oz) caster sugar
100 g (4 oz) sultanas
100 g (4 oz) currants
2 large eggs
175 g (6 oz) self-raising flour
1 rounded tablespoon chunky
    marmalade

TO FINISH
1 tablespoon chunky
    marmalade, or a little
    caster sugar for sprinkling

1 Pre-heat the oven to 160°C/Fan 140°C/Gas 3. Grease a 900 g (2 lb) loaf tin and line the base with baking parchment.

2 Cut the cherries into quarters, put in a sieve and rinse under running water. Drain well then dry thoroughly on kitchen paper. Measure all the remaining ingredients together into a large bowl, add the cherries and mix well until blended. Turn into the prepared tin and level the top.

3 Bake in the pre-heated oven for about 1½ hours or until a skewer inserted into the centre of the cake comes out clean. Leave to cool in the tin for 10 minutes then turn out, peel off the parchment and finish cooling on a wire rack.

4 To finish, warm the marmalade in a small pan and then spoon over the top of the cake and leave to set. Or simply sprinkle the top of the cake with caster sugar before serving.

TIP
Store dried fruits in the freezer, well wrapped, and use within two years.

Strawberry Dessert Cake

This is absolutely delicious served warm with cream, when it tends to be more of a dessert. Served cold, it is more of a cake.

225 g (8 oz) self-raising flour
1½ level teaspoons baking
    powder
225 g (8 oz) caster sugar
2 large eggs
1 teaspoon vanilla extract
150 g (5 oz) butter, melted
350 g (12 oz) sliced
    strawberries
25 g (1 oz) flaked almonds

1 Pre-heat the oven to 160°C/Fan 140°C/Gas 3. Grease a 20 cm (8 in) loose-bottomed 5 cm (2 in) deep fluted flan tin or a 20 cm (8 in) loose-bottomed cake tin and line the base with baking parchment.

2 Measure the flour, baking powder and sugar into a bowl. In a separate bowl, beat the eggs and vanilla extract together, then stir them into the dry ingredients along with the melted butter. Stir until thoroughly mixed, then spread half the mixture in the prepared tin.

3 Arrange the strawberries on top to within 1 cm (½ in) of the edge. Spoon the remaining mixture on top of the strawberries, then spread to cover the surface. It does not matter if there are a few gaps; the mixture will melt and spread to fill them in the heat of the oven. Sprinkle with almonds.

4 Bake in the pre-heated oven for 1½ hours or until the cake is golden brown and shows signs of shrinking from the side of the tin. Leave to cool in the tin for 15 minutes then turn out and peel off the parchment. Serve warm, with cream.

TIPS

The unbaked cake can be covered and kept in the fridge for up to 24 hours, but it will need time to come back up to room temperature before baking, following the recipe above.

This cake is easily adaptable. Try fresh, sliced peaches instead of strawberries and add almond extract instead of vanilla. It is also excellent with apples, but with these I add grated lemon rind rather than vanilla extract.

English Cherry Cake

Wash and dry the quartered cherries thoroughly before adding them to the cake mixture. This prevents them from sinking to the bottom during baking.

200 g (7 oz) red or natural glacé cherries
275 g (10 oz) self-raising flour
75 g (3 oz) ground almonds
2 level teaspoons baking powder
225 g (8 oz) softened butter
225 g (8 oz) caster sugar
4 large eggs

1 Pre-heat the oven to 160°C/Fan 140°C/Gas 3. Grease a 20 cm (8 in) deep round cake tin then line the base with baking parchment.

2 Cut the cherries into quarters, put in a sieve and rinse under running water. Drain well then dry thoroughly on kitchen paper.

3 Measure all the remaining ingredients into a large bowl and beat for 1 minute to mix thoroughly. Lightly fold in the cherries. Turn into the prepared tin and level the surface.

4 Bake in the pre-heated oven for 1½–1¾ hours or until a skewer inserted into the centre of the cake comes out clean. Leave to cool in the tin for 10 minutes then turn out, peel off the parchment and finish cooling on a wire rack.

CHAPTER THREE

Spiced Cakes

Spices such as cinnamon, cloves, ginger and nutmeg are all synonymous with warmth and comfort, and have been used in cooking and baking ever since they were introduced to Europe from the East over ten centuries ago. Spices have long been used for their therapeutic and medicinal properties, as much as for their flavour, and some, like ginger, are particularly useful in cooking as they act as a natural preservative.

There are some traditional favourites in this chapter, including **Parkin** (opposite) from the North of England, and a recipe for **Classic Sticky Gingerbread** (page 82). Fruit complement spices very well and my **Apple and Cinnamon Cake** (page 89) and **Sticky Ginger and Orange Cake** (page 86) demonstrate this perfectly. These are recipes to enjoy with tea or hot chocolate in winter months, after a day spent outdoors.

I have included one no-cook recipe here, **Ginger Cream Roll** (page 91), which you might consider a cheat. You could make the ginger biscuits for the centre yourself if you are feeling very virtuous, but good-quality bought biscuits are the simplest and quickest base for this recipe. Although it's not a baking recipe in the strictest sense, I've found it a handy recipe to have on standby for dinner parties, or whenever you need to whip up a dessert at short notice. You can buy the biscuits in advance and store them in your cupboard, ready to be pulled out when needed.

Ground and whole spices don't go off in the same sense as other cake ingredients, but their pungent flavours do deteriorate over time. Store your spices in a cool, dry, dark cupboard to preserve their flavour, and use them within a year.

Traditional Parkin

This is old-fashioned parkin, using black treacle. A favourite from the North of England, Parkin definitely improves with keeping, so try to store it for a week before cutting.

175 g (6 oz) black treacle
150 g (5 oz) butter
100 g (4 oz) dark muscovado sugar
175 g (6 oz) plain flour
2 level teaspoons ground ginger
1 level teaspoon ground cinnamon
1 level teaspoon freshly grated nutmeg
275 g (10 oz) porridge oats
1 large egg
150 ml (5 fl oz) milk
1 level teaspoon bicarbonate of soda

1 Pre-heat the oven to 180°C/Fan 160°C/Gas 4. Grease an 18 cm (7 in) deep square cake tin then line the base with baking parchment.

2 Measure the treacle, butter and sugar into a medium pan and heat gently until the butter has melted and the sugar has dissolved. Allow to cool slightly.

3 Sift the flour and spices into a large bowl and add the porridge oats. Mix together the egg and milk and stir in the bicarbonate of soda. Add to the dry ingredients along with the treacle mixture and stir well to mix. Pour into the prepared tin.

4 Bake in the pre-heated oven for about 1 hour or until firm to the touch. Leave to cool in the tin for 10 minutes then turn out, peel off the parchment and finish cooling on a wire rack.

5 Wrap the cold parkin in baking parchment and store in a cake tin for a week before cutting into 16 squares.

Classic Sticky Gingerbread

This keeps and freezes extremely well. Sometimes you get a dip in the middle of the gingerbread, which indicates that you have been a bit heavy-handed with the syrup and treacle. It just means it tastes even more moreish!

225 g (8 oz) butter
225 g (8 oz) light muscovado
   sugar
225 g (8 oz) golden syrup
225 g (8 oz) black treacle
225 g (8 oz) self-raising flour
225 g (8 oz) wholemeal
   self-raising flour
4 level teaspoons ground
   ginger
2 large eggs
300 ml (½ pint) milk

1 Pre-heat the oven to 160°C/Fan 140°C/Gas 3. Grease a 30 x 23 cm (12 x 9 in) traybake or roasting tin then line the base and sides with baking parchment.

2 Measure the butter, sugar, golden syrup and black treacle into a medium pan and heat gently until the mixture has melted evenly. Allow to cool slightly.

3 Put the flours and ground ginger into a large mixing bowl and stir together lightly. Beat the eggs into the milk. Pour the cooled butter and syrup mixture into the flour along with the egg and milk mixture and beat until smooth. Pour the mixture into the prepared tin and tilt gently to level the surface.

4 Bake in the pre-heated oven for 50 minutes, until well risen, golden and springy to the touch. Leave to cool in the tin for a few minutes then turn out, peel off the parchment and finish cooling on a wire rack. When cold, cut into 16 squares.

Iced Gingerbread with Stem Ginger

Gingerbread is said to be one of the oldest forms of cake in the world. Most European countries have their own version. One of the major advantages of homemade gingerbread is that it improves with keeping.

100 g (4 oz) softened butter

100 g (4 oz) light muscovado sugar

2 large eggs

150 g (5 oz) black treacle

150 g (5 oz) golden syrup

225 g (8 oz) plain flour

1 level teaspoon ground ginger

1 level teaspoon ground mixed spice

½ level teaspoon bicarbonate of soda

2 tablespoons milk

FOR THE ICING

175 g (6 oz) icing sugar

3 tablespoons stem ginger syrup

about 3 teaspoons water

2.5 cm (1 in) piece stem ginger

1 Pre-heat the oven to 160°C/Fan 140°C/Gas 3. Grease an 18 cm (7 in) deep square cake tin then line the base with baking parchment.

2 Measure the butter, sugar, eggs, treacle and golden syrup into a bowl and beat until thoroughly mixed. Sift the flour with the spices and fold into the mixture. Add the bicarbonate of soda to the milk and then stir this into the mixture. Pour into the prepared tin.

3 Bake in the pre-heated oven for 1 hour. Reduce the oven temperature to 150°C/Fan 130°C/Gas 2 and bake for a further 15–30 minutes until well risen and firm to the touch. Leave to cool in the tin for 10 minutes then turn out, peel off the parchment and finish cooling on a wire rack.

4 For the icing, sift the icing sugar into a bowl and add the stem ginger syrup and enough water to make a spreading consistency. Mix to give a smooth icing. Finely chop the stem ginger and add to the icing. Pour the icing over the cake and leave to set before cutting into 16 squares.

Almond Spice Cake

A thin layer of sweet almond paste is baked through the centre of this cake and works very well with the warming flavours of cinnamon and clove.

100 g (4 oz) almond paste
  or marzipan (see page 388
  for almond paste recipe)
175 g (6 oz) softened butter
175 g (6 oz) caster sugar
3 large eggs
225 g (8 oz) self-raising flour
2 level teaspoons baking
  powder
½ level teaspoon ground
  cinnamon
¼ level teaspoon ground
  cloves
75 g (3 oz) toasted flaked
  almonds

FOR THE TOPPING
50 g (2 oz) butter
100 g (4 oz) light muscovado
  sugar
2 tablespoons double cream
25 g (1 oz) toasted flaked
  almonds, to sprinkle

1 Pre-heat the oven to 180°C/Fan 160°C/Gas 4. Grease an 18 cm (7 in) deep round cake tin then line the base with baking parchment.

2 Roll out the almond paste to an 18 cm (7 in) circle, then set aside. Measure the butter, sugar, eggs, flour, baking powder and spices into a bowl and beat until thoroughly blended. Fold in 75 g (3 oz) of the toasted flaked almonds.

3 Spoon half of the cake mixture into the prepared cake tin and level the surface. Lightly place the circle of almond paste on top, then add the remaining cake mixture and level the surface.

4 Bake in the pre-heated oven for about 1–1¼ hours or until well risen and golden brown and the surface springs back when lightly pressed with a finger. Leave to cool in the tin for 5 minutes then turn out, peel off the parchment and finish cooling on a wire rack.

5 For the topping, heat the butter, sugar and cream in a saucepan until blended, then bring to the boil. Stand the wire rack on a baking tray to catch any drips, then drizzle the icing over the cake. Sprinkle with the remaining 25 g (1 oz) of toasted flaked almonds, then leave to set for 10–15 minutes.

Sticky Ginger and Orange Cake

If possible store the cake for 2 days, wrapped in baking parchment and foil, before icing. This allows the cake to mature and become moist and sticky.

100 g (4 oz) golden syrup
100 g (4 oz) black treacle
250 ml (9 fl oz) water
100 g (4 oz) softened butter
100 g (4 oz) caster sugar
grated rind of 1 orange
1 large egg, beaten
275 g (10 oz) plain flour
1½ level teaspoons
    bicarbonate of soda
1 level teaspoon ground
    cinnamon
1 level teaspoon ground
    ginger

FOR THE ICING
100 g (4 oz) icing sugar
juice of 1 orange

1 Pre-heat the oven to 180°C /Fan 160°C/Gas 4. Grease a 23 cm (9 in) deep round cake tin then line the base and sides with baking parchment.

2 Measure the golden syrup and treacle into a pan along with the water and bring to the boil. Meanwhile, put the remaining ingredients into a mixing bowl and beat well until thoroughly blended. Add the syrup and treacle mixture and beat again until smooth. Pour the mixture into the prepared tin.

3 Bake in the pre-heated oven for about 50 minutes or until a skewer inserted into the centre comes out clean. Leave to cool in the tin for 10 minutes then turn out, peel off the parchment and finish cooling on a wire rack.

4 To make the icing, sift the icing sugar into a bowl and add enough orange juice to make a smooth, fairly thick mixture. Stand the wire rack on a baking tray to catch any drips, then spoon the icing over the top of the cake and leave to set for about 1 hour.

Wholemeal Ginger Cake

Don't be over-generous with the marmalade, otherwise the cake will sink!

175g (6 oz) softened butter
350 g (12 oz) golden syrup
120 g (4½ oz) granulated
   sugar
1½ level tablespoons orange
   marmalade
200 ml (7 fl oz) milk
175 g (6 oz) self-raising flour
1½ level teaspoons ground
   ginger
1½ level teaspoons ground
   mixed spice
½ level teaspoon bicarbonate
   of soda
175 g (6 oz) wholemeal
   self-raising flour
3 large eggs, beaten

FOR THE ICING
3 tablespoons lemon juice
225 g (8 oz) sifted icing sugar
stem ginger, to decorate
   (optional)

1 Pre-heat the oven to 160°C/Fan 140°C/Gas 3. Grease a 30 x 23 cm (12 x 9 in) traybake or roasting tin then line the base with baking parchment.

2 Gently heat the butter, syrup, sugar, marmalade and milk together in a saucepan until the sugar has dissolved. Allow to cool a little. Meanwhile, sift the self-raising flour with the spices and bicarbonate of soda into a mixing bowl. Add the brown flour and mix together.

3 Stir the melted butter and golden syrup mixture into the flours along with the beaten eggs. Stir well to form a smooth batter. Pour into the prepared tin and bake in the pre-heated oven for about 1½ hours or until it has shrunk slightly from the sides of the tin and is springy to the touch. Leave to cool in the tin for a few minutes then turn out, peel off the parchment and finish cooling on a wire rack.

4 To make the icing, mix together the lemon juice and icing sugar and beat until smooth. Spread out evenly over the cake and leave to set. Decorate with chopped stem ginger, if you like.

Apple and Cinnamon Cake

This is the sort of cake that you would expect to find in a first-class coffee shop or tearoom. It's great for school fêtes and charity events – sell it in wedges, ideally warmed and with dollop of clotted cream.

225 g (8 oz) softened butter
225 g (8 oz) light muscovado sugar
3 large eggs
100 g (4 oz) chopped walnuts
100 g (4 oz) sultanas
225 g (8 oz) self-raising flour
2 level teaspoons baking powder
400 g (14 oz) cooking apples, peeled, cored and grated
1 level teaspoon ground cinnamon

TO FINISH
light muscovado sugar, for sprinkling
extra chopped walnuts, for sprinkling
icing sugar, for dusting

1 Pre-heat the oven to 180°C/Fan 160°C/Gas 4. Grease a 23 cm (9 in) deep round cake tin then line the base with baking parchment.

2 Measure the butter, sugar, eggs, chopped walnuts, sultanas, flour and baking powder into a large bowl and beat for about 2 minutes until thoroughly blended.

3 Spoon half the mixture into the prepared tin then spread the grated apple and ground cinnamon in an even layer on top. Spoon the remaining cake mixture on top, level the surface then sprinkle generously with light muscovado sugar and walnuts.

4 Bake in the pre-heated oven for about 1¼–1½ hours or until the cake is well risen and golden brown. Leave to cool in the tin for a few minutes then turn out, peel off the parchment and finish cooling on a wire rack. Dust with icing sugar to serve.

Cut and Come Again Cake

This is a traditional name for a cake that is so delicious that everyone will come back for another slice. Good for a hungry family, this is not a rich cake so it is best eaten as fresh as possible.

350 g (12 oz) self-raising flour
1 level teaspoon ground
   mixed spice
175 g (6 oz) softened butter
175 g (6 oz) caster sugar
3 large eggs, beaten
175 g (6 oz) currants
100 g (4 oz) sultanas
100 g (4 oz) raisins
3 tablespoons milk

1 Pre-heat the oven to 180°C/Fan 160°C/Gas 4. Grease a 20 cm (8 in) deep round cake tin then line the base with baking parchment.

2 Measure all the ingredients into a large bowl and beat until thoroughly mixed. Turn into the prepared tin and level the surface.

3 Bake in the pre-heated oven for about 1¼–1½ hours or until a skewer inserted into the centre of the cake comes out clean. Leave to cool in the tin for 10 minutes then turn out, peel off the parchment and finish cooling on a wire rack.

Ginger Cream Roll

This is a no-cook pudding, but I've included it in here as it is such an easy but impressive-looking pudding to make. It does have to be made a day before serving to allow the brandy, biscuits and cream to meld together. Serve at a winter dinner party.

425 ml (¾ pint) whipping
    cream
225 g (8 oz) ginger biscuits
4 tablespoons brandy
stem ginger slices, to decorate

1 Measure half the whipping cream into a bowl and whisk until it forms fairly stiff peaks. Quickly dip each biscuit in a little brandy, then sandwich together with the cream, shaping the sandwiched biscuits into a long roll. Place on a serving dish, cover and leave in the fridge overnight.

2 The next day, whip the remaining cream and use it to cover the roll completely. Pipe rosettes down the length of the roll using a piping bag. If you don't have a piping bag, use two plastic food bags put inside each other for strength, and cut off one corner to create a funnel. Decorate with slices of stem ginger. To serve, cut the roll into diagonal slices.

CHAPTER FOUR

Chocolate Cakes

The expression 'chocoholic' might be relatively new, but the passion for chocolate is much older and widespread throughout the world. It is a rich, irresistible ingredient used in both sweet and savoury cooking.

The versatility of chocolate in baking is clear in this chapter; from the all-American **Devil's Food Cake** (page 96) with a contrasting white frosting to **Chocolate Rum Cake** (page 101) and **Almond and Chocolate Chip Cake** (page 106), the range of flavours that complement chocolate is vast.

As explained in more detail in the main introduction to this book (page 29), the quality of chocolate varies considerably between brands, so it is important to always check the cocoa-solids and cocoa-butter content in the chocolate you are using. Not only do they all taste very different, but they also have different melting points and cooking properties.

I have always found a plain chocolate with **39 per cent cocoa solids** the best for baking. For milk and white chocolate, choose a Belgian cooking chocolate.

Death by Chocolate Cake

I have given a generous amount of icing to fill and ice this cake, as death by chocolate should be sheer luxury and a complete indulgence! The icing is very easy to make, but take care not to overheat it or it will lose its shine. For the same reason, don't store the cake in the fridge – a cool place is fine.

275 g (10 oz) plain flour

3 level tablespoons cocoa powder

1½ level teaspoons bicarbonate of soda

1½ level teaspoons baking powder

215 g (7½ oz) caster sugar

3 tablespoons golden syrup

3 large eggs, beaten

225 ml (8 fl oz) sunflower oil

225 ml (8 fl oz) milk

FOR THE ICING

450 g (1 lb) plain chocolate (39 per cent cocoa solids)

200 g (7 oz) unsalted butter

TO FINISH

50 g (2 oz) Belgian white chocolate and plain chocolate, each coarsely grated

1 Pre-heat the oven to 160°C/Fan 140°C/Gas 3. Grease two 20 cm (8 in) deep loose-bottomed cake tins then line the base of each tin with baking parchment.

2 Sift the flour, cocoa powder, bicarbonate of soda and baking powder into a large bowl. Add the sugar and mix well. Make a well in the centre of the dry ingredients and add the golden syrup, eggs, oil and milk. Beat well, using a wooden spoon, until smooth and then pour into the prepared tins.

3 Bake in the pre-heated oven for about 35 minutes or until well risen and the tops of the cakes spring back when lightly pressed with a finger. Leave to cool in the tins for a few minutes then turn out, peel off the parchment and finish cooling on a wire rack. When cold, cut each cake in half horizontally.

4 To make the icing, break the chocolate into pieces and gently heat in a heatproof bowl set over a pan of simmering water for about 10 minutes or just until the chocolate has melted, stirring occasionally. Remove from the heat, add the butter and leave to melt into the chocolate.

5 Stand the wire rack on a baking tray to catch any drips, then sandwich the cake layers together with the icing. Pour the remaining icing over the top of the cake and use a small palette knife to smooth it evenly over the top and around the sides. Leave to set then decorate with the coarsely grated plain and white chocolates.

Devil's Food Cake

This classic American cake is moist dark, and slightly bitter in flavour. The frosting is very sweet, crisp on the top and like marshmallow underneath. American frosting usually requires the use of a sugar thermometer, but in this version, I use a frosting that doesn't require one.

50 g (2 oz) cocoa powder
225 ml (8 fl oz) water
100 g (4 oz) softened butter
275 g (10 oz) caster sugar
2 large eggs
175 g (6 oz) plain flour
¼ level teaspoon baking powder
1 level teaspoon bicarbonate of soda

FOR THE FROSTING
175 g (6 oz) caster sugar
1 large egg white
2 tablespoons hot water
a pinch cream of tartar

1 Pre-heat the oven to 180°C/Fan 160°C/Gas 4. Grease two 20 cm (8 in) sandwich tins then line the base of each tin with baking parchment.

2 Blend the cocoa and the water until smooth then set aside. Put the butter in a bowl and gradually beat in the sugar until the mixture is pale and fluffy. Lightly whisk the eggs, then gradually beat into the creamed mixture until evenly blended.

3 Sift the flour with the baking powder and bicarbonate of soda and fold into the creamed mixture alternately with the cocoa and water. Divide the mixture between the tins and level the surface.

4 Bake in the pre-heated oven for 30–35 minutes or until well risen and the tops of the cakes spring back when lightly pressed with a finger. Leave to cool in the tins for a few minutes then turn out, peel off the parchment and finish cooling on a wire rack.

5 To make the frosting, measure all the ingredients into a bowl set over a pan of hot water and whisk for 10–12 minutes until thick. Sandwich the cake layers together with a little of the frosting, then use the remainder to cover the top and sides of the cake, swirling the icing to form soft peaks. Work quickly as the icing sets rapidly. Leave to set in a cool place, but not in the fridge.

If you have a sugar thermometer, try the alternative American frosting recipe on page 393.

Mississippi Mud Pie

The origin of this pie is rather uncertain but it has become a very popular dessert in cafés and bistros. Like many American recipes it is rich, so it serves 6–8 in small slices.

FOR THE CRUMB
CRUST BASE
100 g (4 oz) crushed
digestive biscuits
50 g (2 oz) butter, melted
25 g (1 oz) demerara sugar

FOR THE FILLING
200 g (7 oz) plain chocolate
(39 per cent cocoa solids)
100 g (4 oz) butter
1 level tablespoons instant
coffee granules
1 tablespoons boiling water
300 ml (½ pint) single cream
175 g (6 oz) dark muscovado
sugar
6 large eggs, beaten

TO FINISH
150 ml (¼ pint) whipping or
double cream, whipped

1 Pre-heat the oven to 180°C/Fan 160°C/Gas 4. Grease a 20 cm (8 in) deep loose-bottomed cake tin or springform tin.

2 To make the base, mix together the crushed digestive biscuits, the melted butter and the sugar and spoon into the prepared tin. Press the biscuit mixture out in an even layer, using the back of a metal spoon.

3 To make the filling, break the chocolate into pieces and gently heat in a large pan along with the butter, instant coffee granules and water until the butter and chocolate have melted, stirring occasionally. Remove from the heat and beat in the cream, sugar and eggs. Pour the mixture on to the biscuit crust.

4 Bake for about 1¼ hours or until set. Leave to cool completely in the tin then turn out and decorate the top with whipped cream.

Dark Indulgent Chocolate and Walnut Brownies

With a little coffee, some chopped walnuts and the addition of plain chocolate chips, these brownies have a rich, 'grown-up' flavour. Cooked brownie mixture, like gingerbread, is likely to dip in the middle, but this all adds to the charm!

350 g (12 oz) plain chocolate (39 per cent cocoa solids)
225 g (8 oz) butter
2 level teaspoons instant coffee granules
2 tablespoons hot water
3 large eggs
225 g (8 oz) caster sugar
1 teaspoon vanilla extract
75 g (3 oz) self-raising flour
175 g (6 oz) chopped walnuts
225 g (8 oz) plain chocolate chips

1 Pre-heat the oven to 190°C/Fan 170°C/Gas 5. Grease a 30 x 23 cm (12 x 9 in) traybake or roasting tin then line the base with baking parchment.

2 Break up the chocolate into pieces and melt slowly with the butter in a bowl set over a pan of hot water, stirring occasionally. Leave to cool. Dissolve the coffee in the hot water.

3 In another bowl, mix together the coffee, eggs, sugar and vanilla extract. Gradually beat in the chocolate mixture. Fold in the flour, walnuts and chocolate chips, and then pour the mixture into the prepared tin.

4 Bake in the pre-heated oven for about 40–45 minutes or until the brownies have a crusty top and a skewer inserted into the centre comes out clean. Leave the brownies to cool in the tin and then cut into 24 squares. Store in an airtight tin.

Chocolate Chip Brownies

A really simple brownie recipe – just measure all the ingredients into a bowl and give it a good mix! Be careful not to overcook your brownies: they should have a slightly gooey texture. The outside crust should be on the crisp side though, thanks to the high proportion of sugar.

275 g (10 oz) softened butter
375 g (13 oz) caster sugar
4 large eggs
75 g (3 oz) cocoa powder
100 g (4 oz) self-raising flour
100 g (4 oz) plain chocolate
    chips

1 Pre-heat the over to 180°C/Fan 160°C/Gas 4. Grease a 30 x 23 cm (12 x 9 in) traybake or roasting tin then line the base and sides with baking parchment.

2 Measure all the ingredients into a large bowl and beat until evenly blended. Spoon the mixture into the prepared tin, scraping the sides of the bowl with a plastic spatula to remove all of it. Spread the mixture gently to the corners of the tin and level the top with the back of the spatula.

3 Bake in the pre-heated oven for 40–45 minutes or until the brownies have a crusty top and a skewer inserted into the centre comes out clean. Cover loosely with foil for the last 10 minutes if the mixture is browning too much. Leave the brownies to cool in the tin and then cut into 24 squares. Store in an airtight tin.

Chocolate Rum Cake

This moist chocolate cake is laced with rum, then filled and covered with a glossy chocolate icing that melts in the mouth. It is irresistible to chocoholics, and can be served as an afternoon cake, or as a pudding with single cream.

200 g (7 oz) plain chocolate (39 per cent cocoa solids)
100 g (4 oz) cubed unsalted butter
3 large eggs, separated
100 g (4 oz) dark muscovado sugar
50 ml (2 fl oz) dark rum
75 g (3 oz) sifted self-raising flour
50 g (2 oz) ground almonds

FOR THE FILLING AND ICING
225 g (8 oz) plain chocolate (39 per cent cocoa solids)
100 g (4 oz) diced unsalted butter
4 tablespoons apricot jam

FOR THE CHOCOLATE GANACHE (OPTIONAL)
175 g (6 oz) plain chocolate (39 per cent cocoa solids)
4 tablespoons single cream
50 g (2 oz) diced butter
2 large egg yolks
1 tablespoon dark rum

1 Pre-heat the oven to 180°C/Fan 160°C/Gas 4. Grease a 20 cm (8 in) deep round cake tin then line the base with baking parchment.

2 Break the chocolate into pieces and melt with the butter gently in a bowl set over a pan of hot water, stirring occasionally, then allow to cool slightly. Put the egg yolks and the sugar into a large bowl and whisk until pale and creamy. Add the cooled chocolate mixture and the rum and mix well. Gently fold in the flour and the ground almonds.

3 In a separate bowl, whisk the egg whites until stiff but not dry, then lightly fold into the mixture. Turn into the prepared tin and gently level the surface.

4 Bake in the pre-heated oven for about 45 minutes or until well risen and the top of the cake springs back when lightly pressed with a finger. Leave to cool in the tin for a few minutes then turn out, peel off the parchment and finish cooling on a wire rack.

5 To make the filling and icing, break the chocolate into pieces and melt gently in a bowl set over a pan of hot water, stirring occasionally. Add the cubed butter and stir until the mixture has the consistency of thick pouring cream. Slice the cake in half horizontally and use a little of the icing to fill it. Warm the apricot jam then push through a sieve. Brush this over the cake top and sides and allow to set. Smooth the icing over and leave to set.

6 To make the chocolate ganache (if using), break the chocolate into pieces and melt with the cream in a bowl set over a pan of hot water, stirring occasionally. Cool slightly then beat in the butter a little at a time. Beat in the egg yolks and rum and then leave until cool and firm, stirring occasionally. When firm enough to hold its shape, spoon into a piping bag fitted with a star nozzle and pipe rosettes of the ganache to decorate the cake.

Chocolate Mousse Cake

There are quite a few stages to this cake, so it's not one to tackle if you're in a hurry, but you can make the cake in advance and freeze it. Be very light-handed when folding in the flour and melted butter, or the butter will sink and result in a heavy cake. Eat as a dessert, with a fork.

25 g (1 oz) butter
6 large eggs
175 g (6 oz) caster sugar
100 g (4 oz) self-raising flour
25 g (1 oz) cocoa powder
2 tablespoons cornflour

FOR THE MOUSSE FILLING
175 g (6 oz) plain chocolate
    (39 per cent cocoa solids)
2 tablespoons brandy
1 level teaspoon powdered
    gelatine
2 large eggs, separated
300 ml (½ pint) double cream

FOR THE CARAQUE
    (SEE PAGE 392)
200 g (7 oz) plain chocolate
    (39 per cent cocoa solids)
150 g (5 oz) Belgian white
    chocolate
150 ml (¼ pint) double cream

TO FINISH
icing sugar, for dusting

1 Pre-heat the oven to 180°C/Fan 160°C/Gas 4. Grease a 23 cm (9 in) deep loose-bottomed cake tin then line the base with baking parchment.

2 Put the butter in a small pan and heat gently until melted, then leave to cool slightly.

3 Beat the eggs and sugar together at full speed until the mixture is pale and creamy and thick enough to leave a trail when the whisk is lifted from the mixture. Sift the flour, cocoa and cornflour together.

4 Carefully fold half the flours into the egg mixture. Pour half the cooled butter around the edge of the mixture and carefully fold in. Gradually fold in the remaining flours and then the remaining butter. Pour the mixture into the prepared tin.

5 Bake in the pre-heated oven for about 35–40 minutes or until well risen and the top of the cake springs back when lightly pressed with a finger. Leave to cool in the tin for a few minutes then turn out, peel off the parchment and finish cooling on a wire rack.

6 Wash the cake tin and then, when the cake is cold, cut it in half horizontally and put the bottom half back in the cleaned tin.

7 To make the mousse filling, break the chocolate into pieces and melt with the brandy gently in a bowl set over a pan of hot water, stirring occasionally. Meanwhile sprinkle the gelatine over 1 tablespoon cold water in a small bowl and leave to 'sponge' for about 10 minutes. Stand the bowl in a pan of hot water and allow to dissolve gently.

8 Leave the melted chocolate to cool slightly and then stir in the egg yolks. Whip the cream until it just stands in soft peaks, then fold into the chocolate. Stir the dissolved gelatine into the chocolate mixture.

9 Whisk the egg whites until stiff but not dry, and gently fold in. Pour the mousse on top of the cake in the tin, gently level the surface and top with the remaining cake. Cover and leave to set in the fridge.

10 While the mousse is setting, melt the decoration chocolates separately, and use to make caraque (see page 392). When the mousse is set, ease around the sides of the mousse with a small palette knife and then stand the base of the cake tin on a large can. Ease the sides of the tin down, then slip the cake off the cake tin base and on to a serving plate.

11 Whip the cream and cover the top and sides of the cake with it. Arrange the white and plain chocolate caraque to cover the cake completely, in any pattern you like! Finish with a little dusting of icing sugar.

Very Best Chocolate Fudge Cake

This will become your favourite chocolate cake recipe – it is the best! It is speedy to make and the easy filling doubles as an icing. The cake is moist and has a 'grown-up' chocolate flavour.

50 g (2 oz) sifted cocoa powder
6 tablespoons boiling water
3 large eggs
50 ml (2 fl oz) milk
175 g (6 oz) self-raising flour
1 rounded teaspoon baking
  powder
100 g (4 oz) softened butter
275 g (10 oz) caster sugar

**FOR THE ICING
   AND FILLING**

3 tablespoons apricot jam
150 g (5 oz) plain chocolate
   (39 per cent cocoa solids)
150 ml (¼ pint) double cream

1 Pre-heat the oven to 180°C/Fan 160°C/Gas 4. Grease two 20 cm (8 in) deep sandwich tins then line the base of each tin with baking parchment.

2 Blend the cocoa and boiling water in a large bowl then add the remaining cake ingredients and beat until the mixture has become a smooth, thickish batter. Divide the cake mix equally between the prepared tins and level the surface.

3 Bake in the pre-heated oven for about 25–30 minutes or until well risen and the tops of the cakes spring back when lightly pressed with a finger. Leave to cool in the tins for a few minutes then turn out, peel off the parchment and finish cooling on a wire rack.

4 To make the icing, warm the apricot jam in a very small pan, then spread a little over the base of one cake and the top of the other. Break the chocolate into pieces and gently heat with the cream in a heatproof bowl set over a pan of simmering water for about 10 minutes or just until the chocolate has melted, stirring occasionally.

5 Remove the bowl from the heat and stir the chocolate mixture to make sure it has completely melted. Leave to cool until it is on the point of setting then spread on top of the apricot on both cakes. Sandwich the cakes together and use a small palette knife to smooth the icing on the top. Keep in a cool place until ready to serve.

TIP
The cake can be frozen (iced or un-iced) for up to 1 month. Store in a round freezer-proof container about 2.5 cm (1 in) bigger than the diameter of the cake. Sit the cake on the inside of the lid and place the container over the top. Seal, label and freeze. If the cake is frozen iced, the icing will not be quite as shiny once thawed. To defrost, release the lid but leave in position and thaw for 4 hours at room temperature.

Almond and Chocolate Chip Cake

This is a lovely cake that makes a great family treat.

175 g (6 oz) self-raising flour
175 g (6 oz) softened butter
175 g (6 oz) caster sugar
3 large eggs
50 g (2 oz) ground almonds
175 g (6 oz) plain chocolate
   chips
1 teaspoon vanilla extract
flaked almonds, for sprinkling

1 Pre-heat the oven to 180°C/Fan 160°C/Gas 4. Grease an 18 cm (7 in) deep round cake tin then line the base with baking parchment.

2 Measure the flour, butter, sugar, eggs, ground almonds, chocolate chips and vanilla extract into a large bowl and beat for about 2 minutes until thoroughly mixed. Turn the mixture into the prepared tin and level the surface. Sprinkle the top liberally with flaked almonds.

3 Bake in the pre-heated oven for about 1–1¼ hours or until well risen and the top of the cake springs back when lightly pressed with a finger. Leave to cool in the tin for 10 minutes then turn out, peel off the parchment and finish cooling on a wire rack.

Date and Chocolate Loaf

A rich loaf that's so moist it doesn't need to be buttered. The dates give the cake a lovely toffee flavour and texture.

150 g (5 oz) stoned dried dates
150 ml (¼ pint) boiling water
150 g (5 oz) plain chocolate
    (39 per cent cocoa solids)
40 g (1½ oz) softened butter
150 g (5 oz) Brazil nuts
225 g (8 oz) plain flour
40 g (1½ oz) caster sugar
1 level teaspoon baking
    powder
1 level teaspoon bicarbonate
    of soda
1 large egg
150 ml (5 fl oz) milk
demerara sugar, for
    sprinkling

1 Pre-heat the oven to 180°C/Fan 160°C/Gas 4. Grease a 900 g (2 lb) loaf tin then line the base with baking parchment.

2 Roughly chop the dates and place in a small bowl. Pour over the boiling water and leave to soak for about 30 minutes. Break up the chocolate and melt with the butter in a small bowl, set over a pan of simmering water, stirring occasionally. Roughly chop the Brazil nuts and reserve about 2 tablespoons for decoration.

3 In a bowl mix together the flour, caster sugar, baking powder and bicarbonate of soda. Mix together the egg and milk and beat this into the dry ingredients, adding the nuts, dates and their soaking liquid, and the chocolate mixture. Spoon into the prepared tin, level the surface and sprinkle over the reserved nuts along with the demerara sugar.

4 Bake in the pre-heated oven for about 1¼ hours or until a skewer inserted into the centre comes out clean. Cover loosely with foil towards the end of the cooking time if the cake is becoming too brown. Leave to cool in the tin for 10 minutes then turn out, peel off the parchment and finish cooling on a wire rack.

Marbled Chocolate Ring Cake

This family weekend cake has a nice texture and looks spectacular, marbled with white and brown. It must be eaten fresh.

225 g (8 oz) softened butter
225 g (8 oz) caster sugar
4 large eggs
225 g (8 oz) self-raising flour
2 level teaspoons baking
    powder
1½ level tablespoons
    cocoa powder
1½ tablespoons hot water

FOR THE ICING
150 g (5 oz) plain chocolate
    (39 per cent cocoa solids)
2 tablespoons water
100g (4 oz) butter
50 g (2 oz) Belgian milk
    chocolate

1 Pre-heat the oven to 180°C/Fan 160°C/Gas 4. Grease a 1.75 litre (3 pint) ring mould then line with strips of baking parchment.

2 Measure all the cake ingredients, except the cocoa and water, into a large bowl. Beat until thoroughly blended. Dot about half of this mixture, in teaspoons, into the base of the prepared tin.

3 Mix the cocoa and hot water together in a small bowl and then mix into the remaining cake mixture. Dot this mixture over and between the plain mixture in the tin until all is used up. Swirl a little with a knife, then carefully level the surface.

4 Bake in the pre-heated oven for about 40 minutes or until well risen and the top of the cake springs back when lightly pressed with a finger. Leave to cool in the tin for a few minutes then turn out, peel off the parchment and finish cooling on a wire rack.

5 To make the icing, break the plain chocolate into pieces, then melt it gently with the water and the butter in a bowl set over a pan of hot water, stirring occasionally. Pour over the cake and then leave to set for about 1 hour. Break the milk chocolate into pieces then melt it in a small bowl set over a pan of hot water. Spoon into a paper piping bag, cut off the tip of the bag and drizzle the chocolate over the top of the plain chocolate icing. Leave to set.

TIP
If you don't have a piping bag, use two plastic food bags, which have been put inside each other for strength and snip off one corner to create a funnel.

CHAPTER FIVE

Cupcakes and other Small Bakes

I love the variety of small cakes, from everyday bakes like cupcakes, fairy cakes and muffins to pastry-based Eccles Cakes, coconut-covered English Madeleines and shell-shaped, elegant French Madeleines.

Once a basic recipe has been mastered, it can be reinvented with just a few extra ingredients: it can be flavoured with orange, chocolate, vanilla or coffee, the sponge or icing can be tinted with natural food colouring and the cake can be covered in butter icing, fondant or glacé icing then topped with little sweets.

Ordinary cakes can be transformed into special treats, such as dainty **Iced Fairy Cakes** (page 114) and **Butterfly Cakes** (page 118) for children's parties, as well as beautifully iced **Cupcakes** (page 121) piled high on cake stands for birthday and wedding celebrations.

As well as looking attractive, small cakes have the added bonuses of being quick to make and taking less time to cook in the oven. They are perfect for children to help make, to go in lunch boxes and to take on picnics.

One of the main advantages of small cakes as far as I am concerned, is that they can be frozen. If you have a small family, then make one or two batches and then, when the cakes are completely cold, freeze the surplus in freezer bags. You can keep them frozen for up to 3 weeks, taking out as many as you need and leaving the rest for another time.

Fairy Cakes

Classic little cakes that are simple enough for children to make, these are made from a Victoria sponge mixture but baked in individual paper cake cases. This makes 12 fairy cakes.

100 g (4 oz) softened butter
100 g (4 oz) caster sugar
2 large eggs
100 g (4 oz) self-raising flour
1 level teaspoon baking
    powder

1 Pre-heat the oven to 200°C/Fan 180°C/Gas 6. Place fairy cake cases into a 12-hole bun tin, to keep a good even shape as they bake.

2 Measure all the ingredients into a large bowl and beat for 2–3 minutes until the mixture is well blended and smooth. Fill each paper case with the mixture.

3 Bake in the pre-heated oven for about 15–20 minutes until the cakes are well risen and golden brown. Lift the paper cases out of the bun tin and cool the cakes on a wire rack.

To make Queen Cakes, follow the recipe above and add 25 g (1 oz) currants to the whisked mixture in step 2.

To make Chocolate Fairy Cakes, follow the recipe above but replace the quantity of self-raising flour with 75g (3 oz) self-raising flour and 25 g (1 oz) sifted cocoa powder.

Iced Fairy Cakes

This makes special little cakes, ideal for childrens' parties.

100 g (4 oz) softened butter
100 g (4 oz) caster sugar
2 large eggs
100 g (4 oz) self-raising flour
1 level teaspoon baking
    powder

FOR THE ICING
225 g (8 oz) sifted icing sugar
2–3 tablespoons warm water
sweets, to decorate

1 Pre-heat the oven to 200°C/Fan 180°C/Gas 6. Place fairy cake cases into a 12-hole bun tin, to keep a good even shape as they bake.

2 Measure all the ingredients into a large bowl and beat for 2–3 minutes until the mixture is well blended and smooth. Fill each paper case with the mixture.

3 Bake in the pre-heated oven for about 15–20 minutes until the cakes are well risen and golden brown. Lift the paper cases out of the bun tin and cool the cakes on a wire rack.

4 Put the icing sugar in a bowl and gradually blend in the warm water until you have a fairly stiff icing. Spoon over the top of the cakes and decorate with sweets.

To make Orange Fairy Cakes, follow the recipe above and add the grated rind of 1 orange in step 2. To make the icing, gradually blend 225 g (8 oz) sifted icing sugar with the juice of 1 orange until you have a fairly stiff icing. Spoon over the tops of the cakes.

Eccles Cakes

These spicy little currant cakes, enclosed in a flaky pastry, come from the north of England. You can use ready-made puff pastry, if you wish, and follow the recipe from step 4. This makes about 8 cakes.

FOR THE FLAKY PASTRY
225 g (8 oz) plain flour
175 g (6 oz) butter
a squeeze of lemon juice
8 tablespoons cold water

FOR THE FILLING
50 g (2 oz) softened butter
50 g (2 oz) light muscovado sugar
½ level teaspoon ground mixed spice
50 g (2 oz) chopped candied peel
100 g (4 oz) currants

TO FINISH
1 large egg white, beaten
a little caster sugar

1 First make the flaky pastry. Measure the flour into a bowl. Divide the butter into 4 equal portions and rub one portion of it into the flour, using the fingertips, until the mixture resembles fine breadcrumbs. Add the lemon juice and water to the flour and mix with a round-bladed knife to form a soft dough.

2 On a lightly floured work surface, gently knead the dough until smooth. Roll out into an oblong three times as long as it is wide (see figure 1). Dot a second portion of the butter in small pieces over the top two-thirds of the pastry (see figure 2). Fold the bottom third of the pastry up over the middle third and the top third down (see figures 3 and 4), then seal the edges well with the edge of your hand (see figure 5). Wrap the pastry in clingfilm and put into the fridge to relax for about 15 minutes.

3 Re-roll the pastry as before, always starting with the folds of the dough to the left, until the remaining portions of butter have been used up. Wrap the pastry again in clingfilm and leave in the fridge for at least 30 minutes before using.

4 Pre-heat the oven to 220°C/Fan 200°C/Gas 7. To make the filling, mix together the butter, sugar, spice, candied peel and

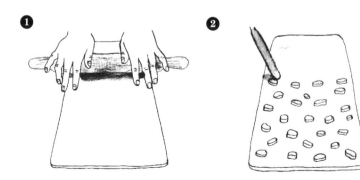

currants. Roll out the pastry thinly and cut into eight rounds about 15 cm (6 in) in diameter (use a saucer as a guide). If using ready-made puff pastry, remember to roll it out very thinly otherwise it will be too thick when cooked.

5 Place a good tablespoon of the filling into the centre of each round, dampen the pastry edges with water and then draw together to enclose the filling. Turn the pastry over and flatten gently with the rolling pin so that the currants just show through. Re-shape to a round with the hands if necessary. Make 3 small cuts in the top of each cake, brush with the beaten egg white and sprinkle with caster sugar. Transfer to a baking tray.

6 Bake in the pre-heated oven for about 10–15 minutes until golden. Leave to cool on the baking tray for a few minutes before lifting on to a wire rack to cool completely.

TIP
For light pastry, incorporate as much air as possible by sifting flour from a height, cutting in small pieces of butter with a knife, and lifting your hands well above the bowl when rubbing in.

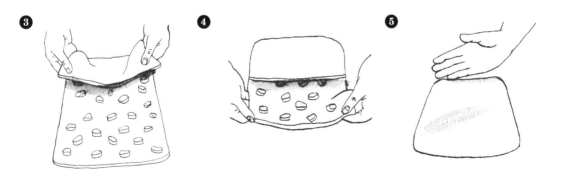

Butterfly Cakes

Butterfly cakes are quick and easy to make and very effective for a children's party.

100 g (4 oz) softened butter
100 g (4 oz) caster sugar
2 large eggs
100 g (4 oz) self-raising flour
1 level teaspoon baking
    powder

FOR THE ICING
175 g (6 oz) softened butter
350 g (12 oz) sifted icing sugar

TO FINISH
sifted icing sugar, to dust

1 Pre-heat the oven to 200°C/Fan 180°C/Gas 6. Place fairy cake cases into a 12-hole bun tin, to keep a good even shape as they bake.

2 Measure all the ingredients into a large bowl and beat well for 2–3 minutes until the mixture is well blended and smooth. Fill each paper case with the mixture.

3 Bake in the pre-heated oven for about 15–20 minutes until the cakes are well risen and golden brown. Lift the paper cases out of the bun tin and cool the cakes on a wire rack.

4 To make the icing, beat the butter and icing sugar together until well blended. Cut a slice from the top of each cake and cut this slice in half. Pipe a swirl of butter cream into the centre of each cake and place the half slices of cake on top to resemble butterfly wings. Dust the cakes with icing sugar to finish.

To make Chocolate Butterfly Cakes, follow the recipe opposite, then make chocolate icing by mixing 2 tablespoons cocoa with 3 tablespoons hot water. Allow to cool slightly, then beat in 175 g (6 oz) softened butter and 350 g (12 oz) sifted icing sugar until well blended.

To make these butterfly cakes really chocolatey, you can replace 25 g (1 oz) of self-raising flour from the cake ingredients with 25 g (1 oz) cocoa to make the cakes chocolate flavour too.

To make Orange or Lemon Butterfly Cakes add the grated rind of 1 orange or lemon to the cake mixture in step 2. Ice them with a butter cream made from butter, icing sugar and a little orange or lemon juice, then dust with icing sugar.

Cupcakes

Cupcakes are great for teatime, or arranged stacked on a cake stand instead of a large traditional birthday cake or even a wedding cake. Cupcakes are a different shape to fairy cakes – the cases they are baked in are deeper and have less angular sides.

100g (4oz) softened butter
150g (5oz) self-raising flour
150g (5oz) caster sugar
3 tablespoons milk
2 large eggs
½ teaspoon vanilla extract

FOR THE ICING
(choose one type of icing or
    halve the ingredients and
    make a mixture of both)

BUTTER ICING
100g (4oz) softened butter
225g (8oz) sifted icing sugar
½ teaspoon vanilla extract

GLACÉ ICING
225g (8oz) sifted icing sugar
juice of 1 lemon, warmed

TO DECORATE
plain or white chocolate
    curls or shavings,
silver hearts,
100 and 1000's,
silver balls,
coloured sweets, to decorate

1 Pre-heat the oven to 180°C/Fan 160°C/Gas 4. Put muffin cases into a 12-hole muffin tin, to keep a good even shape as they bake.

2 Measure all the cupcake ingredients into a large bowl and beat until blended and smooth. Spoon evenly between the paper cases.

3 Bake in the pre-heated oven for about 20–25 minutes until risen and golden brown. Lift the paper cases out of the tin and cool the cakes on a wire rack until completely cold before icing.

4 To make the butter icing, beat together all the ingredients to give a creamy thick icing, then smooth over the cold cupcakes. To make the glacé icing, gradually add the warmed lemon juice to the icing sugar to give a glossy icing. If decorating with chocolate curls, allow the chocolate bar to reach room temperature then shave using a vegetable peeler.

To make Fruity Celebration Cupcakes, follow the ingredients and method for Rich Fruit Cake (see page 64) and cook at 160°C/Fan 140°C/Gas 3 for about 1 hour. Ice with fondant icing (see page 390).

TIP
If you are making a double quantity of cupcakes or are using a smaller tin, you can prepare your cupcake mixture in one go and spoon it into the paper cases ready to go into the oven. They will come to no harm, as raising agents react more slowly nowadays. Bake only one tray of cupcakes at a time though.

Try adding 2 tablespoons of cocoa powder or 1 teaspoon of coffee essence to the butter icing to make chocolate or coffee icing. When making the glacé icing, it helps to warm the lemon juice before mixing with the icing sugar as it then sets better.

Apricot Swiss Cakes

Traditionally a red jam is used for the centre of these cakes, which are buttery and very delicious.

225 g (8 oz) butter
75 g (3 oz) sifted icing sugar
200 g (7 oz) self-raising flour
50 g (2 oz) cornflour

TO FINISH
a little apricot jam
icing sugar

1 Pre-heat the oven to 180°C/Fan 160°C/Gas 4. Place fairy cake cases into a 12-hole bun tin.

2 Soften the butter in a large bowl. Add the icing sugar and beat well until really soft and fluffy. Stir in the flours and mix until smooth. Spoon the mixture into a large piping bag fitted with a large star nozzle. Pipe circles of the mixture into the base of each paper case until all the mixture is used up.

3 Bake in the pre-heated oven for about 15–20 minutes or until pale golden brown. Remove the paper cases from the tin and cool the cakes on a wire rack. Put a small amount of apricot jam on to the centre of each cake. Dust lightly with sifted icing sugar.

French Madeleines

These shell-shaped cakes are made using a madeleine tin, available from specialist kitchen shops and department stores. It is worth greasing and flouring the tins well so that the cakes come out cleanly. They are best on the day of making and, in France, are traditionally dipped into tea to eat. This recipe makes about 30 madeleines.

150 g (5 oz) butter
3 large eggs
150 g (5 oz) caster sugar
150 g (5 oz) self-raising flour
½ level teaspoon baking
    powder
grated rind of 1 lemon

1 Pre-heat the oven to 220°C/Fan 200°C/Gas 7. Grease a madeleine tray, dust with flour and shake off any excess.

2 Melt the butter in a small pan and allow to cool slightly. Measure the eggs and sugar into a large bowl and whisk until pale and thick.

3 Sift in half the flour with the baking powder along with the lemon rind and fold in gently. Pour in half the melted butter around the edge of the bowl and fold in. Repeat the process with the remaining flour and butter. Spoon the mixture into the prepared moulds so that it is just level with the tops.

4 Bake in the pre-heated oven for about 8–10 minutes until well risen, golden and springy to the touch. Ease out of the tins with a small palette knife and cool on a wire rack. Grease and flour the tins again and repeat until all the mixture has been used up.

English Madeleines

For this recipe, you will need dariole moulds, which are available from specialist cook shops and department stores. If you don't have ten, make the madeleines in two batches.

100 g (4 oz) softened butter
100 g (4 oz) caster sugar
2 large eggs
100 g (4 oz) self-raising flour
1 level teaspoon baking
    powder
2–3 drops vanilla extract

TO FINISH
4 tablespoons raspberry
    or strawberry jam
50 g (2 oz) desiccated coconut
5 red or natural glacé cherries

1 Pre-heat the oven to 180°C/Fan 160°C/Gas 4. Grease 10 dariole moulds then line the base of each mould with baking parchment. Stand the tins on a baking tray.

2 Measure the cake ingredients into a large bowl and beat until the mixture is well blended and smooth. Spoon the mixture into the dariole moulds, filling them about half full.

3 Bake in the pre-heated oven for about 20 minutes until well risen and firm to the touch. Leave to cool in the moulds for 5 minutes then turn out, peel off the parchment and finish cooling on a wire rack.

4 When the cakes are cool, trim the bases so that they stand firmly. Push the raspberry or strawberry jam through a sieve, then put into a small pan and warm through. Spread the coconut out on a large plate. Use a fork to spear the bases of the cakes to hold them. Brush them with the warm jam, then roll in the coconut to coat. Cut the glacé cherries in half and decorate each madeleine with a half.

Chocolate Chip American Muffins

These large muffins look quite impressive. They're best eaten on the day of baking.

250 g (9 oz) self-raising flour
1 level teaspoon baking powder
50 g (2 oz) softened butter
75 g (3 oz) caster sugar
175 g (6 oz) plain chocolate chips
2 large eggs
1 teaspoon vanilla extract
250 ml (9 fl oz) milk

1 Pre-heat the oven to 200°C/Fan 180°C/Gas 6. Place muffin cases into a 12-hole muffin tin.

2 Measure the flour and baking powder into a large bowl, then add the butter and rub into the flour until the mixture resembles fine breadcrumbs. Stir in the sugar and chocolate chips.

3 Mix together the eggs, vanilla extract and milk, then pour the mixture all in one go into the dry ingredients. Mix quickly with a wooden spoon to blend. The mixture should have a lumpy consistency. Spoon the mixture into the paper cases in the tin, filling almost to the top.

4 Bake in the pre-heated oven for about 20–25 minutes or until well risen and firm to the touch. Leave to cool for a few minutes in the tray, then lift out the paper cases and cool the muffins for a little longer on a wire rack.

St Clements Muffins

Not breakfast muffins and, therefore, sweeter, these are delicious at any time and children love them, too. This recipe makes 24 mini muffins or 12 large muffins.

1 thin-skinned orange, washed
grated rind of 1 lemon
100 g (4 oz) caster sugar
1 large egg
100 ml (3½ fl oz) milk
50 g (2 oz) butter, melted and cooled slightly
1 level teaspoon baking powder
175 g (6 oz) self-raising flour
icing sugar, for dusting

1 Pre-heat the oven to 200°C/Fan 180°C/Gas 6. Line two 12-hole mini muffin tins or one 12-hole muffin tin with appropriately-sized muffin cases. If you don't have any cases, grease the tins well.

2 Cut the whole orange into chunks and remove any pips with the point of a knife. Process the orange in a food processor until finely chopped. Put all the remaining ingredients except the icing sugar into a mixing bowl and beat quickly until just mixed. Gently stir in the chopped orange. Spoon the mixture into the prepared tins, filling them almost to the top.

3 If making mini muffins, bake for about 15 minutes, until well risen, golden and firm to the touch. The large muffins will take a little longer to cook about 20–25 minutes. Lift the paper cases out of the tin and leave the muffins to cool on a wire rack. If you didn't use cases, leave the muffins to cool before trying to remove them – if you try to remove them when they are hot, they tend to come apart. Dust with icing sugar to serve.

Blueberry Muffins

The American muffin has increased in popularity in Britain. These are best served warm, traditionally at breakfast time.

250 g (9 oz) self-raising flour
1 level teaspoon baking
   powder
50 g (2 oz) softened butter
75 g (3 oz) caster sugar
175 g (6 oz) blueberries
grated rind of 1 lemon
2 large eggs
250 ml (9 fl oz) milk

1 Pre-heat the oven to 200°C/Fan 180°C/Gas 6. Place muffin cases in a 12-hole muffin tin.

2 Measure the flour and baking powder into a large bowl. Rub in the butter with the fingertips until the mixture resembles fine breadcrumbs. Stir in the sugar, blueberries and the grated lemon rind.

3 Mix together the eggs and milk, then pour the mixture all in one go into the dry ingredients. Mix quickly to blend. The mixture should have a lumpy consistency. Spoon the mixture into the prepared tins or paper cases, filling almost to the top.

4 Bake in the pre-heated oven for about 20–25 minutes until well risen, golden and firm to the touch. Leave to cool for a few minutes in the tray, then lift out the paper cases and cool the muffins for a few minutes on a wire rack. Serve warm.

CHAPTER SIX

Celebration Cakes

For me Christmas wouldn't be complete without a **Christmas cake** (page 136), or Easter without **Simnel Cake** (page 146). Celebrations – whether a major calendar celebration like New Year or a more personal occasion like a birthday, an anniversary, a wedding or a christening – call for special cakes.

Everyone has their own idea of what a celebration should be, and many families have their favourite celebration cakes. Bearing this in mind I've chosen my most popular celebration cakes here, including a mixture of sponge and fruit cakes that I hope will appeal to everyone.

If you are trying out a celebration cake for the first time, there are recipes here that should guarantee you success. My **Classic Rich Christmas Cake** (page 134) is virtually foolproof and you'll find this recipe easy to follow. I've also worked out all the ingredient quantities and timings for a wide range of round and square cake tins, so you simply have to choose the instructions that suit your tins. If you haven't got enough time before Christmas to mature a traditional Christmas Cake, I've also included delicious, lighter versions that can be made at short notice as they don't require feeding.

I think my recipe for **Christening Cake** (page 149) is really special, made with a light sponge that's split into three and sandwiched together with cream and lemon curd then covered in fondant icing. And I couldn't leave out two enduring favourites that I am asked for time and again: my rich **Divine Chocolate Birthday Cake** (opposite) and **American Chocolate Wedding Cake** (page 143). Whichever recipes you choose to bake, I hope they make your celebration even more memorable.

Divine Chocolate Birthday Cake

This is a very close-textured 'fudgy' cake that needs no filling. There is no flour in this recipe; ground almonds give the flavour and texture. Decorate the cake with crystallized flowers (see page 393) and candles, if you like. This recipe serves about 10 people.

6 large eggs, 5 of them
   separated
215 g (7½ oz) caster sugar
265 g (9½ oz) plain chocolate
   (39 per cent cocoa solids)
1 level teaspoon instant coffee
   granules
1 teaspoon hot water
150 g (5 oz) ground almonds

FOR THE ICING
4 tablespoons apricot jam
225 g (8 oz) plain chocolate
   (39 per cent cocoa solids)
100 g (4 oz) unsalted butter

1 Pre-heat the oven to 190°C/Fan 170°C/Gas 5. Grease a 23 cm (9 in) deep round cake tin then line the base with baking parchment.

2 Place the egg yolks and whole egg in a large bowl with the sugar and beat together until thick and light in colour. Melt the chocolate gently in a heatproof bowl set over a pan of simmering water, stirring occasionally. Dissolve the coffee granules in the water and add to the melted chocolate. Cool slightly, then stir into the egg mixture along with the ground almonds.

3 In a separate bowl, whisk the egg whites until stiff but not dry. Carefully fold into the egg and chocolate mixture. Turn into the prepared tin and gently level the surface.

4 Bake in the pre-heated oven for about 50 minutes or until well risen, and a skewer inserted into the centre comes out clean. Leave to cool in the tin for 10 minutes then turn out, peel off the parchment and finish cooling on a wire rack.

5 Measure the apricot jam into a small saucepan and allow to melt over a low heat. Brush over the cake. To make the icing, melt the chocolate gently in a bowl set over a pan of hot water, stirring occasionally. Add the butter and stir until the icing has the consistency of thick pouring cream, cooling if necessary.

6 Stand the wire rack on a baking tray to catch any drips, then pour the icing over the cake smoothing it over the top and sides with a palette knife. Allow to set, then decorate if you like.

Classic Rich Christmas Cake

This is a wonderful, rich traditional fruit cake. It can be made up to three months in advance. Make sure you allow plenty of time to 'feed' the cake with brandy and let it mature.

100 g (4 oz) red or natural
   glacé cherries
100 g (4 oz) ready-to-eat
   dried apricots
275 g (10 oz) currants
175 g (6 oz) sultanas
175 g (6 oz) raisins
50 g (2 oz) finely chopped
   candied peel
3 tablespoons brandy
225 g (8 oz) plain flour
¼ level teaspoon freshly
   grated nutmeg
½ level teaspoon ground
   mixed spice
225 g (8 oz) softened butter
225 g (8 oz) dark
   muscovado sugar
4 large eggs
50 g (2 oz) chopped almonds
1 scant tablespoon
   black treacle
grated rind of 1 lemon
grated rind of 1 orange

TO FINISH
brandy, to feed
675 g (1½ lb) almond paste
   or marzipan (see page 388
   for almond paste recipe)
675 g (1½ lb) fondant or
   ready-to-roll icing (see
   page 390)

1 Begin this cake the night before you want to bake it. Cut the cherries into quarters, put in a sieve and rinse under running water. Drain well then dry thoroughly on kitchen paper. Snip the apricots into pieces. Measure the fruits into a large bowl, mix in the brandy, cover and leave in a cool place overnight.

2 Pre-heat the oven to 140°C/Fan 120°C/Gas 1. Grease a 20 cm (8 in) deep round cake tin then line the base and sides with a double layer of baking parchment.

3 Measure the flour, spices, butter, sugar, eggs, almonds, treacle and lemon and orange rinds into a large bowl. Beat well, then fold in the soaked fruits. Spoon the mixture into the prepared tin and spread out evenly with the back of a spoon. Cover the top of the cake loosely with a double layer of baking parchment.

4 Bake in the pre-heated oven for about 4½–4¾ hours or until the cake feels firm to the touch and a skewer inserted into the centre comes out clean. Leave the cake to cool in the tin.

5 When cool, pierce the cake at intervals with a fine skewer and feed with a little brandy. Wrap the completely cold cake in a double layer of baking parchment, and again in foil, and store in a cool place, feeding at intervals with more brandy. Don't remove the lining parchment when storing as this helps to keep the cake moist. Cover the cake with almond paste about a week before icing.

6 Cover the cake with fondant or ready-to-roll icing. Colour the almond paste (left over from putting the almond paste on to the cake) dark green. Roll out on a board that has been lightly sprinkled with icing sugar and cut into 2.5 cm (1 in) wide strips. Cut these into diamonds and then, with the base of an icing nozzle, remove half circles from the sides of the diamonds to give holly-shaped leaves. Make vein marks on the leaves with a sharp knife, bend the leaves over the handles of wooden spoons and

TO DECORATE
almond paste (leftover from
    putting over the cake)
green food colouring
ribbon, holly or your
    favourite decorations

leave to dry. Decorate the top of the cake with the almond-paste holly leaves and finish by tying a ribbon around the sides of the cake.

Below is a table of ingredients needed for various cake tin sizes. Simply choose the size then follow the recipe for Classic Rich Christmas Cake using the ingredients quantities listed below.

	15 cm (6 in) round / 12.5cm (5 in) square	18 cm (7 in) round / 15 cm (6 in) square	20 cm (8 in) round / 18 cm (7 in) square	23 cm (9 in) round / 20 cm (8 in) square	25 cm (10 in) round / 23 cm (9 in) square	28 cm (11 in) round / 25 cm (10 in) square	30 cm (12 in) round / 28 cm (11 in) square	33 cm (13 in) round / 30 cm (12 in) square
Glacé cherries	50 g (2 oz)	75 g (3 oz)	100 g (4 oz)	150 g (5 oz)	175 g (6 oz)	225 g (8 oz)	275 g (10 oz)	350 g (12 oz)
Ready-to-eat dried apricots	50 g (2 oz)	75 g (3 oz)	100 g (4 oz)	150 g (5 oz)	175 g (6 oz)	225 g (8 oz)	275 g (10 oz)	350 g (12 oz)
Currants	150 g (5 oz)	200 g (7 oz)	275 g (10 oz)	400 g (14 oz)	450 g (1 lb)	550 g (1¼ lb)	750 g (1½ lb)	800 g (1¾ lb)
Sultanas	75 g (3 oz)	100 g (4 oz)	175 g (6 oz)	225 g (8 oz)	275 g (10 oz)	350 g (12 oz)	450 g (1 lb)	550 g (1¼ lb)
Raisins	75 g (3 oz)	100 g (4 oz)	175 g (6 oz)	225 g (8 oz)	275 g (10 oz)	350 g (12 oz)	450 g (1 lb)	550 g (1¼ lb)
Candied peel	25 g (1 oz)	40 g (1½ oz)	50 g (2 oz)	65 g (2½ oz)	75 g (3 oz)	100 g (4 oz)	150 g (5 oz)	175 g (6 oz)
Brandy	1½ tbsp	2 tbsp	3 tbsp	4 tbsp	5 tbsp	6 tbsp	7 tbsp	8 tbsp
Plain flour	100 g (4 oz)	175 g (6 oz)	225 g (8 oz)	275 g (10 oz)	400 g (14 oz)	450 g (1 lb)	500 g (1 lb 2 oz)	550 g (1¼ lb)
Grated nutmeg	⅛ tsp	scant ¼ tsp	¼ tsp	scant ½ tsp	½ tsp	½ tsp	¾ tsp	1 tsp
Ground mixed spice	¼ tsp	scant ½ tsp	½ tsp	¾ tsp	¾ tsp	1 tsp	1¼ tsp	1½ tsp
Softened butter	100 g (4 oz)	175 g (6 oz)	225 g (8 oz)	275 g (10 oz)	400 g (14 oz)	450 g (1 lb)	500 g (1 lb 2 oz)	550 g (1¼ lb)
Dark musc. sugar	100 g (4 oz)	175 g (6 oz)	225 g (8 oz)	275 g (10 oz)	400 g (14 oz)	450 g (1 lb)	500 g (1 lb 2 oz)	550 g (1¼ lb)
Large eggs	2	3	4	5	7	8	9	10
Chopped almonds	25 g (1 oz)	40 g (1½ oz)	50 g (2 oz)	65 g (2½ oz)	75 g (3 oz)	100 g (4 oz)	150 g (5 oz)	175 g (6 oz)
Black treacle	½ tbsp	rounded ½ tbsp	scant 1 tbsp	1 tbsp	1½ tbsp	2 tbsp	3 tbsp	4 tbsp
Rind lemon	½	½	1	1½	2	2	3	3
Rind orange	½	½	1	1½	2	2	3	3
Baking times (approx.)	3½ hrs	4 hrs	4½ hrs	4¾ hrs	5 hrs	5½ hrs	6 hrs	6½ hrs

Victorian Christmas Cake

Unlike traditional Christmas cakes, this mixture produces a light, yet succulent cake.

350 g (12 oz) red or natural
   glacé cherries
225 g (8 oz) can pineapple
   in natural juice
350 g (12 oz) ready-to-eat
   dried apricots
100 g (4 oz) blanched almonds
finely grated rind of 2 lemons
350 g (12 oz) sultanas
250 g (9 oz) self-raising flour
250 g (9 oz) caster sugar
250 g (9 oz) softened butter
75 g (3 oz) ground almonds
5 large eggs

TO DECORATE
blanched almonds
red or natural glacé cherries
glacé pineapple (available
   from health-food shops)
100 g (4 oz) sifted icing sugar

1 Pre-heat the oven to 160°C/Fan 140°C/Gas 3. Grease a 23 cm (9 in) deep round cake tin then line the base and sides with a double layer of baking parchment.

2 Cut the cherries into quarters, put in a sieve and rinse under running water then drain well. Drain and roughly chop the pineapple, then dry the pineapple and cherries very thoroughly on kitchen paper. Snip the apricots into pieces. Roughly chop the almonds. Place the prepared fruit and nuts in a bowl with the grated lemon rind and sultanas and gently mix together.

3 Measure the remaining ingredients into a large bowl and beat well for 1 minute until smooth. Lightly fold in the fruit and nuts then turn the mixture into the prepared cake tin. Level the surface and decorate the top with blanched whole almonds, halved glacé cherries and pieces of glacé pineapple.

4 Bake in the pre-heated oven for about 2¼ hours or until golden brown. A skewer inserted into the centre of the cake should come out clean. Cover the cake loosely with foil after 1 hour to prevent the top becoming too dark. Leave to cool in the tin for 30 minutes then turn out, peel off the parchment and finish cooling on a wire rack. Mix the icing sugar with a little water, and drizzle over the cake to glaze.

Fast Mincemeat Christmas Cake

I've often been asked for this recipe, which doesn't have to be made in advance or fed with brandy. The cake is light and moist. Cover it with royal icing, as this is the simplest and quickest decoration for a Christmas cake, and finish with a ribbon and bow.

150 g (5 oz) softened butter
150 g (5 oz) light muscovado
    sugar
2 large eggs
225 g (8 oz) self-raising flour
400 g (14 oz) luxury
    mincemeat
175 g (6 oz) currants
50 g (2 oz) chopped almonds

TO DECORATE
25 cm (10 in) round silver
    cake board
675 g (1½ lb) almond paste
    or marzipan (see page 388
    for almond paste recipe)
1 quantity of royal icing
    (see page 391)
ribbon, to decorate

1 Pre-heat the oven to 160°C/Fan 140°C/Gas 3. Grease a 20 cm (8 in) deep round cake tin then line the base and sides with baking parchment.

2 Measure all the cake ingredients into a large bowl and beat well for 1 minute until thoroughly mixed. Turn into the prepared tin and level the surface.

3 Bake in the pre-heated oven for about 1¾ hours or until a skewer inserted into the centre comes out clean and the cake is shrinking from the sides of the tin. Cover the cake with foil after 1 hour if beginning to brown too much. Leave to cool in the tin for 10 minutes then turn out, peel off the parchment and finish cooling on a wire rack.

4 Cover the cake with almond paste about a week before icing. Make up the royal icing (see page 391) and spread some of the icing thickly over the sides of the cake, smoothing with a palette knife. Spoon more royal icing on to the top of the cake, smooth a strip in the centre (this is where the ribbon will go) then pull the remainder into peaks with the back of a spoon. Leave the icing to harden for a few hours, then decorate the cake with ribbon.

Bûche de Noël

**This is a version of the French Christmas log, which is suitable
for serving as a dessert or with coffee. This recipe serves 8.**

1 unfilled Chocolate Swiss
Roll (see page 47)

FOR THE FILLING
1 tablespoon coffee essence
4 tablespoons hot milk
225 g (8 oz) unsweetened
chestnut purée
50 g (2 oz) caster sugar
150 ml (¼ pint) whipping or
double cream, whipped
2 tablespoons brandy

FOR THE TOPPING
300 ml (½ pint) whipping or
double cream, whipped
cocoa powder, to dust
holly leaves, to decorate

1 First make the Chocolate Swiss Roll (page 47). Roll with baking
parchment inside and leave to cool.

2 While it is cooling, make the filling. Mix the coffee essence with
the milk. Sieve the chestnut purée into a bowl and beat in the
coffee mixture and the sugar until the mixture is smooth. Fold the
whipped cream into the chestnut purée along with the brandy.

3 Carefully unroll the Swiss roll, remove the parchment and
spread the chestnut filling all over the cake, then re-roll. Cut a
small slice off at an angle from one of the ends of the Swiss roll,
place the Swiss roll on to a serving plate or board, and attach
the slice to look like a branch.

4 Spread the whipped cream over the cake to cover completely,
using a small palette knife in long strokes to give the bark effect.
Dust lightly with cocoa and decorate with holly leaves.

New Year Tipsy Cake

A 'tipsy' cake seems quite appropriate for a New Year's celebration. I've filled and topped the cake with orange segments, but you can make this cake with various fruits. It's also very nice with red summer berries, if made in warmer months. Potato flour is available from health-food shops and good delicatessens. This recipes serves 8–10 people.

5 large eggs, 2 of them
   separated
275 g (10 oz) caster sugar
65 g (2½ oz) sifted
   self-raising flour
65 g (2½ oz) sifted potato
   flour (fecule) or cornflour
grated rind of 1 lemon

FOR SOAKING THE CAKE
50 g (2 oz) granulated sugar
3 tablespoons water
150 ml (¼ pint) sweet
   white wine
1 tablespoon brandy

FOR THE FILLING
   AND DECORATION
225 g (8 oz) orange segments
450 ml (¾ pint) whipping or
   double cream, whipped
1 oranges, thinly sliced,
   to decorate

1 Pre-heat the oven to 180°C/Fan 160°C/Gas 4. Grease a 23 cm (9 in) deep round cake tin then line the base with baking parchment.

2 Put the 3 whole eggs, the 2 egg yolks and the sugar into a large bowl and beat over hot water until thick and mousse-like, and the mixture leaves a trail when the whisk is lifted.

3 In a separate bowl, whisk the egg whites until stiff but not dry and fold into the mixture, along with the flours and the grated lemon rind. Turn into the prepared tin.

4 Bake in the pre-heated oven for about 45–50 minutes or until the cake is well risen, golden and the surface springs back when lightly pressed with the fingertip. Leave to cool in the tin for 10 minutes then turn out, peel off the parchment and finish cooling on a wire rack.

5 In a small pan, gently dissolve the granulated sugar in the water over a low heat. When the sugar has completely dissolved, bring the syrup to the boil and allow to boil for 2 minutes. Allow to cool, then add the wine and the brandy.

6 When the cake is cold, use a serrated knife to make a cut in the top around the cake about 2.5 cm (1 in) in from the edge and about 4 cm (1½ in) deep. Holding the knife almost horizontally, cut towards the centre of the cake to remove a 'lid' of sponge, leaving a sponge flan case shape. Put the lid to one side.

7 Soak the cake with two-thirds of the sugar syrup and fill with the orange segments and half the whipped cream. Replace the 'lid' and moisten with the remaining syrup. Smooth the remaining cream over the top and sides of the cake and decorate with thin slices of orange.

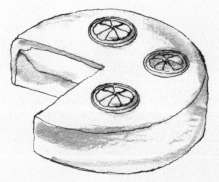

American Chocolate Wedding Cake

This cake serves about 100 people and makes a super dessert for a wedding breakfast served with raspberry coulis (see page 391). You can make this recipe all in one go, but you will need huge bowls. The separate quantities needed to make each layer individually have also been included (overleaf), which some might find an easier method – also useful if you want to make one of the layers for a practice run. The cakes can be frozen for up to 2 months, but the icing should be made the day before the wedding.

THE TOTAL INGREDIENTS NEEDED

1.6 kg (3 lbs 9 oz) plain chocolate (39 per cent cocoa solids), broken into pieces
30 large eggs, separated
8 large eggs, whole
1.25 kg (2½ lb) caster sugar
840 g (1 lb 14 oz) ground almonds
7½ teaspoons freshly made black coffee
225 g (8 oz) apricot jam

FOR THE ICING

1.25 kg (2½ lb) plain chocolate (39 per cent cocoa solids)
450 g (1 lb) unsalted butter

TO DECORATE

foliage and flowers

To make the complete cake in one go, follow the method below, using the total ingredients list. To make each layer separately, follow the separate ingredients lists (overleaf) and use the appropriate cooking time for each cake size.

1 Pre-heat the oven to 190°C/Fan 170°C/Gas 5. Lightly grease a 15 cm (6 in), a 23 cm (9 in) and a 30 cm (12 in) deep round cake tin then line the base and sides of each tin with baking parchment.

2 Melt the chocolate in a bowl set over a pan of simmering water, stirring occasionally, then leave to cool slightly. Measure the yolks, whole eggs and sugar into a large bowl and beat until thick and light. Add the melted chocolate along with the almonds and the coffee. In a separate bowl, whisk the egg whites until stiff but not dry. Fold carefully into the chocolate mixture, then divide the mixture between the prepared tins.

3 Bake in the pre-heated oven (they can all go into the oven at once, put the large cake on the middle shelf and the two smaller cakes on the top shelf). The small cake will take about 45 minutes, the medium cake about 1–1¼ hours and the large cake about 1½ –1¾ hours (cover loosely with foil after 1 hour). Test the centre of each with a skewer, which should come out just about clean. Leave to cool in the tins for a few minutes then turn out, peel off the baking parchment and finish cooling on a wire rack. At this point, the cakes can be frozen.

continued overleaf

15 CM (6 IN) CAKE

175 g (6 oz) plain chocolate (39 per cent
    cocoa solids), broken into pieces
3 large eggs, separated
1 large egg, whole
150 g (5 oz) caster sugar
75 g (3 oz) ground almonds
½ teaspoon freshly made black coffee
2 tablespoons apricot jam

FOR THE ICING

225 g (8 oz) plain chocolate (39 per cent
    cocoa solids)
75 g (3 oz) unsalted butter

23 CM (9 IN) CAKE

525 g (1 lb 3 oz) plain chocolate (39 per cent
    cocoa solids), broken into pieces
10 large eggs, separated
2 large eggs, whole
425 g (15 oz) caster sugar
275 g (10 oz) ground almonds
2½ teaspoons freshly made black coffee
75 g (3 oz) apricot jam

FOR THE ICING

350 g (12 oz) plain chocolate (39 per cent
    cocoa solids)
150 g (5 oz) unsalted butter

30 CM (12 IN) CAKE

900 g (2 lb) plain chocolate (39 per cent
    cocoa solids), broken into pieces
17 large eggs, separated
5 large eggs, whole
700 g (1 lb 9 oz) caster sugar
475 g (1 lb 1 oz) ground almonds
4½ teaspoons freshly made black coffee
100 g (4 oz) apricot jam

FOR THE ICING

550 g (1¼ lb) plain chocolate (39 per cent
    cocoa solids)
225 g (8 oz) unsalted butter

4 Turn the cold cakes upside down so that
the flat side is uppermost. Push the apricot
jam through a sieve, then brush over the tops
and sides of the cakes. For the icing, break
the chocolate into pieces and melt gently in a
bowl over a pan of simmering water, stirring
occasionally, then add the butter and stir until
the butter has melted. Stand each cake on the
wire rack on a baking tray to catch any drips,
then pour over the chocolate icing. Smooth the
top and sides with a palette knife and then
leave to set in a cool place.

5 Transport the cake as separate layers
and assemble and decorate *in situ*. Place the
largest cake on a cake board or serving plate
then carefully stack the other two cakes on top.
Decorate, with fresh flowers and foliage
to match the wedding bouquet. Serve with
Raspberry Coulis (page 391).

TIPS
The cake will freeze un-iced for up to a month
or can be made up to 7 days ahead. It is normal
for the cakes to have crusty tops when baked
– trim if necessary. Use a good-quality
chocolate for the icing. I find better quality
chocolates give a smoother finish. The high
chocolate and sugar content make the cakes
susceptible to burning, so do keep an eye on
them. You may need to cover them with foil or
baking parchment. The cakes are firm enough
to stack as they are but use thin cake boards
slightly smaller than each layer if you feel
happier. Don't ice the cake more than a day
before the wedding to prevent it loosing its
sheen. Once iced, keep the cake in a cool place,
but not in the fridge.

Tiny Fruit Cakes

Individual fruit cakes are particularly welcome gifts for those who live on their own or have small appetites. This recipes makes 3 cakes. Small 220 g baked bean cans are an ideal size, but you can also use English muffin rings.

40 g (1½ oz) red or natural glacé cherries
50 g (2 oz) raisins
50 g (2 oz) sultanas
50 g (2 oz) currants
25 g (1 oz) ready-to-eat dried apricots
15 g (½ oz) chopped candied peel
2 teaspoons brandy, rum or sherry, plus extra for feeding the cake
15 g (½ oz) chopped blanched almonds
15 g (½ oz) ground almonds
grated rind of ¼ lemon
75 g (3 oz) plain flour
½ level teaspoon mixed ground spice
50 g (2 oz) dark muscovado sugar
50 g (2 oz) softened butter
2 teaspoons black treacle
1 large egg
1 tablespoon flaked almonds

FOR THE ICING
3 tablespoons apricot jam
225 g (8 oz) almond paste or marzipan (see page 388 for almond paste recipe)
225 g (8 oz) fondant or ready-to-roll icing (see page 390)

1 Cut the cherries into quarters, put in a sieve and rinse under running water. Drain well then dry thoroughly on kitchen paper. Measure all the dried fruits into a large bowl, add the brandy, rum or sherry, cover the bowl tightly and leave overnight.

2 Pre-heat the oven to 160°C/Fan 140°C/Gas 3. Remove the labels, wash and thoroughly dry three empty 220g (7½ oz) baked bean cans. Grease the cans then line the base and sides of each can with baking parchment.

3 Measure the chopped and ground almonds, lemon rind, flour, mixed spice, sugar, butter, treacle and egg into large bowl and mix together. Beat thoroughly for about 2 minutes until the mixture is smooth. Add the soaked fruit and any liquid to the bowl and stir to mix in thoroughly. Spoon the mixture into the prepared cans, spreading it evenly. Level the surfaces and then sprinkle with flaked almonds.

4 Bake in the pre-heated oven for about 1–1¼ hours or until a fine skewer inserted into the centre comes out clean. Allow the cakes to cool in the tins. Pierce the top of the cakes in several places with a skewer and spoon in a little brandy, rum or sherry.

5 Remove the cakes from the cans but do not remove the baking parchment as this helps to keep the cakes moist. Wrap in more baking parchment and then some foil, and store in a cool place for a week.

6 Sieve the apricot jam and warm it slightly, then brush it over the surface of the cakes. Cover with almond paste and icing in the usual way. Decorate as liked.

Easter Simnel Cake

This has become the traditional Easter cake, but originally it was given by servant girls to their mothers when they went home on Mothering Sunday. The almond-paste balls represent the eleven apostles (not including Judas).

100 g (4 oz) red or natural
   glacé cherries
225 g (8 oz) softened butter
225 g (8 oz) light muscovado
   sugar
4 large eggs
225 g (8 oz) self-raising flour
225 g (8 oz) sultanas
100 g (4 oz) currants
50 g (2 oz) chopped
   candied peel
grated rind of 2 lemons
2 level teaspoons ground
   mixed spice

FOR THE FILLING
   AND TOPPING
450 g (1 lb) almond paste
   or marzipan (see page 388
   for almond paste recipe)
2 tablespoons apricot jam
1 large egg, beaten, to glaze

1 Pre-heat the oven to 150°C/Fan 130°C/Gas 2. Grease a 20 cm (8 in) deep round cake tin then line the base and sides with baking parchment.

2 Cut the cherries into quarters, put in a sieve and rinse under running water. Drain well then dry thoroughly on kitchen paper. Measure all the cake ingredients into a large mixing bowl and beat well until thoroughly blended. Place half the mixture into the prepared tin and level the surface.

3 Take one-third of the almond paste and roll it out to a circle the size of the tin and then place on top of the cake mixture. Spoon the remaining cake mixture on top and level the surface.

4 Bake in the pre-heated oven for about 2½ hours until well risen, evenly brown and firm to the touch. Cover with foil after 1 hour if the top is browning too quickly. Leave to cool in the tin for 10 minutes then turn out, peel off the parchment and finish cooling on a wire rack.

5 When the cake is cool, brush the top with a little warmed apricot jam and roll out half the remaining almond paste to fit the top. Press firmly on the top and crimp the edges to decorate. Mark a criss-cross pattern on the almond paste with a sharp knife. Form the remaining almond paste into 11 balls.

6 Brush the almond paste with beaten egg and arrange the almond paste balls around the edge of the cake. Brush the tops of the balls with beaten egg, too, and then place the cake under a hot grill to turn the almond paste golden.

Sponge Christening Cake

A lemon cake is perfect for a christening. Colour the icing pale pink for or pale blue, if you like, or maybe a pale primrose yellow.

75 g (3 oz) butter
6 large eggs
175 g (6 oz) caster sugar
150 g (5 oz) self-raising flour
2 level tablespoons cornflour

FOR THE FILLING
300 ml (½ pint) whipping or
    double cream, whipped
4 tablespoons lemon curd

TO FINISH
900 g (2 lb) fondant or
    ready-to-roll icing,
    crystallized flowers
    and ribbon, to decorate
    (see page 390 for
    fondant icing and page
    393 for crystallized
    flowers recipes)

1 Pre-heat the oven to 180°C/Fan 160°C/Gas 4. Grease a 23 cm (9 in) deep round cake tin then line the base with baking parchment.

2 Melt the butter in a small pan and then leave it to cool slightly. Measure the eggs and sugar into a large bowl and whisk over hot water with an electric whisk on high speed until the mixture becomes pale and creamy and thick enough to leave a trail on the surface when the whisk is lifted. Remove the bowl from the pan and continue to whisk until the mixture is cold.

3 Sift the flours together into a bowl. Fold half the flour into the egg mixture with a metal spoon, then carefully pour half the cooled butter around the edge of the mixture and lightly fold in. Fold in the remaining flour and butter in the same manner. Pour into the prepared tin and level the surface.

4 Bake in the pre-heated oven for about 40 minutes or until well risen, firm to the touch and beginning to shrink away from the sides of the tin. Leave to cool in the tin for a few minutes then turn out, peel off the parchment and finish cooling on a wire rack.

5 Cut the cake into 3 horizontally. Reserve 3–4 tablespoons of the whipped cream then mix the remainder with the lemon curd and use to sandwich the cake slices. Put the cake on a serving plate or board. Spread the reserved cream around the sides and over the top of the cake, just enough to make them sticky.

6 Dust the work surface with icing sugar and roll out the icing large enough to cover the cake completely. Fold the icing over the rolling pin and carefully lift on to the cake, gently smoothing the sides. Trim the extra icing from the base of the cake. Decorate with ribbon and crystallized flowers (see page 393).

CHAPTER SEVEN

Special Cakes

The recipes here are called 'special cakes' because they are more complicated to make, but look very impressive. Most require more steps and processes, employing a variety of cooking techniques that can test even a seasoned cook. These recipes should be attempted when you have plenty of time and patience but, if you make them successfully, you will be rewarded with beautiful, patisserie-style cakes.

The majority of the recipes in this chapter originated on the Continent. During the eighteenth century, a number of European countries enjoyed a rise in affluence. As special cake ingredients, such as fine flour, became more widely available cookery was elevated to an art.

To show off their skills, pastry cooks vied with each other to produce ever more elaborate confections and sold them in all the European capitals, particularly Paris, Vienna and Budapest. I have included here some of the famous cakes that date from this time, such as **Gâteau Saint Honoré** (page 157) and **Doboz Torte** (page 155).

Other cakes in this chapter are not as complicated to make but are more special than everyday cakes, like my recipe for the German **Nusskuchen** (opposite), which translates as 'nut cake'. There are many varieties of Nusskuchen and this one is filled with cooked apple and topped with chocolate. I've included my **Wimbledon Cake** (page 160) here too, which is made with polenta instead of flour, then filled with strawberries and cream, an appropriate combination to mark a great sporting occasion!

Nusskuchen

Nusskuchen comes in many forms, but always contains hazelnuts. This one is filled with a delicious apple mixture and topped with melted chocolate. This recipe serves 6.

40 g (1½ oz) shelled hazelnuts
100 g (4 oz) softened butter
100 g (4 oz) caster sugar
2 large eggs, separated
1 level teaspoon instant
    coffee granules
1 tablespoon warm milk
100 g (4 oz) self-raising flour

FOR THE FILLING
450 g (1 lb) dessert apples
2 tablespoons apricot jam
grated rind and juice of
    ½ lemon

TO FINISH
50 g (2 oz) plain chocolate
    (39 per cent cocoa solids)

1 Pre-heat the oven to 190°C/Fan 170°C/Gas 5. Grease a 20 cm (8 in) deep round cake tin then line the base with baking parchment.

2 To prepare the hazelnuts, place them on a baking tray and put into the oven for about 10 minutes. Tip on to a clean tea towel and rub the nuts together to remove the skins. (Some stubborn ones may need to go back into the oven but don't worry about getting every last bit of skin off, it's not necessary.) Place the nuts into a food processor and grind.

3 Measure the softened butter and the sugar into a bowl and beat together until light and fluffy. Gradually beat in the egg yolks and stir in the prepared nuts. Dissolve the coffee in the warm milk then stir it into the mixture. Carefully fold in the flour.

4 In a separate clean bowl, whisk the egg whites until they form soft peaks and then gently fold into the mixture. Turn the cake mixture into the prepared tin.

5 Bake in the pre-heated oven for about 25 minutes or until well risen and the top of the cake springs back when lightly pressed with a finger. Leave to cool in the tin for a few minutes then turn out, peel off the parchment and finish cooling on a wire rack.

6 Meanwhile, prepare the filling. Peel, core and slice the apples and put them in a pan with the apricot jam, lemon rind and juice. Cover and cook very gently until the apples are soft but still retain their shape. Leave to cool.

7 Cut the cake in half horizontally and sandwich the slices together with the cooled apple mixture. Melt the chocolate gently in a bowl set over a pan of hot water, stirring occasionally. Spread over the top of the cake and leave to set. Serve with cream or crème fraîche.

Sachertorte

This chocolate cake is said to have been invented in Vienna by the chef Franz Sacher in 1832. It improves if left a day or two before cutting. It is quite dense and rich, so this recipe easily serves 12. Serve in small wedges only, with coffee or tea.

150 g (5 oz) plain chocolate
(39 per cent cocoa solids)
150 g (5 oz) softened
unsalted butter
100 g (4 oz) caster sugar
½ teaspoon vanilla extract
5 large eggs, separated
75 g (3 oz) ground almonds
40 g (1½ oz) plain flour

**FOR THE TOPPING
AND ICING**
6 tablespoons apricot jam
150 g (5 oz) plain chocolate
(39 per cent cocoa solids)
200 ml (7 fl oz) double cream
25 g (1 oz) milk chocolate

1 Pre-heat the oven to 180°C/Fan 160°C/Gas 4. Grease a 23 cm (9 in) deep round cake tin then line the base with baking parchment.

2 Break the chocolate into pieces, melt gently in a bowl set over a pan of hot water, stirring occasionally, then cool slightly. Beat the butter until really soft and gradually beat in the sugar until the mixture is light and fluffy. Add the cooled chocolate and the vanilla extract and beat again. Add the egg yolks, one at a time, beating between each addition, then fold in the ground almonds and flour. The mixture will be quite thick at this stage.

3 In a separate bowl, whisk the egg whites until they are stiff but not dry. Add about one-third to the chocolate mixture and stir in vigorously. Gently fold in the remaining egg whites. Pour the mixture into the prepared tin and level the surface.

4 Bake in the pre-heated oven for about 45–50 minutes until well risen and the top of the cake springs back when lightly pressed with a finger. Leave to cool in the tin for a few minutes then turn out, peel off the parchment and finish cooling on a wire rack.

5 To make the topping, heat the apricot jam in a small pan and then brush evenly over the top and sides of the cold cake. Allow to set. Make the icing by breaking the plain chocolate into pieces and melting gently with the double cream, in a small bowl set over a pan of hot water. Stir occasionally. Allow to cool for a couple of minutes to thicken slightly, then pour the icing on to the centre of the cake. Spread it gently over the top and down the sides, and leave to set.

6 For the icing 'writing', break the milk chocolate into pieces then melt gently in a bowl set over a pan of hot water. Spoon into a small paper icing bag or polythene bag and snip off the corner. Pipe 'Sacher' across the cake and leave to set.

Doboz Torte

This Hungarian cake is not the quickest to make, but it does look spectacular when finished. The caramel topping will eventually soften due to the moisture from the cake, so serve the torte within 12 hours. This cake serves 8.

FOR THE SPONGE LAYERS
4 large eggs
175 g (6 oz) caster sugar
150 g (5 oz) sifted self-
 raising flour

FOR THE CHOCOLATE
 BUTTER CREAM
2 large egg whites
100 g (4 oz) icing sugar
225 g (8 oz) softened
 unsalted butter
100 g (4 oz) plain chocolate
 (39 per cent cocoa solids)

FOR THE CARAMEL
175 g (6 oz) granulated
 or caster sugar
5 tablespoons water

1 Pre-heat the oven to 220°C/Fan 200°C/Gas 7. Mark six 20 cm (8 in) circles on baking parchment and lay on baking trays.

2 To make the sponge layers, break the eggs into a large bowl and add the sugar. Whisk until the mixture is light and foamy and the whisk just leaves a trail when lifted out of the mixture. Lightly fold in the flour, a little at a time. Divide the mixture between the 6 marked circles, spreading the mixture out evenly.

3 Bake a few at a time, if you have room, in the pre-heated oven for about 6–8 minutes until pale golden and springy to the touch. With a sharp knife, trim the circles. Peel off the parchment and leave to cool on a wire rack.

4 To make the chocolate butter cream, whisk the egg whites and icing sugar in a bowl set over a pan of simmering water until the mixture holds its shape. Cream the butter until really soft then add the egg white mixture to it a little at a time. Melt the chocolate gently in a bowl set over a pan of hot water, stirring occasionally. Cool slightly then add to the butter cream and mix well until evenly blended.

5 Take one of the sponge circles and place it on a sheet of baking parchment, ready to be topped with caramel. Lay out another sheet of baking parchment ready for the leftover caramel, which will be crushed once set.

6 To make the caramel, dissolve the sugar in the water over a low heat, then increase the heat and boil the syrup until it reaches a deep straw colour. Allow it to cool slightly then pour just over half of it over the sponge circle. Pour the remainder on to the second sheet of parchment.

continued overleaf

7 When the caramel on top of the sponge is just beginning to set, mark it and then cut into 16 portions with an oiled knife. Once the caramel on the second sheet of parchment is completely set, crush it up with a rolling pin.

8 Sandwich the remaining five circles of sponge together with butter cream. Spread butter cream around the sides, leaving some for piping, and press the crushed caramel on to the sides to decorate. Pipe 16 rosettes of the chocolate butter cream around the top and place a caramel-topped wedge of cake at an angle on top of each rosette to form the top layer.

Gâteau Saint Honoré

A Parisian speciality, this gâteau was named in honour of Saint Honoré, the patron saint of bakers. It's an absolute classic but does take time and skill to make. The different stages (but not the caramel and spun sugar) can be made ahead of time, and the gâteau assembled two hours before serving. This recipes serves 6.

FOR THE PÂTE SUCRÉE
100 g (4 oz) plain flour
50 g (2 oz) softened butter
50 g (2 oz) caster sugar
2 large egg yolks

FOR THE CHOUX PASTRY
50 g (2 oz) butter
150 ml (¼ pint) water
65 g (2½ oz) plain flour
2 large eggs, beaten

FOR THE CRÈME
    PÂTISSIÈRE
600 ml (1 pint) milk
1 vanilla pod
4 large eggs
100 g (4 oz) caster sugar
50 g (2 oz) plain flour
150 ml (¼ pint) whipping or
    double cream

FOR THE CARAMEL
225 g (8 oz) granulated sugar
75 ml (2½ fl oz) water

FOR THE SPUN SUGAR
    (OPTIONAL)
100 g (4 oz) granulated sugar
50 ml (2 fl oz) water

1 Pre-heat the oven to 190°C/Fan 170°C/Gas 5. Grease 3 baking trays.

2 To make the *pâte sucrée* (sweet pastry), measure the flour into a bowl and rub in the softened butter with your fingertips until the mixture resembles fine breadcrumbs. Stir in the sugar, then add the egg yolks and mix until the ingredients form a dough. Knead the mixture gently until smooth. Wrap in clingfilm and leave to rest in the fridge for about 30 minutes. You can process the flour, butter and sugar briefly in the food processor, add the egg yolks and process until *just* blended, then knead and wrap as before.

3 Roll out the *pâte sucrée* on to a lightly floured work surface to an 18 cm (7 in) round. Place on one of the prepared baking trays, crimp the edges and prick all over with a fork.

4 Bake in the pre-heated oven for about 15–20 minutes or until the pastry is a pale golden brown. Leave to cool in the baking tray for a few minutes then turn out and finish cooling on a wire rack. Increase the oven temperature to 220°C/Fan 200°C/Gas 7.

5 Next make the choux pastry. Measure the butter and water into a medium pan, heat gently until the butter had melted then bring slowly to the boil. Remove the pan from the heat, add the flour all at once and beat until the mixture forms a soft ball. Allow the flour mixture to cool slightly, then gradually beat in the eggs, beating well between each addition to give a smooth shiny paste.

6 Spoon the choux pastry dough into a piping bag fitted with a 1 cm (½ in) plain nozzle. Pipe an 18 cm (7 in) ring of choux pastry on to the second baking tray and pipe the remaining choux pastry into pieces about the size of a walnut.

continued overleaf

7 Bake in the pre-heated oven for about 10 minutes, then reduce the temperature to 190°C/Fan 170°C/Gas 5 and cook for a further 20 minutes until well risen, golden brown and crisp. Remove from the oven and pierce the choux ring and the buns at intervals underneath, to allow the steam to escape. Return to the oven for about 5 minutes to dry out completely. Cool on a wire rack.

8 To make the *crème pâtissière* (vanilla egg custard), measure the milk into a small pan and add the vanilla pod. Bring to just below boiling point then turn off the heat and leave to infuse for about 10 minutes. Strain and discard the vanilla pod. In a bowl, beat the eggs, sugar and flour together with a little of the strained milk. Pour the remaining milk on to the egg mixture, stir and then pour back into the pan. Cook over a gentle heat, stirring continously, until thickened. Pour into a clean bowl and cover the surface tightly with clingfilm to prevent a skin forming. Allow to cool, stirring occasionally.

9 Whip the cream until it forms soft peaks. Whisk the cooled *crème pâtissière* until smooth and fold in the cream. Cover tightly with clingfilm and chill thoroughly before using.

10 Pipe or spoon a little of the *crème pâtissière* into the choux ring and the buns, through the holes made in the bases to allow the steam to escape. Leave in a cool place while making the caramel.

11 To make the caramel, measure the sugar and water into a heavy-based pan. Heat gently until the sugar has dissolved, brushing down the sides of the pan with hot water from time to time. Bring to the boil and boil the syrup until it turns a golden colour. Immediately plunge the base of the pan into cold water to stop the caramel darkening further. Place the pan in a large bowl and fill the bowl with boiling water, to keep the caramel fluid.

12 Put the *pâte sucrée* on a plate and position the choux ring on top. One by one, dip the base of each choux bun in the caramel and place on the choux ring, holding it in place for a few seconds to secure. Continue with the remaining choux buns, placing them close together to form a ring. Spoon a little caramel over the top of each choux bun.

13 To make the spun sugar, cover your working area with sheets of oiled foil, and cover a rolling pin with foil and oil it lightly. Have ready 2 forks taped together back to back. Measure the sugar and water into a small heavy-based pan and heat gently until melted. Bring to the boil until the sugar syrup is a pale golden colour. Immediately dip the base of the pan into cold water and cool for 30 seconds only. Dip the prongs of the forks in the syrup and, holding the covered rolling pin in the other hand, flick the forks back and forth over the rolling pin (see illustration below), to form long strands of sugar. Repeat with the remaining syrup, then place on an oiled baking sheet until needed.

14 Spoon the remaining *crème pâtissière* into the choux case and decorate with the spun sugar, if using. If you have decorated the gâteau with spun sugar, serve it within the hour, as the sugar will gradually start to disintegrate due to the moisture.

NB The sugar syrup used to make the caramel and spun sugar can easily burn skin. Please take extra care when handling the caramel and spun sugar, particularly if there are children in the house at the time.

Wimbledon Cake

This cake is perfect not just for Wimbledon, but for all summer occasions. It uses no flour, and the semolina used instead gives it a slightly crunchy, close texture. The cake must be eaten on the day of filling.

3 large eggs, separated
100 g (4 oz) caster sugar
grated rind and juice of
   1 orange
75 g (3 oz) semolina

FOR THE FILLING
AND TOPPING

100 g (4 oz) strawberries
1 passion fruit
150 ml (¼ pint) whipping or
   double cream, whipped
icing sugar, to finish

1 Pre-heat the oven to 180°C/Fan 160°C/Gas 4. Grease a 20 cm (8 in) deep round cake tin then line the base with baking parchment.

2 Measure the egg yolks, sugar, grated orange rind and juice and the semolina into a bowl and beat until thoroughly blended. In a separate clean bowl, whisk the egg whites until they are stiff but not dry, then gently fold into the orange and semolina mixture. Turn into the prepared tin.

3 Bake in the pre-heated oven for about 30–35 minutes or until well risen and the top of the cake springs back when lightly pressed with a finger. Leave to cool in the tin for a few minutes then turn out, peel off the parchment and finish cooling on a wire rack.

4 Reserve a few strawberries to decorate the top of the cake, then slice the remainder. Halve the passion fruit and scoop out the pulp. To fill the cake, cut it in half horizontally and sandwich the slices together with the sliced strawberries, passion fruit pulp and whipped cream. Just before serving, decorate with the reserved strawberries, sliced or left whole, and sieve some icing sugar over the top.

Gâteau Moka aux Amandes

This is one of my favourite coffee cakes, and it looks spectacular, too. Add a little brandy to the filling, if you like.

3 large eggs
100 g (4 oz) caster sugar
75 g (3 oz) self-raising flour

FOR THE CRÈME AU
BEURRE MOKA
75 g (3 oz) caster sugar
4 tablespoons water
2 large egg yolks
175 g (6 oz) softened butter
1–2 tablespoons coffee
  essence

TO FINISH
175 g (6 oz) shredded or
  flaked toasted almonds
icing sugar, for dusting
  (optional)

1 Pre-heat the oven to 190°C/Fan 170°C/Gas 5. Grease a 23 cm (9 in) deep round cake tin then line the base with baking parchment.

2 Measure the eggs and sugar into a large bowl and whisk at full speed until the mixture is pale in colour and thick enough to just leave a trail when the whisk is lifted. Sift the flour over the surface of the mixture and gently fold in with a metal spoon or spatula. Turn into the prepared tin.

3 Bake in the pre-heated oven for about 30 minutes or until well risen and the top of the cake springs back when lightly pressed with a finger. Leave to cool in the tin for a few minutes then turn out, peel off the parchment and finish cooling on a wire rack.

4 To make the *crème au beurre moka* (coffee butter cream), measure the sugar and water into a small heavy-based pan. Heat very gently until the sugar has dissolved. Bring to the boil then boil steadily for 2–3 minutes until it has reached a temperature of 107°C on a sugar thermometer, or until the syrup forms a slim thread when pulled apart between 2 teaspoons.

5 Place the egg yolks into a bowl and give them a quick stir to break them up. Pour the syrup in a thin stream on to the egg yolks, whisking all the time. Continue to whisk until the mixture is thick and cold. In another bowl, cream the butter until very soft and gradually beat in the egg yolk mixture. Stir in the coffee essence to flavour.

6 Cut the cake in half horizontally and sandwich the slices together with a thin layer of the coffee butter cream. Spread butter cream over the top and sides of the cake as well, retaining some for decoration, then press the toasted almonds all over the cake. Dust lightly with icing sugar and finish the cake by piping rosettes of the remaining coffee butter cream around the top.

Lemon Griestorte

Made with semolina and ground almonds instead of flour, this cake has a lovely light but 'short' texture. It keeps better than an ordinary sponge cake, and is delicious with different fruits. For an even more luscious cake, double the quantities of cream and lemon curd to smooth over the top of the cake as well as fill it. This recipe serves 6.

3 large eggs, separated
100 g (4 oz) caster sugar
grated rind and juice of
    ½ lemon
50 g (2 oz) fine semolina
15 g (½ oz) ground almonds

FOR THE FILLING
150 ml (¼ pint) whipping
    or double cream
4 tablespoons lemon curd
100 g (4 oz) fresh raspberries
    (optional)

TO FINISH
icing sugar

1 Pre-heat the oven to 180°C/Fan 160°C/Gas 4. Grease a 20 cm (8 in) deep round cake tin and line the base and sides with baking parchment.

2 Measure the egg yolks and sugar into a bowl and whisk until pale and light in texture. Add the lemon juice and continue to whisk until the mixture is thick. Fold in the grated lemon rind, semolina and ground almonds. In a separate bowl, whisk the egg whites until they form soft peaks, then fold into the mixture until evenly blended. Turn into the prepared tin.

3 Bake in the pre-heated oven for about 30–35 minutes or until well risen and a pale golden brown. Leave to cool in the tin for a few minutes then turn out, peel off the parchment and finish cooling on a wire rack.

4 Cut the cake in half horizontally. Whisk the cream until it holds its shape, then fold in the lemon curd. Sandwich the cake together with the lemon cream and raspberries, if liked, and dust the top with icing sugar to serve.

TIP
Flours, porridge oats and semolina should all be used within four months once the bags or packets have been opened.

Chocolatines

These small cakes can be fiddly to make, but are delicious, made with a sponge that is moist and light. They are the sort of cake that would be on sale in the very best of French patisseries. This recipe makes 9 Chocolatines.

FOR THE GENOESE SPONGE
40 g (1½ oz) butter
3 large eggs
75 g (3 oz) caster sugar
65 g (2½ oz) self-raising flour
1 level tablespoon cornflour

FOR THE CRÈME AU
   BEURRE CHOCOLAT
50 g (2 oz) granulated sugar
4 tablespoons water
2 large egg yolks
175 g (6 oz) softened
   unsalted butter
100 g (4 oz) plain chocolate
   (39 per cent cocoa solids),
   melted

TO FINISH
75 g (3 oz) toasted
   chopped mixed nuts

1 Pre-heat the oven to 180°C/Fan 160°C/Gas 4. Grease an 18 cm (7 in) shallow square cake tin then line the base with baking parchment.

2 To make the sponge, gently melt the butter in a pan, then set aside to cool slightly. Measure the eggs and sugar into a large bowl and whisk at full speed until the mixture is pale and mousse-like, and thick enough so that a trail is left when the whisk is lifted from the mixture.

3 Sift the flours together into a bowl. Carefully fold half the flour into the egg mixture then gently pour half the cooled butter around the edge of the mixture and fold in. Repeat with the remaining flour and butter. Pour the mixture into the prepared tin.

4 Bake in the pre-heated oven for about 35–40 minutes or until well risen and the top of the cake springs back when lightly pressed with a finger. Leave to cool in the tin for a few minutes then turn out, peel off the parchment and finish cooling on a wire rack.

5 To make the *crème au beurre chocolat* (chocolate butter cream), measure the sugar and water into a small heavy-based pan. Heat very gently until the sugar has dissolved. Bring to the boil then boil steadily for 2–3 minutes until the syrup is still clear and forms a slim thread when pulled apart between 2 teaspoons.

continued overleaf

6 Put the egg yolks into a bowl and give them a quick stir to break them up. Pour the syrup in a thin stream on to the egg yolks, whisking all the time. Continue to whisk until the mixture is thick and cold. In another bowl, cream the butter until very soft and gradually beat in the egg yolk mixture. Stir in the cooled, melted chocolate to flavour.

7 Cut the cold sponge in half horizontally and sandwich the slices together with a thin layer of the chocolate butter cream, then trim the cake edges and cut neatly into 5 cm (2 in) squares. Spread the top and sides of each cake with most of the remaining chocolate butter cream and press the chopped, toasted nuts around the sides. Finish the tops of the cakes by piping with tiny rosettes of the remaining chocolate butter cream.

TIP
Leftover egg whites can be stored in a covered container in the fridge for up to three weeks, or frozen for up to six months.

Mokatines

These are a coffee-flavoured variation of Chocolatines. I've often seen them in smart Parisian patisseries. The recipe traditionally does not use self-raising flour, but I always do, because it gets a better result. This recipes makes 8 Mokatines.

FOR THE GENOESE SPONGE

40 g (1½ oz) butter
3 large eggs
75 g (3 oz) caster sugar
65 g (2½ oz) self-raising flour
1 level tablespoon cornflour

FOR THE CRÈME AU
BEURRE MOKA

40 g (1½ oz) caster sugar
2 tablespoons water
1 large egg yolk
75 g (3 oz) softened butter
1 tablespoon coffee essence

FOR THE SOFT
COFFEE ICING

3 tablespoons apricot jam
50 g (2 oz) butter
3 tablespoons milk
1 level tablespoon instant
   coffee granules
225 g (8 oz) sifted icing sugar

1 Pre-heat the oven to 180°C/Fan 160°C/Gas 4. Grease an 18 cm (7 in) shallow square cake tin then line the base with baking parchment.

2 To make the sponge, gently melt the butter in a pan, then set to one side to cool slightly. Measure the eggs and sugar into a large bowl and whisk at full speed until the mixture is pale and mousse-like, and thick enough so that a trail is left when the whisk is lifted from the mixture.

3 Sift the flours together into a bowl. Carefully fold half the flour carefully into the egg mixture, gently pour half the cooled butter around the edge of the mixture and then fold in. Repeat with the remaining flour and butter. Pour the mixture into the prepared tin.

4 Bake in the pre-heated oven for about 35–40 minutes or until well risen and the top of the cake springs back when lightly pressed with a finger. Leave to cool in the tin for a few minutes then turn out, peel off the parchment and finish cooling on a wire rack.

5 To make the *crème au beurre moka* (coffee butter cream), measure the sugar and water into a small heavy-based pan. Heat very gently until the sugar has dissolved. Bring to the boil then boil steadily for 2–3 minutes until the syrup is still clear and forms a slim thread when pulled apart between 2 teaspoons.

continued overleaf

6 Put the egg yolks into a bowl and give them a quick stir to break them up. Pour the syrup in a thin stream over the yolks, whisking all the time. Continue to whisk until the mixture is thick and cold. In another bowl, cream the butter until very soft and gradually beat in the egg yolk mixture. Stir in the coffee essence to flavour.

7 Cut the cold cake in half horizontally and sandwich the slices together with a thin layer of the coffee butter cream. Trim the cake edges and then neatly cut in half, and then cut each half into 4 to give 8 oblongs. Sieve the apricot jam into a small pan and warm gently. Brush the top and sides of the cakes with the hot apricot jam.

8 To make the coffee icing, measure the butter, milk and coffee into a small pan and heat gently until the butter has melted. Add the sifted icing sugar and beat until smooth and glossy. Leave to thicken slightly, then use most of the cream to pour over each cake, smoothing the sides quickly if necessary. Leave to set and then decorate with the remaining piped coffee butter cream.

TIP
Store eggs in a cool place, larder or fridge, pointed end down, and away from strong-smelling foods such as fish. Bring them to room temperature before using.

Swiss Wild Strawberry and Walnut Cake

This is a light walnut sponge filled with wild strawberries and cream, often served on the Continent as a pudding. For a lighter filling, you can use full-fat crème fraîche and you can use regular strawberries when wild strawberries are out of season.

3 large eggs
100 g (4 oz) caster sugar
75 g (3 oz) self-raising flour
50 g (2 oz) roughly chopped
    walnuts

**FOR THE FILLING
AND TOPPING**
300 ml (½ pint) whipping or
    double cream, whipped
450 g (1 lb) wild strawberries
extra wild strawberries, for
    decoration

1 Pre-heat the oven to 180°C/Fan 160°C/Gas 4. Grease a 20 cm (8 in) deep round cake tin then line the base with baking parchment.

2 Measure the eggs and sugar into a large bowl and beat until the mixture is thick and mousse-like and leaves a trail when the whisk is lifted out of the mixture. Sift the flour on to the mixture and lightly fold in along with the chopped walnuts. Turn into the prepared cake tin.

3 Bake in the pre-heated oven for about 40–45 minutes or until well risen and the top of the cake springs back when lightly pressed with a finger. Leave to cool in the tin for a few minutes then turn out, peel off the parchment and finish cooling on a wire rack.

4 When cold, cut the cake into 3 horizontally. Sandwich the slices together with a good amount of whipped cream and strawberries. Spread the remaining cream over the top and the sides of the cake and decorate with the reserved strawberries.

CHAPTER EIGHT

Traybakes and Flapjacks

Traybakes and flapjacks are some of the easiest bakes to make and are always popular. They are economical in time and energy and require just a few utensils, making them an ideal bake to feed large numbers. A basic traybake mixture can be made in minutes with a free-standing or hand-held food mixer and when cooked, there is no need to turn the cake out on to a wire rack to cool, just ice it and cut it into squares. You can also make a layered cake with traybakes, by sandwiching two together with a filling of your choice, such as jam or butter cream.

I've relied on these effortless recipes for many years when baking to sell at charity events, fêtes and coffee mornings, and have found them invaluable for children's parties. Once you've made the basic mixture, you can create a number of flavoured traybakes with just a few extra ingredients, swiftly turning out racks of lemon, chocolate, sultana and orange, coffee and walnut – the list is endless!

Flapjacks are almost as versatile as traybakes and require just a few storecupboard ingredients. Any leftover porridge oats, syrup and sugar can be stored and used again at a later date. You can freeze leftover butter and defrost it to use another time. Watch your syrup quantities and the length of time the flapjacks spend in the oven as, either made with too much syrup or overcooked, flapjacks will be impossible to get out of the tin and too tough to eat.

All the recipes in this chapter use a 30 x 23 cm (12 x 9 in) traybake tin. If you don't have one, check the size of your roasting tin, as a standard roasting tin is also 30 x 23 cm (12 x 9 in) and works perfectly well. I generally suggest cutting traybakes into 21 pieces and flapjacks in 16 slices or 24 squares for this size tin, but choose a slice size to suit the occasion, such as small triangles or fingers for children's parties.

Basic All-in-one Sponge Traybake

This is the simplest of cakes to make. When cooked and cold, sieve over a little icing sugar to finish, if you like.

225 g (8 oz) softened butter
225 g (8 oz) caster sugar
275 g (10 oz) self-raising flour
2 level teaspoons baking
    powder
4 large eggs
4 tablespoons milk

TO FINISH
a little sifted icing sugar
    (optional)

1 Pre-heat the oven to 180°C/Fan 160°C/Gas 4. Grease a 30 x 23 cm (12 x 9 in) traybake or roasting tin then line the base with baking parchment.

2 Measure all the ingredients into a large bowl and beat until well blended. Turn the mixture into the prepared tin and level the top.

3 Bake in the pre-heated oven for about 35–40 minutes or until the cake has shrunk from the sides of the tin and springs back when pressed in the centre with your fingertips. Leave to cool in the tin, then cut into 21 pieces and peel off the baking parchment.

To make a larger traybake, follow the method above. Grease a 29 x 36 cm (11½ x 14½ in) traybake or roasting tin and line the base with baking parchment. Measure 350 g (12 oz) softened butter, 350 g (12 oz) caster sugar, 450 g (1 lb) self-raising flour, 2 level teaspoons baking powder, 6 large eggs and 6 tablespoons milk into a large bowl and beat until well blended. Bake in the pre-heated oven for about 40–45 minutes or until the cake has shrunk from the sides of the tin and springs back when pressed in the centre with your fingertips. Leave to cool in the tin before cutting into 36 pieces and removing the baking parchment.

Iced Lemon Traybake

You can vary a basic traybake quite simply – in this case by adding a subtle lemon flavour and a lemon glacé icing.

225 g (8 oz) softened butter
225 g (8 oz) caster sugar
275 g (10 oz) self-raising flour
2 level teaspoons baking
   powder
4 large eggs
4 tablespoons milk
grated rind of 2 lemons

FOR THE ICING
3 tablespoons lemon juice
225 g (8 oz) sifted icing sugar

1 Pre-heat the oven to 180°C/Fan 160°C/Gas 4. Grease a 30 x 23 cm (12 x 9 in) traybake or roasting tin then line the base with baking parchment.

2 Measure all the cake ingredients into a large bowl and beat until well blended. Turn the mixture into the prepared tin and level the top.

3 Bake in the pre-heated oven for about 35–40 minutes or until the cake has shrunk from the sides of the tin and springs back when pressed in the centre with your fingertips. Leave to cool in the tin.

4 Mix together the lemon juice and icing sugar to give a runny consistency. Spread out evenly over the cake and leave to set before cutting into 21 pieces.

Iced Chocolate Traybake

Chocolate cakes are always popular, and this is a particularly simple version, which is great for family teas or lunch boxes.

4 level tablespoons cocoa powder
4 tablespoons hot water
225 g (8 oz) softened butter
225 g (8 oz) caster sugar
275 g (10 oz) self-raising flour
2 level teaspoons baking powder
4 large eggs
1 tablespoon milk

FOR THE ICING AND DECORATION
4 tablespoons apricot jam
150 g (5 oz) plain chocolate (39 per cent cocoa solids)
6 tablespoons water
350 g (12 oz) sifted icing sugar
1 teaspoon sunflower oil
chocolate curls (see page 392)

1 Pre-heat the oven to 180°C/Fan 160°C/Gas 4. Grease a 30 x 23 cm (12 x 9 in) traybake or roasting tin then line the base with baking parchment.

2 Blend together the cocoa and hot water then allow to cool slightly. Measure all the cake ingredients into a large bowl and beat until well blended. Turn the mixture into the prepared tin and level the top.

3 Bake in the pre-heated oven for about 35–40 minutes or until the cake has shrunk from the sides of the tin and springs back when pressed in the centre with your fingertips. Leave to cool in the tin.

4 To make the icing, warm the apricot jam in a pan and brush all over the cake. Break the chocolate into pieces and melt in a pan with the water, heating gently until melted and smooth. Leave to cool slightly, then beat in the icing sugar and oil. Pour over the cake and smooth over gently with a palette knife. Leave to set for about 30 minutes, then cut into 21 pieces and decorate with chocolate curls.

TIP
If time allows, do brush the cold cake with apricot jam before icing. It gives the cake a lovely flavour and prevents crumbs from the cake getting into the icing.

Coffee and Walnut Traybake

Coffee and walnuts go particularly well together, but you can use other nuts for this recipe if you prefer.

225 g (8 oz) softened butter
225 g (8 oz) light muscovado sugar
275 g (10 oz) self-raising flour
2 level teaspoons baking powder
4 large eggs
2 tablespoons milk
2 tablespoons coffee essence
75 g (3 oz) chopped walnuts

FOR THE ICING
75 g (3 oz) softened butter
225 g (8 oz) sifted icing sugar
2 teaspoons milk
2 teaspoons coffee essence
walnut halves

1 Pre-heat the oven to 180°C/Fan 160°C/Gas 4. Grease a 30 x 23 cm (12 x 9 in) traybake or roasting tin then line the base with baking parchment.

2 Measure all the cake ingredients into a large bowl and beat until well blended. Turn the mixture into the prepared tin and level the top.

3 Bake in the pre-heated oven for about 35–40 minutes or until the cake has shrunk from the sides of the tin and springs back when pressed in the centre with your fingertips. Leave to cool in the tin.

4 To make the icing, beat together the butter with the icing sugar, milk and coffee essence. Spread evenly over the cold cake using a palette knife, then decorate with the walnut halves and cut 21 pieces.

TIP
If you like, you can use instant coffee granules instead of coffee essence. Mix 2 teaspoons with 2 tablespoons of water.

Devonshire Apple Cake

This apple cake looks a little unappetizing when cold but is quite delicious served warm with cream or fromage frais. This recipe serves 12.

450 g (1 lb) cooking apples
juice of ½ lemon
350 g (12 oz) self-raising flour
2 level teaspoons baking
    powder
350 g (12 oz) caster sugar
4 large eggs
1 teaspoon almond extract
225 g (8 oz) butter, melted
a generous scattering of
    shredded, flaked or
    chopped almonds
caster sugar, to sprinkle

1 Pre-heat the oven to 180°C/Fan 160°C/Gas 4. Grease a 30 x 23 cm (12 x 9 in) traybake or roasting tin then line the base with baking parchment.

2 Peel, core and thinly slice the apples and squeeze the lemon juice over them. Measure the flour, baking powder and sugar into a large bowl. Beat the eggs together with the almond extract and stir into the flour along with the melted butter. Whisk, then spread half this mixture into the tin. Arrange the apples over the top of the cake mixture. Carefully top with the rest of the mixture – but don't worry if the apples show through a little. Sprinkle over the almonds.

3 Bake in the pre-heated oven for about 1¼ hours or until the cake is golden, firm to the touch and slightly shrunk away from the sides of the tin. Leave to cool for 15 minutes and then turn out and remove the parchment. Sprinkle over the caster sugar and serve warm, with cream or fromage frais.

American Spiced Carrot Traybake

Bought mixtures of chopped nuts might include a high proportion of peanuts. I always prefer to make up my own mix from shelled nuts.

275 g (10 oz) self-raising flour
350 g (12 oz) caster sugar
2 level teaspoons baking powder
75 g (3 oz) chopped unsalted mixed nuts
3 level teaspoons ground cinnamon
2 level teaspoons ground ginger
300 ml (½ pint) sunflower oil
275 g (10 oz) grated carrots
4 large eggs
1 teaspoon vanilla extract

FOR THE TOPPING
400 g (14 oz) full-fat soft cheese
4 teaspoons clear honey
2 teaspoons lemon juice
chopped mixed unsalted nuts, to decorate

1 Pre-heat the oven to 180°C/Fan 160°C/Gas 4. Grease a 30 x 23 cm (12 x 9 in) traybake or roasting tin then line the base with baking parchment.

2 Measure all the dry cake ingredients into a large bowl. Add the oil, grated carrots, eggs (one at a time) and vanilla extract, beating between each addition. Pour into the prepared tin and level the surface.

3 Bake in the pre-heated oven for 50–60 minutes or until the cake is well risen, golden brown in colour and firm to the touch. Leave to cool in the tin for 10 minutes then turn out, peel off the parchment and finish cooling on a wire rack.

4 To make the topping, mix together the cheese, honey and lemon juice, adding, if necessary, a little lemon juice to make a spreading consistency. Spread evenly over the cake with a palette knife, then sprinkle over the chopped nuts to decorate and cut into 21 pieces. You can store the iced cake in the fridge for up to 2 weeks.

Sultana and Orange Traybake

Oranges and sultanas go well together in this cake. Sprinkling the cake with demerara sugar gives it a nice crusty, sugary top.

225 g (8 oz) softened butter
225 g (8 oz) caster sugar
275 g (10 oz) self-raising flour
2 level teaspoons baking
    powder
4 large eggs
2 tablespoons milk
275 g (10 oz) sultanas
grated rind of 2 oranges
demerara sugar, to sprinkle

1 Pre-heat the oven to 180°C/Fan 160°C/Gas 4. Grease a 30 x 23 cm (12 x 9 in) traybake or roasting tin then line the base with baking parchment.

2 Measure all the cake ingredients except the demerara sugar into a large bowl and beat until well blended. Turn the mixture into the prepared tin and level the top.

3 Bake in the pre-heated oven for about 25 minutes then sprinkle the top with demerara sugar and return to the oven for a further 10–15 minutes or until the cake has shrunk from the sides of the tin and springs back when pressed in the centre with your fingertips. Leave to cool in the tin, then cut into 21 pieces.

TIP
You can omit the demerara sugar and instead ice the cooked and cooled cake with orange glacé icing made with 225 g (8 oz) sifted icing sugar and about 3 tablespoons of freshly squeezed orange juice.

Lemon Drizzle Traybake

This really is a top favourite. It is always moist and crunchy. The cake needs to be still warm when the topping is added so that it absorbs the lemon syrup easily, leaving the sugar on top. Do allow the cake to cool a little though – if it is too hot, the syrup will tend to run straight through.

225 g (8 oz) softened butter
225 g (8 oz) caster sugar
275 g (10 oz) self-raising flour
2 level teaspoons baking powder
4 large eggs
4 tablespoons milk
finely grated rind of 2 lemons

FOR THE CRUNCHY TOPPING
175 g (6 oz) granulated sugar
juice of 2 lemons

1 Pre-heat the oven to 160°C/Fan 140°C/Gas 3. Grease a 30 x 23 cm (12 x 9 in) traybake or roasting tin then line the base with baking parchment.

2 Measure all the ingredients for the traybake into a large bowl and beat until well blended. Turn the mixture into the prepared tin and level the top gently with the back of a spatula.

3 Bake in the pre-heated oven for 35–40 minutes or until the cake has shrunk from the sides of the tin and springs back when pressed in the centre with your fingertips. Leave to cool in the tin for a few minutes then turn out, carefully peel off the parchment and finish cooling on a wire rack. Stand the wire rack on a tray to catch any drips of the topping.

4 To make the crunchy topping, mix the granulated sugar and lemon juice in a small bowl to give a runny consistency. Spoon this mixture evenly over the traybake while it is still a little warm. Cut into 30 squares when cold.

To make a Lemon Poppy Seed Traybake, add 25 g (1 oz) poppy seeds in step 2.

Cherry and Almond Traybake

In season, you can use fresh stoned cherries instead of glacé, but you must then eat the cake up quickly: it won't keep as well because it will be moister. You'll need about 450 g (1 lb) of sweet black cherries, stoned.

225 g (8 oz) red or natural glacé cherries
275 g (10 oz) self-raising flour
2 level teaspoons baking powder
225 g (8 oz) softened butter
225 g (8 oz) caster sugar
finely grated rind of 2 lemons
75 g (3 oz) ground almonds
5 large eggs
25 g (1 oz) flaked almonds

1 Pre-heat the oven to 180°C/Fan 160°C/Gas 4. Grease a 30 x 23 cm (12 x 9 in) traybake or roasting tin then line the base with baking parchment.

2 Cut the cherries into quarters, put in a sieve and rinse under running water. Drain well then dry thoroughly on kitchen paper.

3 Measure all the remaining cake ingredients, except the flaked almonds, into a large bowl and beat for 1 minute to mix thoroughly. Lightly fold in the cherries. Turn into the prepared tin and sprinkle over the flaked almonds.

4 Bake in the pre-heated oven for about 40 minutes or until the cake has shrunk from the sides of the tin and springs back when pressed in the centre with your fingertips. Leave to cool in the tin, then cut into pieces.

Treacle Spice Traybake

This is one for those who like the rich flavour of treacle in baking. Don't be too worried if the traybake dips in the centre – it just means you were a little generous with the treacle.

225 g (8 oz) softened butter
175 g (6 oz) caster sugar
225 g (8 oz) black treacle
275 g (10 oz) self-raising flour
2 level teaspoons baking powder
2 level teaspoons ground mixed spice
4 large eggs, beaten
4 tablespoons milk

TO FINISH
icing sugar, for dusting

1 Pre-heat the oven to 180°C/Fan 160°C/Gas 4. Grease a 30 x 23 cm (12 x 9 in) traybake or roasting tin then line the base with baking parchment.

2 Measure all the ingredients into a large bowl and beat well for about 2 minutes until well blended. Turn the mixture into the prepared tin and level the top.

3 Bake in the pre-heated oven for 35-40 minutes or until the cake has shrunk from the sides of the tin and springs back when pressed in the centre with your fingertips. Leave to cool in the tin, then cut into 21 pieces. Dust with sifted icing sugar to serve.

Gingerbread Traybake

This gingerbread is equally delicious without the icing, and is perfect for a packed lunch.

275 g (10 oz) golden syrup
275 g (10 oz) black treacle
225 g (8 oz) light muscovado
    sugar
225 g (8 oz) softened butter
450 g (1 lb) self-raising flour
2 level teaspoons ground
    mixed spice
2 level teaspoons ground
    ginger
4 large eggs, beaten
4 tablespoons milk

FOR THE ICING
225 g (8 oz) icing sugar
2 tablespoons water
50 g (2 oz) finely chopped
    crystallized or stem ginger

1 Pre-heat the oven to 160°C/Fan 140°C/Gas 3. Grease a 30 x 23 cm (12 x 9 in) traybake or roasting tin then line the base with baking parchment.

2 Measure the syrup, treacle, sugar and butter into a large pan and heat gently until the butter has melted. Remove from the heat and stir in the flour and spices. Add the lightly beaten eggs and milk, and beat until smooth. Pour into the prepared tin.

3 Bake in the pre-heated oven for 45–50 minutes or until the cake has shrunk from the sides of the tin and springs back when pressed in the centre with your fingertips. Leave to cool in the tin for a few minutes then turn out, peel off the parchment and finish cooling on a wire rack.

4 To make the icing, sift the icing sugar into a bowl, add the water a little at a time, and mix until smooth. Mix in the chopped ginger, spoon over the cake, leave to set, then cut into 21 pieces.

TIP
Heat the syrup and other ingredients through very gently. If they are too hot when the flour is stirred in, it could go lumpy. If it does, you'll have to rub it through a sieve.

Ginger and Treacle Spiced Traybake

Treacle can be difficult to weigh accurately, as it tends to stick to the scale pan. Weighing it on top of the sugar overcomes this problem.

225 g (8 oz) softened butter
175 g (6 oz) light muscovado
    sugar
200 g (7 oz) black treacle
300 g (11 oz) self-raising flour
2 level teaspoons baking
    powder
1 level teaspoon ground
    mixed spice
1 level teaspoon ground
    allspice
4 large eggs
4 tablespoons milk
3 finely chopped bulbs of
    stem ginger from a jar

FOR THE ICING
75 g (3 oz) icing sugar
3 tablespoons stem ginger
    syrup from the jar
3 finely chopped bulbs of
    stem ginger from a jar

1 Pre-heat the oven to 180°C/Fan 160°C/Gas 4. Grease a 30 x 23 cm (12 x 9 in) traybake or roasting tin then line the base with baking parchment.

2 Put all the ingredients for the traybake into a large bowl and beat until well blended. Turn the mixture into the prepared tin, scraping the bowl with a plastic spatula to remove all the mixture. Level the top gently with the back of the spatula.

3 Bake in the pre-heated oven for 35–40 minutes, or until the cake has shrunk from the sides of the tin and springs back when pressed in the centre with your fingertips. Leave to cool in the tin for a few minutes then turn out, peel off the parchment and finish cooling on a wire rack.

4 To make the icing, sift the icing sugar into a bowl, add the ginger syrup and mix until the icing is smooth and has a spreading consistency. Pour the icing over the cake, spread it gently to the edges with a small palette knife and sprinkle with the chopped stem ginger to decorate. Allow the icing to set before slicing the traybake into 15–20 pieces.

TIP
This traybake freezes very well un-iced, and in fact improves with freezing.

Date and Walnut Traybake

This is a deliciously nutty and rich traybake.

250 g (9 oz) stoned and
    chopped dates
40 g (1½ oz) softened butter
350 ml (12 fl oz) boiling water
2 large eggs
200 g (7 oz) dark muscovado
    sugar
150 g (5 oz) ground almonds
150 g (5 oz) chopped walnuts
350 g (12 oz) self-raising flour
1½ level teaspoons ground
    cinnamon

FOR THE ICING
225 g (8 oz) sifted icing sugar
grated rind and juice of
    1 lemon
walnut pieces, to decorate

1 Pre-heat the oven to 180°C/Fan 160°C/Gas 4. Grease a 30 x 23 cm (12 x 9 in) traybake or roasting tin then line the base with baking parchment.

2 Measure the dates and butter into a small bowl and pour over the boiling water. Set aside to cool. Meanwhile, whisk the eggs and sugar together in a large bowl, then add the cooled date mixture and the remaining cake ingredients. Whisk then pour into the prepared tin.

3 Bake in the pre-heated oven for about 1 hour 10 minutes or until the cake is firm to the touch and golden brown in colour. Leave to cool in the tin for 10 minutes then turn out, peel off the parchment and finish cooling on a wire rack.

4 To make the icing, mix the icing sugar with the lemon rind and juice, adding a little hot water to make a spreading consistency. Pour over the cake and gently spread out evenly with a palette knife. Decorate with walnut pieces and leave to set, then cut into 21 pieces.

Marmalade Traybake

Be careful when measuring the marmalade. If you put too much in, the traybake will dip in the centre.

175 g (6 oz) softened butter
175 g (6 oz) caster sugar
175 g (6 oz) sultanas
175 g (6 oz) currants
3 large eggs, beaten
250 g (9 oz) self-raising flour
1½ level teaspoons baking
    powder
50 g (2 oz) quartered red or
    natural glacé cherries
2 tablespoons marmalade
3 tablespoons milk
nibbed sugar, to decorate

1 Pre-heat the oven to 180°C/Fan 160°C/Gas 4. Grease a 30 x 23 cm (12 x 9 in) traybake or roasting tin then line the base with baking parchment.

2 Measure all the ingredients, except the nibbed sugar, into a large bowl and beat until thoroughly blended. Turn into the prepared tin and smooth the top, then sprinkle with nibbed sugar.

3 Bake in the pre-heated oven for 40–45 minutes or until well risen, golden brown and firm to the touch. Leave to cool in the tin for 10 minutes then turn out, peel off the parchment and finish cooling on a wire rack. When cool cut into 24 pieces.

TIP
Instead of nibbed sugar, you could use crushed sugar cubes.

Fast Flapjacks

These flapjacks are crunchy and traditional. Take care not to overbake them, as they can become hard and dark.

225 g (8 oz) butter
225 g (8 oz) demerara sugar
75 g (3 oz) golden syrup
275 g (10 oz) porridge oats

1 Pre-heat the oven to 160°C/Fan 140°C/Gas 3. Grease a 30 x 23 cm (12 x 9 in) traybake or roasting tin.

2 Melt the butter in a large pan along with the sugar and syrup, and then stir in the oats. Mix well and then turn into the prepared tin and press flat with a palette knife or the back of a spoon.

3 Bake in the pre-heated oven for about 35 minutes or until pale golden brown. Remove from the oven and leave to cool for 10 minutes. Mark into 24 squares and leave to finish cooling in the tin.

To make Chocolate Chip Flapjacks (in photo), leave the mixture to cool, after stirring in the oats in step 2. Stir in 100 g (4 oz) plain chocolate chips, then turn into the prepared tin and follow the rest of the method for the above recipe.

To make Muesli Flapjacks, replace 175 g (6oz) of the porridge oats with your favourite muesli, then follow the recipe above. Leave to cool for 10 minutes, then mark into 16 oblongs and leave to finish cooling in the tin. If you like a lot of raisins add 25–50 g (1–2 oz) extra when you make the flapjack mixture.

CHAPTER NINE

Biscuits and Cookies

Biscuits are simple to make – all you need are good-quality ingredients and a reliable recipe. A well-made biscuit can be as satisfying as a slice of cake, and will beat bought biscuits any day! A big plus point for biscuits and cookies is that they are very quick to make and retain their flavour well if kept in an airtight container. All the biscuits in this chapter can be frozen for up to 1 month. When completely cold, carefully pack them into freezer-proof containers or freezer bags and seal tightly. You can also freeze the uncooked dough, tightly wrapped in clingfilm, for up to 6 months, so you can make a batch in advance and quickly whip up some homemade biscuits for unexpected visitors.

With biscuits there's no need for you to expend as much energy in the creaming and mixing process as with cakes, as you only need to soften the fat and sugar sufficiently to allow them to absorb the dry ingredients. You can make the biscuits any size and shape you like, and a basic biscuit recipe can easily be jazzed-up with a few extra ingredients: large **Chocolate Chip Cookies** (page 198) for hungry children, or elegant **Lavender Biscuits** (page 206) or **Fork Biscuits** (opposite) for a special teatime.

Whatever size and shape you choose, just remember to space them well apart on the baking trays as they will spread during baking, and adjust the cooking time accordingly. For biscuits cut from a roll of dough, do make sure they are an even thickness otherwise thinner ones will burn.

Biscuits are ideal for children to make and give as presents too, as they will have more of a sense of involvement and achievement if they have made it themselves. Help your child make **Cheese Straws** (page 210) and then let them decorate the gift box themselves – but make sure they help with the washing up afterwards!

Fork Biscuits

These biscuits first made their appearance in an old red Cordon Bleu cookery book, and I've been making them for years. This recipe makes about 16 biscuits.

100 g (4 oz) softened butter
50 g (2 oz) caster sugar
150 g (5 oz) self-raising flour

1 Pre-heat the oven to 180°C/Fan 160°C/Gas 4. Lightly grease 2 baking trays.

2 Measure the butter into a bowl and beat to soften. Gradually beat in the sugar and then the flour. Bring the mixture together with your hands to form a dough. Form the dough into 16 balls about the size of a walnut and place well apart on the prepared baking trays. Dip a fork in a little water and use this to flatten the biscuits.

3 Bake in the pre-heated oven for 15–20 minutes until a very pale golden. Lift off the baking tray and leave to cool completely on a wire rack.

To make Chocolate Fork Biscuits, follow the recipe above, but use only 120 g (4½ oz) self-raising flour along with 15 g (½ oz) cocoa. Bake until browned.

To make Orange or Lemon Fork Biscuits, follow the recipe above but add the grated rind of 1 small orange or lemon when you beat in the caster sugar. Bake until very pale golden.

Melting Moments

These old-fashioned biscuits are very short in texture. They are best eaten within a couple of days of making. This recipe makes about 36 biscuits.

225 g (8 oz) softened butter
175 g (6 oz) golden caster
    sugar
2 large egg yolks
a few drops of vanilla extract
275 g (10 oz) self-raising flour
50 g (2 oz) porridge oats
12 red or natural glacé
    cherries (optional)

1 Pre-heat the oven to 190°C/Fan 170°C/Gas 5. Line 2 baking trays with baking parchment.

2 Measure the butter, sugar, egg yolks, vanilla extract and flour into a mixing bowl and beat together to form a soft dough.

3 Divide the mixture into about 36 portions. Form each piece into a ball and roll in the oats to cover. Flatten each ball slightly and top each with a quartered glacé cherry, if you like. Place on the prepared baking trays.

4 Bake in the pre-heated oven for about 20 minutes or until golden. Allow to cool slightly on the baking trays for a few minutes before lifting on to a wire rack to cool.

Chocolate Chip Cookies

Don't expect these cookies to be as crisp as traditional biscuits – they should be slightly chewy. For a more adult taste, chop a bar of plain orange chocolate into small cubes and use instead of the chocolate chips. This recipes makes about 20 cookies. They will keep in a tin for a week.

100 g (4 oz) softened butter
75 g (3 oz) caster sugar
50 g (2 oz) light muscovado sugar
½ teaspoon vanilla extract
1 large beaten egg
150 g (5 oz) self-raising flour
100 g (4 oz) plain chocolate chips

1 Pre-heat the oven to 190°C/Fan 170°C/Gas 5. Lightly grease 3 baking trays.

2 Measure the butter and sugars into a medium-sized bowl and beat thoroughly until evenly blended. Add the vanilla extract to the beaten egg and then add a little at a time to the butter and sugar mixture in the bowl, beating well between each addition. Mix in the flour, and lastly stir in the chocolate chips. Spoon large teaspoons of the mixture on to the prepared baking trays, leaving room for the cookies to spread.

3 Bake in the pre-heated oven, on the top shelf, for 8–10 minutes or until the cookies are golden. Watch them like a hawk, as they will turn dark brown very quickly. Leave the cookies to cool on the trays for a few minutes, then lift off with a palette knife or fish slice and place on a wire cooling rack. Leave to cool completely, then store in an airtight tin.

Lime Lattice Cookies

Use the juice of the limes in drinks, or to add sharpness to whipped cream. This recipe makes about 16 cookies.

100 g (4 oz) softened butter
50 g (2 oz) caster sugar
150 g (5 oz) self-raising flour
finely grated rind of 2 limes

1 Pre-heat the oven to 180°C/Fan 160°C/Gas 4. Lightly grease 2 baking trays.

2 Measure the butter and sugar into a bowl and beat together to a creamy consistency. Add the flour and grated lime rind, then bring the mixture together to form a dough. Form the dough into 16 balls the size of a walnut and place on the prepared baking trays. Use a skewer to create a lattice pattern in the top of the biscuits.

3 Bake in the pre-heated oven for 10–15 minutes or until just beginning to turn golden. Lift on to a wire rack and leave to cool.

Double Chocolate Cookies

Dead easy to make, these are wonderful cookies. Expect an irregular shape. They are very soft when they come out of the oven but will harden up considerably on cooling. This recipe make about 36 cookies.

200 g (7 oz) plain chocolate
    (39 per cent cocoa solids)
50 g (2 oz) butter
397 g (14 oz) can
    condensed milk
225 g (8 oz) self-raising flour
65 g (2½ oz) milk or white
    chocolate buttons

1 Lightly grease 3 baking trays. Break up the chocolate and gently melt it along with the butter in a bowl set over a pan of simmering water, stirring occasionally. Stir in the condensed milk then take off the heat and cool.

2 Mix in the flour and the chocolate buttons and chill the mixture until firm enough to handle. Pre-heat the oven to 180°C/Fan 160°C/Gas 4.

3 Place large teaspoonfuls of the mixture spaced well apart on the prepared baking trays. Bake in the pre-heated oven for about 15 minutes. The cookies should still look soft and will glisten. Don't overcook them as they soon become very hard. Carefully remove the cookies with a palette knife and cool on a wire rack.

Shrewsbury Biscuits

These biscuits have a delicate lemony flavour. This recipe makes about 24 biscuits.

100 g (4 oz) softened butter
75 g (3 oz) caster sugar
1 large egg, separated
200 g (7 oz) plain flour
grated rind of 1 lemon
50 g (2 oz) currants
1–2 tablespoons milk
caster sugar, for sprinkling

1 Pre-heat the oven to 200°C/Fan 180°C/Gas 6. Lightly grease 3 baking trays.

2 Measure the butter and sugar into a bowl and cream together until light and fluffy. Beat in the egg yolk. Sieve in the flour and grated lemon rind and mix well. Add the currants and enough milk to give a fairly soft dough.

3 Knead the mixture gently on a lightly floured surface and roll out to a thickness of 5 mm (¼ in). Cut into about 24 rounds using a 6 cm (2½ in) fluted cutter. Place on the prepared baking trays.

4 Bake in the pre-heated oven for 8–10 minutes. Meanwhile, lightly beat the egg whites. Remove the biscuits from the oven, brush with beaten egg white, sprinkle with a little caster sugar and return to the oven for a further 4–5 minutes or until pale golden brown. Lift on to a wire rack to cool and then store in an airtight container.

Dorchester Biscuits

Savoury biscuits are great to go with drinks and these cheesy, nutty ones are delicious. Children like to roll these little balls, and they could give them as a present to a relative. This recipe makes about 30 biscuits.

100 g (4 oz) grated
    mature Cheddar
100 g (4 oz) plain flour
a little salt
100 g (4 oz) softened butter
¼ teaspoon cayenne pepper
50 g (2 oz) chopped unsalted
    mixed nuts, plus a few
    more for sprinkling

1 Pre-heat the oven to 180°C/Fan 160°C/Gas 4. Lightly grease 2 baking trays.

2 Measure all the ingredients, except the nuts for sprinkling, into a bowl and work together with a knife and then your hand to form a dough. Form the dough into 30 balls about the size of a walnut and place well apart on the prepared baking trays.

3 Sprinkle with chopped mixed nuts and then just lightly flatten the balls with your hand. Bake in the pre-heated oven for about 15–20 minutes or until golden brown. Lift on to a wire rack to cool. Serve warm or cold.

TIP
Try whole or halved cashew nuts for the topping, instead of the chopped nuts.

Cornish Fairings

Take care not to bake these spicy biscuits too long as they become hard and too crisp. Banging the baking tray part-way through cooking makes the mixture crack and flatten. This recipe makes about 24 biscuits.

100 g (4 oz) plain flour
¼ level teaspoon ground ginger
¼ level teaspoon ground mixed spice
¼ level teaspoon ground cinnamon
½ level teaspoon bicarbonate of soda
50 g (2 oz) softened butter
50 g (2 oz) caster sugar
75 g (3 oz) golden syrup

1 Pre-heat the oven to 180°C/Fan 160°C/Gas 4. Lightly grease 2 baking trays.

2 Measure the flour, spices and bicarbonate of soda into a bowl. Rub the butter into the flour with your fingertips until the mixture resembles fine breadcrumbs, then mix in the sugar.

3 Gently heat the golden syrup and stir into the mixture to make a soft dough. Roll the dough into 24 balls roughly about the size of a cherry and place on the prepared baking trays, allowing room for them to spread.

4 Bake in the pre-heated oven for about 10 minutes, then take the baking trays out of the oven and carefully hit on a solid surface to make the biscuits crack and spread. Bake for a further 5 minutes until they are a good even brown. Lift off the baking trays and leave to cool on a wire rack.

Yorkshire Gingernuts

Very quick to make and deliciously crunchy, these biscuits look nice stored in an attractive glass jar. This recipe makes about 50 biscuits.

100 g (4 oz) butter
1 generous tablespoon golden syrup
350 g (12 oz) self-raising flour
100 g (4 oz) demerara sugar
100 g (4 oz) light muscovado sugar
1 level teaspoon bicarbonate of soda
1 level tablespoon ground ginger
1 large egg, beaten

1 Pre-heat the oven to 160°C/Fan 140°C/Gas 3. Lightly grease 3 baking trays.

2 Measure the butter and golden syrup into a small pan and gently heat together until the butter has melted. Mix all the dry ingredients together in a large bowl, then add the melted butter mixture and the egg.

3 Form the dough into 50 balls about the size of a walnut and place well apart on the prepared baking trays.

4 Bake in the pre-heated oven for 15–20 minutes or until golden. Lift off the baking trays and leave to cool on a wire rack.

Lavender Biscuits

Both the flowers and the leaves of lavender can be used, although it is best to use young leaves. If you are using fresh lavender, make sure it is unsprayed. Dried lavender is stronger in flavour, so use half the quantity. This recipe makes about 20 biscuits.

175 g (6 oz) softened
    unsalted butter
2 tablespoons fresh,
    unsprayed, finely chopped
    lavender flowers and
    leaves (pick the flowerlets
    and the leaves off the
    stems to measure), or 1
    tablespoon dried lavender
100 g (4 oz) caster sugar
225 g (8 oz) plain flour
25 g (1 oz) demerara sugar

1 Lightly grease 3 large baking trays. Put the softened butter and the lavender into a mixing bowl and beat together (this will obtain the maximum flavour from the lavender).

2 Beat the caster sugar into the butter and lavender and then stir in the flour, bringing the mixture together with your hands and kneading lightly until smooth.

3 Divide the mixture in half and roll out to form 2 sausage shapes 15 cm (6 in) long. Roll the biscuit 'sausages' in the demerara sugar until evenly coated. Wrap in baking parchment or foil and chill until firm.

4 Pre-heat the oven to 160°C/Fan 140°C/Gas 3. Cut each 'sausage' into about 10 slices and put them on the prepared baking trays, allowing a little room for them to spread. Bake in the pre-heated oven for 15–20 minutes, until the biscuits are pale golden brown at the edges. Lift them off the trays with a fish slice or palette knife and leave on a wire rack to cool completely.

Oat Rounds

These biscuits are first cousin to the digestive biscuit, with added oats. They are good with cheese or eaten by themselves with morning coffee and have become a firm favourite in our house. This recipe makes about 16 biscuits.

50 g (2 oz) caster sugar
100 g (4 oz) softened butter
100 g (4 oz) porridge oats
50 g (2 oz) plain flour

1 Pre-heat the oven to 160°C/Fan 140°C/Gas 3. Lightly grease 2 baking trays.

2 Measure the sugar and butter into a bowl and beat together to a creamy consistency. Add the oats and flour and work them into the mixture. Lightly knead the mixture until smooth and then roll out to a thickness of 5 mm (¼ in) on a lightly floured work surface.

3 Cut into rounds using a 6 cm (2½ in) plain cutter and place on the prepared baking trays. Bake in the pre-heated oven for about 20 minutes or until beginning to turn golden. Lift on to a wire rack to cool.

Muesli Cookies

The flavour and consistency will depend on the muesli used. These are good for a lunch box, for a snack at school or work, or to take on a picnic. This recipe makes about 28 cookies.

175 g (6 oz) softened butter
100 g (4 oz) caster sugar
1 large egg
175 g (6 oz) self-raising flour
175 g (6 oz) muesli
demerara sugar, for
    sprinkling

1 Pre-heat the oven to 180°C/Fan 160°C/Gas 4. Lightly grease 3 baking trays.

2 Measure all the ingredients, except the muesli and the demerara sugar, into a large bowl and beat together until well blended and smooth. Stir in the muesli.

3 Spoon 28 teaspoonfuls of the mixture on to the prepared baking trays, leaving room for the cookies to spread. Sprinkle the top of each with a little extra muesli and a little demerara sugar.

4 Bake in the pre-heated oven for 10–15 minutes or until golden brown at the edges. Lift on to a wire rack to cool.

Rich Cheesy Biscuits

Cheesy biscuits always go well with drinks. If you make these ahead of time, they are best just heated again in the oven before serving. This recipe makes about 32 biscuits.

175 g (6 oz) plain flour
¾ level teaspoon salt
¾ level teaspoon dry
    mustard powder
75 g (3 oz) butter
175 g (6 oz) grated mature
    Cheddar
2 large eggs
sesame or poppy seeds,
    for sprinkling

1 Pre-heat the oven to 200°C/Fan 180°C/Gas 6. Lightly grease 3 baking trays.

2 Sieve the flour, salt and mustard powder into a bowl and rub in the butter with your fingertips until the mixture resembles fine breadcrumbs. Stir in the grated cheese. Beat the eggs then stir just enough egg into the flour mixture to form a soft dough (there will be some egg left over for glazing). Wrap the dough in clingfilm and chill for about 15 minutes.

3 Roll the dough out on to a lightly floured work surface to a thickness of about 5 mm (¼ in) and cut into 5 cm (2 in) rounds or triangles. Place on the prepared baking trays and brush with the remaining beaten egg. Sprinkle lightly with sesame or poppy seeds. Re-roll the trimmings once only.

4 Bake in the pre-heated oven for about 10–15 minutes or until crisp and golden. Lift off the baking trays and leave to cool on a wire rack.

Cheese Straws

A lovely gift idea, beautifully presented in a box. They can be made in advance, but do not keep them in the larder; they can quickly go off. Freeze them once cold – they taste good even when freezer-hard! This recipes makes 30 straws.

100 g (4 oz) plain flour
75 g (3 oz) softened butter
50 g (2 oz) grated mature
　　Cheddar
1 large egg yolk
finely grated Parmesan,
　　for sprinkling

1 Pre-heat the oven to 190°C/Fan 170°C/Gas 5. Lightly grease 2 baking trays.

2 Measure the flour into a bowl and rub in the butter with your fingertips until the mixture resembles fine breadcrumbs. Stir in the grated Cheddar. Reserve a tiny bit of the egg yolk for glazing and stir in the remainder. Bring the mixture together to form a dough. Wrap in clingfilm and chill in the fridge for about 30 minutes.

3 Roll the chilled dough out on to a lightly floured work surface to a thickness of about 5 mm (¼ in). Cut into neat strips about 5 mm (¼ in) wide and about 10 cm (4 in) long. Place on the prepared baking trays, brush with the remaining egg yolk and sprinkle generously with grated Parmesan.

4 Bake in the pre-heated oven for 10–15 minutes or until golden. Lift off the baking trays and leave to cool completely on a wire rack. Pack carefully in a gift box and give as fresh as possible, or freeze until ready to offer.

CHAPTER TEN

Fancy Biscuits

A beautiful box of freshly made biscuits is always a welcome present. It shows that you have spent time preparing something for a friend, or even a good cause, instead of just spending money. If you make a note of anything that a relative, friend or guest has especially liked, in the future you can make it again and give them a thoughtful gift you know they will really appreciate.

The biscuits here take more skill and time to make than other biscuits and cookies – **Almond Tuiles** (page 220), **Brandy Snaps** (page 226) and **Sugared Pretzels** (page 223) need to be formed into their familiar shapes; the chocolate cases for the **Chocolate Ganache Petit Fours** (page 219) need to be painted on to the paper cases. But these recipes are worth the extra effort.

Other biscuits in this chapter are not complicated to make, but I've included them here because of their festive importance or special history. For example, **Anzac Biscuits** (page 225) are associated with the memorial holiday Anzac Day in Australia and New Zealand, and were originally sent to soldiers by their loved ones during World War I as they preserve well.

As well as giving traditional food presents at festivals such as Christmas and Easter, I also give food presents for birthdays or anniversaries, when someone has come out of hospital or when I go to stay somewhere for a weekend.

Ovens vary enormously, so if you find that a batch of biscuits takes longer to reach the perfect pale caramel colour, make a note for next time. You may need to rotate the baking trays, if the heat is fiercer at the back of the oven. If the biscuits, once baked, lose their crispiness, pop them back into a moderate oven to refresh.

Viennese Fingers

These biscuits must be made with butter. The mixture holds its shape beautifully for piping, so use it for all shapes of piped biscuits. This recipe makes about 20 biscuits.

100 g (4 oz) softened butter
25 g (1 oz) icing sugar
100 g (4 oz) plain flour
¼ level teaspoon baking
    powder
50 g (2 oz) plain chocolate
    (39 per cent cocoa solids)

1 Pre-heat the oven to 190°C/Fan 170°C/Gas 5. Lightly grease 2 baking trays. Fit a piping bag with a medium star nozzle.

2 Measure the butter and icing sugar into a bowl and beat well until pale and fluffy. Sieve in the flour and baking powder. Beat well until thoroughly mixed. Spoon into the piping bag and pipe out finger shapes about 7.5 cm (3 in) long, spacing them well apart.

3 Bake in the pre-heated oven for 10–15 minutes or until a pale golden brown. Lift off and cool on a wire rack.

4 Break the chocolate into pieces and melt it gently in a bowl set over a pan of hot water, stirring occasionally. Dip both ends of the biscuits into the chocolate and leave to set on the wire rack.

Florentines

Using baking parchment makes it so much simpler to get these biscuits off the baking trays. You can simply use a well-greased baking tray, but be careful not to leave the Florentines for too long or they will harden before you have a chance to lift them off. This recipe makes about 20 Florentines.

50 g (2 oz) butter
50 g (2 oz) demerara sugar
50 g (2 oz) golden syrup
50 g (2 oz) plain flour
4 red or natural glacé cherries, finely chopped
50 g (2 oz) finely chopped candied peel
50 g (2 oz) finely chopped mixed almonds and walnuts
175 g (6 oz) plain chocolate (39 per cent cocoa solids)

1 Pre-heat the oven to 180°C/Fan 160°C/Gas 4. Line 3 baking trays with baking parchment.

2 Measure the butter, sugar and syrup into a small pan and heat gently until the butter has melted. Remove from the heat and add the flour, chopped cherries, candied peel and nuts to the pan and stir well to mix. Spoon teaspoonfuls of the mixture on to the prepared baking trays, leaving plenty of room for them to spread.

3 Bake in the pre-heated oven for 8–10 minutes or until golden brown. Leave the Florentines to cool before lifting on to a cooling rack with a palette knife (if the Florentines have been baked on greased baking trays, then allow them to harden for a few moments only before lifting on to cooling racks to cool completely). If the Florentines become too hard to remove, then pop them back into the oven for a few moments to allow them to soften.

4 Break the chocolate into pieces and melt it in a bowl set over a pan of hot water, stirring occasionally. Spread a little melted chocolate over the flat base of each Florentine, mark a zigzag in the chocolate with a fork and leave to set, chocolate side up, on the cooling rack. Store in an airtight container.

TIP
These are luxurious biscuits, but you do need patience and accurate scales to make them.

Petits Fours
aux Amandes

These make a very special present – petits fours tend to be rather fiddly to make for oneself! Look out for a pretty or unusual plate in an antique shop or car boot sale, and arrange the petits fours on this. Cover with clear cellophane and decorate with a ribbon. The milk and sugar glaze is optional for these petits fours, but it does give a nice shine. This recipe makes 24 petits fours.

2 large egg whites
100 g (4 oz) ground almonds
75 g (3 oz) caster sugar
a little almond extract

TO DECORATE
red or natural glacé cherries,
    chopped

TO FINISH (OPTIONAL)
1 tablespoon caster sugar
2 tablespoons milk

1 Pre-heat the oven to 180°C/Fan 160°C/Gas 4. Line 2 baking trays with baking parchment. Fit a piping bag with a large star nozzle.

2 Whisk the egg whites until stiff. Fold in the ground almonds, sugar and almond extract. Spoon the mixture into the prepared piping bag and pipe the mixture into small rosettes. Decorate each rosette with a small piece of glacé cherry.

3 Bake in the pre-heated oven for about 15 minutes or until golden. Lift on to a wire rack. To finish, mix the caster sugar and milk together and lightly brush over the petits fours.

Chocolate Ganache Petits Fours

These are irresistible, but keep them in a cool place or they'll become very soft. This recipe makes 24 petits fours.

FOR THE CASINGS
175 g (6 oz) plain chocolate
   (39 per cent cocoa solids)
1 teaspoon sunflower oil

FOR THE CHOCOLATE
   GANACHE
150 ml (¼ pint) double cream
100 g (4 oz) plain (39 per cent
   cocoa solids)
a little rum or brandy,
   to flavour

TO DECORATE
chopped pistachio nuts
edible gold leaf (optional)

1 First make the chocolate casings. Break the chocolate into pieces and heat gently along with the oil in a bowl set over a pan of hot water, stirring occasionally until the chocolate has melted.

2 Allow to cool slightly then brush the inside of about 24 petits fours paper cases with a thin layer of chocolate (you can use a fine brush to do this, or even just the fingertip). Leave to set in a cool place. Give the cases a second coat of chocolate and again leave to set.

3 To make the ganache, break the chocolate into pieces. Pour the cream into a small saucepan and bring to the boil. Remove from the heat and add the chocolate pieces and a little rum or brandy. Stir until the chocolate has melted.

4 Return the pan to the heat, bring to the boil and then take off the heat and leave to cool. When firm, spoon the chocolate ganache into a piping bag fitted with a medium star nozzle and pipe rosettes of the ganache into the chocolate cases.

5 Carefully peel off the paper cases. Decorate the top of each petit four with a small piece of pistachio nut or a touch of gold leaf (optional), and chill until required.

Almond Tuiles

These slim, crisp, curled biscuits are wonderful with light mousses, ice-cream and fruit salads. They keep well in an airtight tin or, if made a long time in advance, in the freezer. Store them in a rigid box or tin so they cannot be broken. This recipe makes 20 biscuits.

75 g (3 oz) softened butter
75 g (3 oz) caster sugar
50 g (2 oz) plain flour
1 large egg white
75 g (3 oz) finely chopped
    blanched almonds

TO FINISH
a little icing sugar,
    for dusting

1 Pre-heat the oven to 200°C/Fan 180°C/Gas 6. Lightly grease 2 baking trays.

2 Measure the butter and sugar into a bowl and beat well together until pale and fluffy. Sieve the flour over the egg white, mix and then stir into the butter mixture along with the finely chopped almonds. Place teaspoonfuls of the mixture on to the prepared baking trays, about 4 at a time, leaving ample room for the biscuits to spread.

3 Bake in the pre-heated oven for 6–8 minutes or until they are browned around the edge but not in the middle. Remove from the oven and leave to stand for a second or two then remove from the tray with a palette knife and curl over a rolling pin until set. When cool, store in an airtight container. Serve with a dusting of icing sugar.

Macaroons

Traditionally macaroons were always made on rice paper but, as this is not always easy to get hold of, I've used baking parchment. This recipe makes about 16 macaroons.

2 large egg whites
8 blanched almonds, halved
100 g (4 oz) ground almonds
175 g (6 oz) caster sugar
25 g (1 oz) ground rice or
    semolina
a few drops of almond
    extract

1 Pre-heat the oven to 150°C/Fan 130°C/Gas 2. Line 2 baking trays with baking parchment.

2 Put the egg whites into a bowl, dip in the halved almonds and set them aside. Whisk the egg whites until they form soft peaks. Gently fold in the ground almonds, sugar, ground rice or semolina and almond extract.

3 Spoon the mixture in teaspoonfuls on to the prepared baking trays, and smooth out with the back of a spoon to form circles. Place an almond half in the centre of each.

4 Bake in the pre-heated oven for 20–25 minutes or until a pale golden brown. Leave to cool on the trays for a few minutes, then lift off and finish cooling on a wire rack.

Sugared Pretzels

I use a quick method for making the pastry here rather than the classic way. This recipe makes 16 pretzels.

115 g (4½ oz) plain flour
65 g (2½ oz) butter
25 g (1 oz) caster sugar
1 large egg, beaten
a few drops of vanilla extract

TO FINISH
a little icing sugar,
    for dusting

1 Measure the flour into a large bowl, add the butter and rub in with your fingertips until the mixture resembles fine breadcrumbs. Stir in the sugar and then the egg and vanilla extract and mix until the pastry comes together. Knead very gently on a lightly floured work surface until smooth, then wrap in clingfilm and chill for about 30 minutes, or until firm enough to roll.

2 Pre-heat the oven to 200°C/Fan 180°C/Gas 6. Lightly grease 2 baking trays.

3 Divide the dough into pieces about the size of a walnut. Roll each piece into a thin sausage shape and then twist into the traditional pretzel shape, like a loose knot. Place on the prepared baking trays.

4 Bake in the pre-heated oven for about 8 minutes or until barely changing colour. Lift on to a wire rack and dust thickly with icing sugar while still hot.

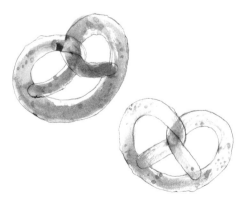

Easter Biscuits

Bought Easter biscuits are usually larger than this. If you like them that way, simply use a larger cutter. This recipe makes about 24 biscuits.

100 g (4 oz) softened butter
75 g (3 oz) caster sugar
1 large egg, separated
200 g (7 oz) plain flour
½ level teaspoon mixed spice
½ level teaspoon ground
  cinnamon
50 g (2 oz) currants
25 g (1 oz) chopped candied
  peel
1–2 tablespoons milk
a little caster sugar, for
  sprinkling

1 Pre-heat the oven to 200°C/Fan 180°C/Gas 6. Lightly grease 3 baking trays.

2 Measure the butter and sugar into a bowl and beat together until light and fluffy. Beat in the egg yolk. Sieve in the flour and spices and mix well. Add the currants and chopped candied peel and enough milk to give a fairly soft dough.

3 Knead the mixture lightly on a lightly floured work surface and roll out to a thickness of 5 mm (¼ in). Cut into rounds using a 6 cm (2½ in) fluted cutter. Place on the prepared baking trays.

4 Bake in the pre-heated oven for 8–10 minutes. Meanwhile, lightly beat the egg white. Remove the biscuits from the oven, brush them with the beaten egg white, sprinkle with a little caster sugar and return to the oven for a further 4–5 minutes or until pale golden brown. Lift on to a wire rack to cool. Store in an airtight container.

TIP
If bought or homemade biscuits have gone a little soft, place them on a baking tray and crisp them in a moderate oven for a few minutes.

Anzac Biscuits

Also known as Diggers, these traditional Australian biscuits are really easy to make. This recipe makes about 45 biscuits.

150 g (5 oz) softened butter
1 tablespoon golden syrup
175 g (6 oz) granulated sugar
75 g (3 oz) self-raising flour
75 g (3 oz) desiccated coconut
100 g (4 oz) porridge oats

1 Pre-heat the oven to 180°C/Fan 160°C/Gas 4. Lightly grease 2 baking trays.

2 Measure the butter, golden syrup and sugar into a medium saucepan and heat gently until the butter has melted and the sugar has dissolved. Stir in the flour, coconut and oats and mix well until evenly blended.

3 Place large teaspoonfuls of the mixture well apart on the prepared baking trays and flatten slightly with the back of the spoon. You should have enough mixture for about 45 mounds, and you will need to bake them in batches.

4 Bake in the pre-heated oven for 8–10 minutes until they have spread out flat and are lightly browned at the edges. Leave to cool on the trays for a few minutes, then carefully lift off with a palette knife and place on a wire rack to cool completely. If the biscuits harden too much to lift off the tray, pop them back in the oven for a few minutes to soften. Store in an airtight container.

Brandy Snaps

I must confess that I rarely make these myself as it is so easy to buy good ones! Serve plain with ice cream or mousses, or fill with whipped cream and serve with fruit. This recipe makes about 24 Brandy Snaps.

50 g (2 oz) butter
50 g (2 oz) demerara sugar
50 g (2 oz) golden syrup
50 g (2 oz) plain flour
½ level teaspoon ground ginger
½ teaspoon lemon juice

1 Pre-heat the oven to 180°C/Fan 160°C/Gas 4. Line 2 baking trays with baking parchment and then oil the handles of 4 wooden spoons.

2 Measure the butter, sugar and syrup into a small pan and heat gently until the butter has melted and sugar has dissolved. Leave the mixture to cool slightly and then sieve in the flour and the ginger. Add the lemon juice and stir well to mix thoroughly. Place teaspoons of the mixture on to the prepared baking trays, at least 10 cm (4 in) apart and only 4 teaspoons at a time.

3 Bake in the pre-heated oven for about 8 minutes or until the mixture is well spread out and a dark golden colour. Remove from the oven and leave for a few minutes to firm, then lift from the baking parchment using a fish slice. Turn over and roll around the handle of the wooden spoons. Leave to set on a wire rack and then slip out the spoons. Repeat until all the mixture has been used. When cold, store in an airtight tin.

To make Brandy Snap Baskets, mould the cooked mixture around the base of a greased cup or an orange and use your fingers to flute the top. You don't need to grease the orange, as its natural oils will prevent the brandy snap mixture from sticking.

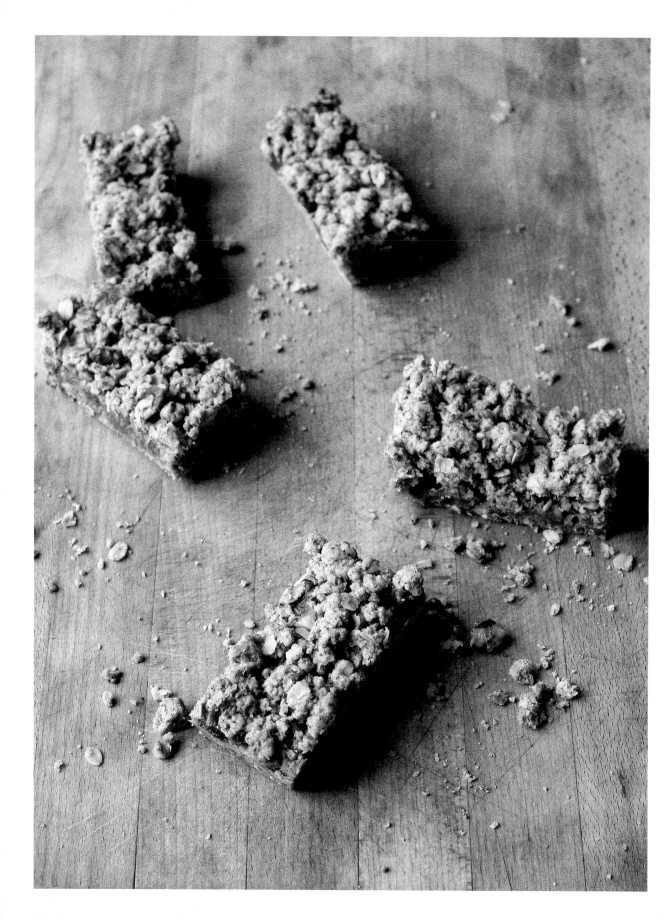

CHAPTER ELEVEN

Shortbreads and Bars

Shortbread is traditionally eaten at Christmas and New Year. It can be made as a round, presented whole or sliced, or made into individual biscuits, and forms the base for familiar bakes, such as schooltime favourite **Millionaires' Shortbread** (page 235) topped with caramel and chocolate.

Shortbread can also be decoratively shaped in wooden or earthenware moulds, adding an extra-special touch to a gift. Once you have made the dough, lightly flour the mould and press the shortbread into the patterned depression. Level with a rolling pin, then turn out on to a baking tray, patterned side up, to bake. New wooden moulds should be seasoned a couple of times before use by rubbing them with a little flavourless salad oil, like vegetable oil. If you are making homemade shortbread as a gift, present it in a decorative box for added impact.

The bars in this chapter, such as **Apricot and Walnut Sandwich Bars** (page 237) are perfect for lunch boxes or for an after-school (or after-work) snack as they contain lots of dried fruit, nuts, seeds, oats and wholemeal flour, making them more wholesome than other bakes – although, of course, they are still cakes, so will never be as healthy as a piece of fresh fruit!

A wonderful bonus when cooking the recipes here is that, if the shortbread or bar mixture is cooked at the edges, but not in the middle, you can put it back in the oven for a few minutes – none of the fears about sinking attached to cake making are relevant to biscuits.

The Very Best Shortbread

For a really good shortbread it is essential to use butter. I like to use semolina as well as flour to give the shortbread crunch, but you can use cornflour or ground rice instead. This recipe cuts into about 30 fingers.

225 g (8 oz) plain flour
100 g (4 oz) semolina
225 g (8 oz) butter
100 g (4 oz) caster sugar
50 g (2 oz) flaked almonds
　　(optional)
25 g (1 oz) demerara sugar,
　　for dusting

1 Lightly grease a 30 x 23 cm (12 x 9 in) traybake or roasting tin. Mix together the flour and the semolina in a bowl or food processor. Add the butter and sugar and rub together with your fingertips until the mixture is just beginning to bind together. Knead lightly until the mixture forms a smooth dough.

2 Press the dough into the prepared tin and level it with the back of a spatula or a palette knife, making sure the mixture is evenly spread. Prick all over with a fork, sprinkle over the flaked almonds if using, and chill until firm. Pre-heat the oven to 160°C/Fan 140°C/Gas 3.

3 Bake in the pre-heated oven for about 35 minutes or until a very pale golden brown. Sprinkle with demerara sugar and leave to cool on the baking tray for a few minutes, then cut in to 30 fingers. Carefully lift the fingers out of the tin with a palette knife and finish cooling on a wire rack. Store in an airtight tin.

To make Orange Shortbread, add the finely grated zest of one large orange to the mixture.

TIPS
Glacé cherries, dried apricots and sultanas make delicious additions to shortbread, but the biscuits then need to be eaten on the day of making as they soon become soggy with the moisture from the fruit.

Bishop's Fingers

If you notice that the underside of the shortbread is not pale gold, return the tray to the oven for a further 5–10 minutes. This recipe makes 12 fingers.

100 g (4 oz) plain flour
25 g (1 oz) ground almonds
25 g (1 oz) semolina
100 g (4 oz) butter
50 g (2 oz) caster sugar
a few drops of almond extract
25 g (1 oz) flaked almonds
a little caster sugar, for
    dusting

1 Pre-heat the oven to 160°C/Fan 140°C/Gas 3. Lightly grease an 18 cm (7 in) shallow square tin.

2 Mix together the flour, ground almonds and semolina in a bowl or food processor. Add the butter, sugar and almond extract and rub together with your fingertips until the mixture is just beginning to bind together. Knead lightly until smooth. Press the dough into the prepared tin and level the surface with the back of a metal spoon or a palette knife. Sprinkle over the flaked almonds.

3 Bake in the pre-heated oven for 30–35 minutes or until a very pale golden brown. Mark the shortbread into 12 fingers with a knife, sprinkle with caster sugar and leave to cool in the tin. When completely cold, cut into fingers, lift out carefully and store in an airtight tin.

Special Shortbread Biscuits

Buy a pretty tin and fill it with a variety of homemade biscuits. Vary the recipe by using caster sugar in place of the light muscovado sugar, if you like. This recipe makes about 30 biscuits.

175 g (6 oz) plain flour
75 g (3 oz) light muscovado
   sugar
100 g (4 oz) butter
a little demerara sugar,
   for sprinkling

1 Pre-heat the oven to 160°C/Fan 140°C/Gas 3. Lightly grease 2 baking trays.

2 Measure the flour and sugar into a large bowl and rub in the butter with your fingertips. Knead gently to bring together to form a dough.

3 Roll out the dough on a lightly floured work surface to a thickness of about 5 mm (¼ in). Cut into circles using a 5 cm (2 in) fluted cutter and transfer the biscuits to the prepared baking trays. Prick the biscuits all over with a fork and sprinkle with demerara sugar.

4 Bake in the pre-heated oven for 15–20 minutes or until pale golden. Lift on to a wire rack and leave to cool.

To make Cherry Shortbread Biscuits, follow the recipe above and then press 25 g (1 oz) of chopped red or natural glacé cherries into the top of each biscuit before baking. Do not sprinkle with demerara sugar as the cherries sweeten the biscuits.

To make Walnut Shortbread Biscuits, follow the recipe above, adding 50 g (2 oz) roughly chopped walnuts in step 2 before kneading the mixture into a dough. Dust generously with sifted icing sugar when cooled.

Millionaires' Shortbread

This shortbread is always popular. The different textures are the principal appeal – the crunch of the shortbread base, the caramel in the middle, and the chunky chocolate on top. This recipe makes about 24 squares.

FOR THE SHORTBREAD
250 g (9 oz) plain flour
75 g (3 oz) caster sugar
175 g (6 oz) softened butter

FOR THE CARAMEL
100 g (4 oz) butter
100 g (4 oz) light
    muscovado sugar
two 397 g (14 oz) cans
    condensed milk

FOR THE TOPPING
200 g (7 oz) plain (39 per
    cent cocoa solids) or milk
    chocolate

1 Pre-heat the oven to 180°C/Fan 160°C/Gas 4. Lightly grease a 33 x 23 cm (13 x 9 in) swiss roll tin.

2 To make the shortbread, mix the flour and caster sugar in a bowl. Rub in the butter with your fingertips until the mixture resembles fine breadcrumbs.

3 Knead the mixture together until it forms a dough, then press into the base of the prepared tin. Prick the shortbread lightly with a fork and bake in the pre-heated oven for about 20 minutes or until firm to the touch and very lightly browned. Cool in the tin.

4 To make the caramel, measure the butter, sugar and condensed milk into a pan and heat gently until the sugar has dissolved. Bring to the boil, stirring all the time, then reduce the heat and simmer very gently, stirring continuously, for about 5 minutes or until the mixture has thickened slightly. It is important to stir the caramel mixture continuously – if you leave it for even a second it will catch on the bottom of the pan and burn. Pour over the shortbread and leave to cool.

5 To make the topping, break the chocolate into pieces and melt gently in a bowl set over a pan of hot water, stirring occasionally. Pour over the cold caramel and leave to set. Cut into squares or bars.

TIP
A marbled chocolate top looks stunning. Simply melt just over 50 g (2 oz) each of plain, milk and white chocolate in separate bowls. Place the chocolate in spoonfuls over the set caramel, alternating the 3 types. Use a skewer to marble the edges of the chocolates together and then leave to set.

Apricot and Walnut Sandwich Bars

These luscious, moist bars are similar to those you can buy in health-food shops, and are quite substantial and wholesome additions to a lunch box. This recipe makes 8 bars.

FOR THE OAT MIXTURE

50 g (2 oz) porridge oats

50 g (2 oz) light muscovado sugar

40 g (1½ oz) chopped walnuts

200 g (7 oz) wholemeal self-raising flour

175 g (6 oz) butter, melted

FOR THE FILLING

175 g (6 oz) ready-to-eat dried apricots

50 ml (2 fl oz) water

2 tablespoons caster sugar

grated rind of 1 lemon

1 Pre-heat the oven to 150°C/Fan 130°C/Gas 2. Grease an 18 cm (7 in) shallow square cake tin then line the base with baking parchment.

2 First prepare the filling. Snip the apricots into pieces and put them in a small pan with the water, caster sugar and lemon rind. Bring to the boil and then simmer very gently until the apricots are really soft and the liquid has evaporated. Set aside to cool.

3 While the apricot filling is cooling, make the oat mixture. Measure the oats, sugar, walnuts and flour into a bowl and add the melted butter. Stir to mix. Divide the oat mixture in half and spread one half into the base of the prepared tin. Spoon the cooled apricot mixture on top and carefully spread it to form an even layer. Cover evenly with the remaining oat mixture.

4 Bake in the pre-heated oven for about 45 minutes or until firm and a golden brown. Cut into bars while still warm.

Date and Cherry Butter Bars

It's important to use butter and not baking margarine in this recipe, to achieve a lovely buttery flavour. This recipe makes 24 bars.

225 g (8 oz) self-raising flour
½ level teaspoon baking powder
75 g (3 oz) butter
100 g (4 oz) caster sugar
75 g (3 oz) chopped dates
25 g (1 oz) chopped red or natural glacé cherries
1 large egg, beaten

1 Pre-heat the oven to 190°C/Fan 170°C/Gas 5. Grease a 30 x 23 cm (12 x 9 in) traybake or roasting tin.

2 Measure the flour and baking powder into a bowl and rub in the butter using your fingertips until the mixture resembles fine breadcrumbs. Stir in the sugar, chopped dates and chopped cherries. Add the beaten egg and bring the mixture together to form a dough. Knead lightly until smooth, then press into the prepared tin.

3 Bake in the pre-heated oven for about 10 minutes then remove from the oven and cut into 24 bars. Return to the oven for about a further 10 minutes until beginning to tinge a golden colour. Re-cut into bars and leave to cool in the tins. When cold, ease the bars out of the tin and store in an airtight container.

Bakewell Slices

Be generous with the raspberry jam, it makes all the difference. As the shortcrust pastry contains a lot of fat and no sugar, there is no need to line the tin with baking parchment.

FOR THE SHORTCRUST PASTRY
175 g (6 oz) plain flour
75 g (3 oz) butter
2–3 tablespoons cold water

FOR THE SPONGE MIXTURE
100 g (4 oz) softened butter
100 g (4 oz) caster sugar
175 g (6 oz) self-raising flour
1 level teaspoon baking powder
2 large eggs
2 tablespoons milk
½ teaspoon almond extract

TO FINISH
about 4 tablespoons raspberry jam
flaked almonds, for sprinkling

1 To make the pastry, measure the flour into a bowl and rub in the butter with your fingertips until the mixture resembles fine breadcrumbs. Add the water gradually, mixing to form a soft dough.

2 Roll out the dough on to a lightly floured work surface and use to line a 30 x 23 cm (12 x 9 in) traybake or roasting tin. Pre-heat the oven to 180°C/Fan 160°C/Gas 4.

3 Measure all the sponge ingredients into a bowl and beat until well blended. Spread the pastry with raspberry jam and then top with the sponge mixture. Sprinkle with the flaked almonds.

4 Bake in the pre-heated oven for about 25 minutes or until the cake has shrunk from the sides of the tin and springs back when pressed in the centre with your fingertips. Leave to cool in the tin and then cut into slices.

CHAPTER TWELVE

Baking for Children

When my own children were small, I loved making cakes with them and found it an effective way of entertaining their friends too! I think it is important to teach children the basics of cooking and to enjoy preparing food. It is never too early to encourage them to experiment with simple recipes, with guidance and supervision. You will also find children are more open to trying new foods, if they have had a hand in their preparation.

Children like to make small, colourful things they can decorate with a little icing and sweets, so you will find recipes here like **Little Gems** (page 256), **Iced Animal Biscuits** (page 257) and **Gingerbread Men** (page 259). There is so much scope for individual creativity with these bakes.

Other recipes here, such as **Chocolate Crispies** (opposite) are the simplest things to make and, although they don't actually require baking in the oven, they are a very good introduction to cake making and the hob.

Although it is easy to buy food for children's parties, this chapter also includes inspiration for party food. The recipes are straightforward and will not only be more cost-effective, but will also ensure that you know that your child is enjoying cakes and bakes free from preservatives and additives.

Doughnuts (page 248) also appear in this chapter because while I don't encourage feeding children deep-fried food, doughnuts have always been a favourite treat with my children and grandchildren and homemade doughnuts are far superior to bought ones.

Chocolate Crispies

This mixture makes 18 small crispies or, for a more generous size, you could make about 12. Keep them cool in warm weather. If you haven't any paper cases, you can spoon the mixture on to baking parchment in mounds and leave to set. When I was small, my mother made them on the waxed paper from inside the cornflake packet!

225 g (8 oz) plain chocolate
   (39 per cent cocoa solids)
1 tablespoon golden syrup
50 g (2 oz) butter
75 g (3 oz) cornflakes

1 Break the chocolate into pieces, and put it into a medium saucepan along with the golden syrup and the butter. Allow to melt over a low heat, stirring occasionally. Meanwhile, put 18 paper cake cases on to a large baking tray.

2 Add the cornflakes to the pan and stir gently until they are all evenly coated in the chocolate mixture. Spoon the mixture into the paper cases and chill in the fridge to set.

Mini Cakes

Simplicity itself to make! You can top the buns with any sweets of your choosing. This recipe makes 32 mini cakes.

40 g (1½ oz) softened butter
1 large egg
50 g (2 oz) self-raising flour
½ level teaspoon baking
    powder
40 g (1½ oz) caster sugar

FOR THE ICING
50 g (2 oz) sifted icing sugar
about ½ tablespoon water
sweets, to decorate

1 Pre-heat the oven to 180°C/Fan 160°C/Gas 4. Arrange about 32 petits fours cases on 2 baking trays.

2 Measure all the cake ingredients into a bowl and beat well until thoroughly blended. Spoon scant teaspoonfuls of the mixture into the cases, being careful not to overfill.

3 Bake in the pre-heated oven for 15–20 minutes until well risen and firm to the touch. Cool on a wire rack.

4 To make the icing, measure the icing sugar into a bowl and add enough water to give a spreading consistency. Spoon a little on top of each cake and spread out with the back of the teaspoon. When the icing has almost set, top with a sweet.

To make Mini Chocolate Cakes, follow the recipe above but replace the 50 g (2 oz) self-raising flour with 40 g (1½ oz) self-raising flour and 15 g (½ oz) sifted cocoa powder. Decorate with fancy chocolate sweets.

Mini Jammy Cakes

These are usually made so the jam is enclosed, but here they are left open so that the jam becomes nice and chewy. The cakes are best served warm. This recipe makes about 24 cakes.

225 g (8 oz) self-raising flour
¼ level teaspoon ground
   mixed spice
50 g (2 oz) softened butter
100 g (4 oz) caster sugar
1 large egg, beaten
3–4 tablespoons milk
a little blackcurrant jam
a little granulated sugar

1 Pre-heat the oven to 200°C/Fan 180°C/Gas 6. Lightly grease 2 baking trays.

2 Measure the flour, spice and butter into a bowl and rub in the butter with your fingertips until the mixture resembles fine breadcrumbs. Stir in the sugar. Mix the egg and milk together and stir into the mixture, adding only enough of the liquid to make a stiff dough. Divide the dough into about 24 pieces and roll each piece into a smooth ball.

3 Using the handle of a wooden spoon, make a hole in the centre of each ball of dough and put about ¼ teaspoon jam into each one. Place the balls of dough – jam side up – on to the prepared baking trays and sprinkle them with a little granulated sugar.

4 Bake in the pre-heated oven for about 10 minutes until they are a pale golden brown. Lift off the tray and allow to cool a little on a wire rack before eating warm.

Chocolate and Vanilla Pinwheel Biscuits

Young children can easily make these – under supervision, of course. They're fun for Bonfire Night. This recipe makes about 20 biscuits.

FOR THE VANILLA
   BISCUIT MIXTURE
50 g (2 oz) softened butter
25 g (1 oz) caster sugar
25 g (1 oz) cornflour
50 g (2 oz) plain flour
½ large egg
a few drops of vanilla extract

FOR THE CHOCOLATE
   BISCUIT MIXTURE
50 g (2 oz) softened butter
25 g (1 oz) caster sugar
25 g (1 oz) corn flour
40 g (1½ oz) plain flour
½ large egg
15 g (½ oz) cocoa powder

1 Lightly grease 2 baking trays.

2 Measure all the ingredients for the vanilla biscuit mixture into a bowl and mix to form a soft dough. Wrap in clingfilm and chill in the fridge for about 30 minutes until firm. Make the chocolate biscuit mixture in the same way, then wrap and chill.

3 On a lightly floured work surface, roll out both pieces of dough to oblongs about 25 x 18 cm (10 x 7 in). Place the vanilla biscuit dough on top of the chocolate dough and then roll up the two together from the narrow edge. Wrap in clingfilm and chill again for about 30 minutes.

4 Pre-heat the oven to 180°C/Fan 160°C/Gas 4. Using a sharp knife, cut the roll into about 20 slices and place on the prepared baking trays.

5 Bake in the pre-heated oven for about 20 minutes until the vanilla biscuit is golden in colour. Lift on to a wire rack and leave to cool.

Doughnuts

Excellent for hungry teenagers, these are best eaten as fresh as possible. This recipe makes 16 doughnuts.

450 g (1 lb) plain flour
7g sachet fast-action yeast
25 g (1 oz) butter
75 g (3 oz) caster sugar
2 large eggs, beaten
6 tablespoons tepid milk
6 tablespoons tepid water
light vegetable oil, for
    deep-frying

FOR THE FILLING
raspberry jam

FOR THE COATING
100 g (4 oz) caster sugar
2 level teaspoons ground
    cinnamon

1 Lightly grease and flour 3 baking trays.

2 Measure the flour into a large bowl and stir in the yeast. Rub in the butter with your fingertips until the mixture resembles fine breadcrumbs, then stir in the sugar. Make a well in the centre of the dry ingredients and pour in the eggs, milk and water. Mix to a smooth dough.

3 Turn out on to a lightly floured work surface and knead for about 5 minutes until the dough is smooth and elastic. Return it to the bowl, cover with oiled clingfilm and leave to rise until doubled in size, about 1–1½ hours in a warm room.

4 Turn the risen dough out of the bowl and knead to knock out the air until the dough is smooth and elastic once more. Divide into 16 equal pieces and shape each into a ball. Flatten each ball, then place a small teaspoon of jam in the centre of each piece. Gather the edges together over the jam and pinch firmly to seal.

5 Place well apart on the prepared baking trays, then cover with oiled clingfilm or put the trays inside large polythene bags and leave to prove for about 30 minutes, until they have doubled in size.

6 Heat 2 cm (5 in) oil in a deep-fat fryer or heavy saucepan until a cube of bread dropped into the fat browns in 30 seconds. Fry the doughnuts a few at a time, turning them once, until they are golden brown all over. This will take about 5 minutes. Lift out with a slotted spoon and drain well on kitchen paper.

7 Put the sugar and cinnamon into a large polythene bag and shake to mix. Then toss the doughnuts, a few at a time, in the sugar mixture until each is well coated. Serve freshly made.

Banana and Chocolate Chip Bars

A really healthy snack. The banana in the middle could be replaced with ready-to-eat dried apricots. This recipe makes 12 bars.

75 g (3 oz) wholemeal self-raising flour
75 g (3 oz) porridge oats
75 g (3 oz) demerara sugar
100 g (4 oz) butter
1 ripe banana, sliced
25 g (1 oz) chocolate chips

1 Pre-heat the oven to 180°C/Fan 160°C/Gas 4. Lightly grease a shallow 18 cm (7in) square cake tin.

2 Mix together the flour, oats and sugar in a large bowl. Rub in the butter with your fingertips until the mixture resembles breadcrumbs. Spread half the mixture over the base of the tin and arrange the sliced banana on top. Sprinkle over the remaining crumb mixture and press down well. Top with the chocolate chips.

3 Bake in the pre-heated oven for about 25 minutes or until golden brown. Leave in the tin until cold and then cut into bars to serve.

Oat and Sunflower Squares

Try to use jumbo oats for this recipe, as these give a crunchier texture than porridge oats.

50 g (2 oz) butter
2 rounded tablespoons
  golden syrup
150 g (5 oz) jumbo oats
50 g (2 oz) sunflower seeds

1 Pre-heat the oven to 180°C/Fan 160°C/Gas 4. Lightly grease an 18 cm (7 in) shallow square cake tin.

2 Heat the butter and syrup together gently until evenly blended. Mix the oats and sunflower seeds together in a bowl and pour on the syrup mixture. Stir thoroughly to mix. Spoon into the prepared tin and press the mixture down well with the back of a spoon.

3 Bake in the pre-heated oven for 20–25 minutes or until golden brown and just firm to the touch. Cut into 16 squares then leave to cool in the tin before carefully lifting out.

Chocolate Chip and Vanilla Marble Cake

This is a popular traybake for parties, and children particularly enjoy the fun of making marble cakes. This recipe cuts into about 21 small pieces.

225 g (8 oz) softened butter
225 g (8 oz) caster sugar
275 g (10 oz) self-raising flour
2 level teaspoons baking
  powder
4 large eggs
2 tablespoons milk
½ teaspoon vanilla extract
1½ level tablespoons cocoa
  powder
2 tablespoons hot water
50 g (2 oz) plain chocolate
  chips

FOR THE ICING
50 g (2 oz) plain chocolate
  (39 per cent cocoa solids)
50 g (2 oz) Belgian white
  chocolate

1 Pre-heat the oven to 180°C/Fan 160°C/Gas 4. Grease a 30 x 23 cm (12 x 9 in) traybake or roasting tin and line the base with baking parchment.

2 Measure the butter, sugar, flour, baking powder, eggs, milk and vanilla extract into a large bowl and beat well for about 2 minutes until well blended. Spoon half the mixture into the prepared tin, dotting the spoonfuls apart.

3 In a small bowl, blend the cocoa and hot water. Cool slightly, then add it to the remaining cake mixture along with the chocolate chips. Spoon this chocolate mixture in between the plain cake mixture to fill the gaps.

4 Bake in the pre-heated oven for 35–40 minutes or until the cake has shrunk from the sides of the tin and springs back when pressed in the centre with your fingertips. Leave to cool in the tin.

5 To make the icing, break the plain and white chocolate into pieces and melt them separately. Spoon into two separate small plastic bags, snip off a corner of each bag and drizzle the chocolates all over the top of the cake to decorate. Leave to set for about 30 minutes before cutting into squares.

Bunny Rabbit Birthday Cake

You can use this basic shape to make other animals, such as a cat, a teddy bear, a koala bear or an owl. Chocolate sprinkles can be used in place of the coconut, if preferred.

FOR THE CAKE
275 g (10 oz) softened butter
275 g (10 oz) caster sugar
5 large eggs
275 g (10 oz) self-raising flour
1 level teaspoon baking powder

FOR THE BUTTER CREAM
225 g (8 oz) softened butter
450 g (1 lb) sifted icing sugar
juice of ½ lemon

FOR THE DECORATION
about 350 g (12 oz) desiccated coconut
sweets for eyes, nose and whiskers

1 Pre-heat the oven to 180°C/Fan 160°C/Gas 4. Grease two 18 cm (7 in) and one 20 cm (8 in) shallow sandwich tins and line the bases with baking parchment.

2 Measure all the ingredients for the cake into a large bowl and beat well for about 2 minutes until blended and smooth. Divide the mixture between the cake tins.

3 Bake in the pre-heated oven for 25–30 minutes for the 18 cm (7 in) cakes, and 30–35 minutes for the 20 cm (8 in) cake. When cooked the cakes will be well risen and the tops should spring back when lightly pressed with a finger. Leave the cakes to cool in their tins for a few minutes then turn out, peel off the parchment and finish cooling on a wire rack.

4 While the cakes are cooling, make the butter cream by mixing the butter, icing sugar and lemon juice thoroughly together. Toast three-quarters of the coconut for the decoration until golden brown.

5 To make the rabbit shape, cut one 18 cm (7 in) cake to form the ears, paw and tail. For the ears, cut 2 oval pieces from each side of the cake and then 1 smaller oval to form the hind paw and a circle for the tail (left). The 20 cm (18 in) cake becomes the body and the second 18 cm (7 in) cake becomes the head. Assemble the rabbit on a large cake board or a foil covered baking tray, positioning the ears, paw and tail.

6 Cover with the butter cream then sprinkle all over with the toasted coconut except the tail, inner ear and tummy. Use the untoasted coconut to fill the inner ear and to cover the tummy and tail. Finish by adding the sweets to make the eyes, nose and whiskers. (I used thinly sliced liquorice sweets to create the whiskers.)

Jumbles

It is usual to shape this mixture into 'S' shapes, but of course you can shape it into any letter or number of your own choice. This recipe makes about 32 Jumbles.

150 g (5 oz) softened butter
150 g (5 oz) caster sugar
a few drops vanilla extract
finely grated rind of 1 lemon
1 large egg
350 g (12 oz) plain flour
clear honey, to glaze
demerara sugar, for dusting

1 Lightly grease 3 baking trays. Measure all the ingredients except the honey and demerara sugar into a bowl and work together by hand until a dough is formed. This can also be done in a food processor or with an electric mixer.

2 Divide the dough into 32 pieces. Roll each piece of dough into a strip about 10 cm (4 in) long, then twist them into 'S' shapes. Put them on the baking trays and chill for about 30 minutes. Pre-heat the oven to 190°C/Fan 170°C/Gas 5.

3 Bake the jumbles in the pre-heated oven for 10–15 minutes until they are a pale golden colour, then remove from the oven. Turn the oven up to 220°C/Fan 200°C/Gas 7 and, while the jumbles are still warm, brush them well with honey and sprinkle with demerara sugar. Return to the oven for 2–3 minutes until the sugar has caramelised. Cool on a wire rack.

Coconut Pyramids

You can use dariole moulds or eggcups for these easy-to-make little cakes, or you can buy pyramid moulds for a more pointed shape. This recipes makes 12 Pyramids.

225 g (8 oz) desiccated coconut
100 g (4 oz) caster sugar
2 large eggs, beaten
a little pink food colouring
    (optional)

1 Pre-heat the oven to 180°C/Fan 160°C/Gas 4. Line 2 baking trays with baking parchment.

2 Measure the coconut and sugar into a bowl and mix together. Beat in enough egg to bind the mixture together and add a few drops of pink colouring, if you like.

3 Dip each mould or egg cup into cold water and drain it well. Fill with the coconut mixture and press down lightly. Turn the moulded coconut out on to the baking tray and continue with the remaining mixture.

4 Bake in the pre-heated oven for about 20 minutes or until the pyramids are tinged with pale golden brown. Lift off the baking tray and leave to cool on a wire rack.

Little Gems

Children love to help by putting their favourite sweets on top of these tiny cakes. This recipes makes 65 gems, which sounds like a lot, but they are very tiny as they are made in sweetie or petits fours cases.

75 g (3 oz) softened butter
2 large eggs
100 g (4 oz) self-raising flour
1 level teaspoon baking
    powder
75 g (3 oz) caster sugar
1 tablespoon milk

FOR THE DECORATION
100 g (4 oz) sifted icing sugar
about 1 tablespoon lemon
    juice
small sweets, to decorate

1 Pre-heat the oven to 180°C/Fan 160°C/Gas 4. Arrange about 65 petits fours cases on baking trays.

2 Measure all the cake ingredients into a bowl and beat well until thoroughly blended. Spoon scant teaspoonfuls of the mixture into the cases, being careful not to overfill.

3 Bake in the pre-heated oven for 15–20 minutes until well risen and pale golden brown. Cool on a wire rack.

4 To make the icing, measure the icing sugar into a bowl and add enough lemon juice to give a spreading consistency. Spoon a little on top of each cooled gem and spread out with the back of a teaspoon. When the icing has almost set, top with a sweet.

Iced Animal Biscuits

Let the children ice the animals themselves with their favourite colours. Animal cutters are available from good cook shops. This recipe makes about 50 biscuits.

100 g (4 oz) softened butter
225 g (8 oz) self-raising flour
few drops of vanilla extract
100 g (4 oz) caster sugar
1 large egg, beaten
1 tablespoon milk

FOR THE ICING
100 g (4 oz) sifted icing sugar
about 1 tablespoon lemon
    juice
food colouring (red, green,
    blue, yellow)
silver balls, for eyes

1 Pre-heat the oven to 190°C/Fan 170°C/Gas 5. Lightly grease 2 baking trays.

2 Rub the butter into the flour with your fingertips until the mixture resembles fine breadcrumbs. Add the vanilla extract, sugar, beaten egg and milk and mix to form a fairly stiff dough. Roll out thinly on to a lightly floured work surface, and cut into animal shapes using the cutters. Place on the prepared baking trays.

3 Bake in the pre-heated oven for 10–15 minutes until golden brown. Cool on a wire rack.

4 To make the icing, measure the icing sugar into a bowl and add enough lemon juice to give a spreading consistency. Divide the icing between 2–3 small bowls (cups would do) and add a drop of different food colourings to each bowl, mixing well. Spoon a little icing on to each of the biscuits and spread out with the back of the teaspoon. Finish by adding silver balls for the eyes.

Gingerbread Men

Children love to cut out and decorate these biscuits. I used a 13.5 cm (5½ in) gingerbread man cutter to make 20 gingerbread men from this mixture.

350 g (12 oz) plain flour
1 level teaspoon
    bicarbonate of soda
2 level teaspoons ground
    ginger
100 g (4 oz) butter
175 g (6 oz) light
    muscovado sugar
4 tablespoons golden syrup
1 large egg, beaten
currants, to decorate

1 Pre-heat the oven to 190°C/Fan 170°C/Gas 5. Lightly grease 3 baking trays.

2 Measure the flour, bicarbonate of soda and ginger into a bowl. Rub in the butter with your fingertips until the mixture resembles fine breadcrumbs, then stir in the sugar. Add the golden syrup and beaten egg and mix to form a smooth dough, kneading lightly with the hands towards the end.

3 Divide the dough in half and roll out one half on to a lightly floured work surface to a thickness of about 5 mm (¼ in). Cut out gingerbread men using a gingerbread man cutter, and place them on to the prepared baking trays. Use the currants for eyes and buttons. Repeat with the remaining dough.

4 Bake in the pre-heated oven for about 10–12 minutes until they become a slightly darker shade. Cool slightly then lift on to a wire rack and leave to cool completely.

CHAPTER THIRTEEN

Tarts and Pastries

A classic tart, like a **Tarte Tatin** (opposite), makes a delightful ending to a dinner or an impressive present for a friend. I've always found my **Glazed Lemon Tart** (page 264), **French Apple Tart** (page 271) and **Deep Treacle Tart** (page 272) particularly well-received gifts!

Making tarts and pastries might seem like hard work, but they really don't have to be. Even patisserie-style pastries, such as **Danish Pastries** (page 277), **Chocolate Éclairs** (page 274) and **Profiteroles** (page 276) are simpler to make than you might realise. And, even if these recipes require a little effort to make, it is worth it as homemade versions are always far superior to bought alternatives.

There is now a large selection of good-quality, ready-made pastries available, which make homebaking really simple. Filo pastry in particular can be tricky to make, and in my recipe for **Filo Apple Strudels** (see page 266) I suggest using ready-made filo pastry as it is not necessary to make your own from scratch. Look for ready-made pastry made with butter, in the refrigerated and freezer sections of the supermarket. Remember frozen dough, once thawed, should not be refrozen.

Tarte Tatin

This classic 'upside-down' French tart is usually served warm, as a pudding, rather than as a cold cake. This recipe serves 6.

FOR THE PASTRY
100 g (4 oz) self-raising flour
50 g (2 oz) diced butter
1 level tablespoon sifted
    icing sugar
1 large egg yolk
scant tablespoon cold water

FOR THE TOPPING
900 g (2 lb) dessert apples
finely grated rind and juice
    of 1 lemon
75 g (3 oz) butter
75 g (3 oz) demerara sugar

TO FINISH
75 g (3 oz) demerara
    sugar (optional)

1 First prepare the pastry. Measure the flour, butter and icing sugar into a bowl and rub in the butter with your fingertips until the mixture resembles fine breadcrumbs. Add the egg yolk and enough water to bring the mixture together to a firm but not sticky dough. Knead lightly, wrap in clingfilm and chill for about 30 minutes.

2 Pre-heat the oven to 200°C/Fan 180°C/Gas 6. Peel, core and slice the apples and sprinkle with the lemon juice and rind. Measure the butter and sugar into a small pan and heat gently until the butter has melted and the sugar has dissolved. Pour into the base of a 23 cm (9 in) sandwich tin. Arrange a single layer of the best apples slices in a circular pattern over mixture. Cover with the remainder of the apple slices.

3 Roll out the chilled dough on to a lightly floured work surface and use to cover the apples. Bake in the pre-heated oven for about 20 minutes or until the pastry is crisp and golden brown (it will have shrunk a little when cooked).

4 Tip the juices from the cake tin into a small pan. Turn the tart out on to a plate, with the pastry on the bottom. Boil the juices to reduce to a syrupy caramel and pour over the apple. If there is very little juice – the amount will depend on the apples used – add 2 tablespoons demerara sugar, dissolved in the pan with the juices and cook until syrupy. Serve warm, with cream, crème fraîche or yoghurt.

Glazed Lemon Tart

Another classic tart with a crisp sweet pastry case and a sharp lemon filling. The sliced lemon topping is optional, but it does make it look special. This recipe serves 6.

FOR THE PÂTE SUCRÉE

175 g (6 oz) plain flour
75 g (3 oz) softened butter
75 g (3 oz) caster sugar
3 large egg yolks

FOR THE FILLING

2 large eggs
90 g (3½ oz) caster sugar
150 g (5 oz) ground almonds
85 ml (3½ fl oz) whipping or
    double cream
4 lemons

TO FINISH

150 g (5 oz) caster sugar
135 ml (4½ fl oz) water
2 lemons
about 3 tablespoons
    apricot jam

1 First make the *pâte sucrée* (sweet pastry). Measure the flour into a bowl. Rub in the butter with your fingertips until the mixture resembles fine breadcrumbs. Stir in the sugar, then add the egg yolks and mix until the ingredients come together to form a dough. Knead the mixture gently until smooth. Wrap the dough in clingfilm and leave to rest in the fridge for about 30 minutes.

2 Pre-heat the oven to 180°C/Fan 160°C/Gas 4. Roll out the pastry on to a lightly floured work surface and use to line a 23 cm (9 in) loose-bottomed flan tin. Prick the pastry all over with a fork. Chill while preparing the filling.

3 To make the filling, beat together the eggs, sugar, ground almonds and cream. Add the finely grated rind of all 4 lemons and the juice of 2. Pour the filling into the pastry case and bake in the pre-heated oven for about 30–35 minutes until the filling is golden and firm to the touch.

4 Meanwhile, prepare the lemon slices to finish the top of the tart. Measure the sugar and water into a pan and heat gently until the sugar dissolves, then boil for 1 minute. Slice the lemons thinly, discard any pips, and place into the hot syrup. Bring the syrup back to the boil, then remove the pan from the heat, pour into a bowl and leave to soak for at least 2 hours.

5 Drain the lemon slices and arrange overlapping on the tart. Sieve the apricot jam into a small pan and heat until boiling. Brush liberally over the tart and leave to set.

Glazed Fruit Tartlets

These little tarts look best if each one is filled with a single type of fruit. Use redcurrant glaze for red fruits, and apricot glaze for orange or green fruits such as green grapes and kiwi fruit. Fill the pastry cases at the last moment as they soften quickly. This recipe makes 12 tartlets.

FOR THE PÂTE SUCRÉE
100 g (4 oz) plain flour
50 g (2 oz) softened butter
50 g (2 oz) caster sugar
2 large egg yolks

FOR THE FILLING
 AND GLAZE
150 g (¼ pint) double cream
225 g (8 oz) fresh fruits
   (such as raspberries
   and blueberries)
about 4 tablespoons
   redcurrant jelly (or
   apricot jam)

1 First make the *pâte sucrée* (sweet pastry). Measure the flour into a bowl. Rub in the butter with your fingertips until the mixture resembles fine breadcrumbs. Stir in the sugar, then add the egg yolks and mix until the ingredients come together to form a dough. Knead the mixture gently until smooth. Wrap the dough in clingfilm and leave to rest in the fridge for about 30 minutes.

2 Pre-heat the oven to 190°C/Fan 170°C/Gas 5. Roll out the pastry on to a lightly floured work surface and cut out about 12 rounds using a 7.5 cm (3 in) fluted pastry cutter. Re-roll the trimmings once only. Ease the pastry rounds into patty tins and prick lightly with a fork. Place a small piece of baking parchment or foil into each pastry case and fill with baking beans.

3 Bake the pastry cases in the pre-heated oven for about 15 minutes or until golden brown. Turn out on to a wire rack, remove the paper and baking beans, and leave to cool.

4 To make the filling, whip the cream until it forms soft peaks and spoon a little into each tartlet case. Arrange the fruits on top. Warm the redcurrant jelly or apricot jam in a small pan and brush liberally over the fruits to glaze.

Filo Apple Strudels

I've used ready-made filo pastry in this recipe, for ease. Try to find the shorter packets of filo pastry as then you won't need to trim the pastry to size. Any leftover filo will keep in the fridge for 2 days, alternatively, you can wrap it carefully, put it into the freezer straight away and use within 1 month.

FOR THE FILLING
350g (12 oz) peeled, cored and roughly chopped cooking apples
juice of ½ lemon
75 g (3 oz) demerara sugar
25 g (1 oz) fresh breadcrumbs
50 g (2 oz) sultanas
1 level teaspoon ground cinnamon
8 sheets filo pastry 18 x 33 cm (7 x 13 in)
100 g (4 oz) butter, melted

FOR THE TOPPING
2 tablespoons caster sugar
2 tablespoons water
icing sugar, for dusting

1 Pre-heat the oven to 200°C/Fan 180°C/Gas 6. Lightly grease 2 baking trays.

2 First prepare the filling. Mix together the apples, lemon juice, sugar, breadcrumbs, sultanas and cinnamon in a bowl.

3 Unfold 1 sheet of filo pastry and brush liberally with melted butter. Spoon one-eighth of the apple mixture to cover the middle third of the longest edge of the pastry, leaving a small border. Fold in this border, then bring the two short sides over the apple to cover it. Roll the filled pastry over and over to form a neat strudel. Put it on one of the prepared baking trays, then repeat the process with the remaining 7 pastry sheets and apple mixture.

4 Brush the strudels with the melted butter then bake in the pre-heated oven for about 15–20 minutes or until golden brown and crisp. Meanwhile, blend the caster sugar and water together in a small pan and heat gently until all the sugar has dissolved. Spoon the syrup over the warm strudels and dust with icing sugar to serve.

Lemon Cream Tartlets

These lovely little shortbread cases can actually be filled with anything you like – a good way of spinning out a small amount of fruit, like the first strawberries of the season, for instance. They are quite crumbly to eat. This recipe makes about 10 tartlets.

FOR THE SHORTBREAD
100 g (4 oz) softened butter
50 g (2 oz) caster sugar
50 g (2 oz) semolina
100 g (4 oz) plain flour

FOR THE FILLING
about 3 tablespoons
 good lemon curd
150 ml (¼ pint) double cream,
 whipped
a few sliced strawberries

1 First make the shortbread. Soften the butter in a bowl, add the sugar, semolina and flour and work together to form a smooth dough. Wrap in clingfilm and chill in the fridge for about 15 minutes.

2 Pre-heat the oven to 150°C/Fan 130°C/Gas 2. On a lightly floured work surface, roll out the shortbread to just under 5 mm (¼ in) in thickness. Cut out circles using a 7.5 cm (3 in) fluted cutter, then press the circles gently into a 12-hole bun tin. Prick the bases well.

3 Bake in the pre-heated oven for 20–25 minutes or until firm and golden. Leave the shortbread in the tins to harden slightly then ease out of the tins and leave to cool completely on a wire rack.

4 To make the filling, mix together the lemon curd and the whipped cream. Just before serving, spoon a little of the filling into each shortbread case and top with sliced strawberries.

TIP
The shortbread cases can be made ahead, and they can be frozen for up to 2 months. Once filled, however, they go soft very quickly, so serve and eat straight away.

Frangipane Tartlets

Pâte sucrée is the classic French sweet pastry. I make mine in the food processor, or in a bowl, which is easier than the traditional way, where the flour is sifted on to a work surface, and the other ingredients are placed into a well in the flour and worked together to a paste before the flour is gently worked in. This recipe makes 12 tartlets.

FOR THE PÂTE SUCRÉE
100 g (4 oz) plain flour
50 g (2 oz) softened butter
50 g (2 oz) caster sugar
2 large egg yolks

FOR THE FRANGIPANE
50 g (2 oz) softened butter
50 g (2 oz) caster sugar
1 large egg, beaten
65 g (2½ oz) ground almonds
a few drops of almond extract
50 g (2 oz) flaked almonds

TO FINISH
3 tablespoons apricot jam
2 tablespoons ground
  almonds

1 First make the *pâte sucrée* (sweet pastry). Measure the flour into a bowl. Rub in the butter with your fingertips until the mixture resembles fine breadcrumbs. Stir in the sugar, then add the egg yolks and mix until the ingredients come together to form a dough. Knead the mixture gently until smooth. Wrap the dough in clingfilm and leave to rest in the fridge for about 30 minute.

2 Pre-heat the oven to 190°C/Fan 170°C/Gas 5. Roll out the pastry on to a lightly floured work surface and cut out about 12 rounds using a 7.5 cm (3 in) plain pastry cutter. Re-roll the trimmings once only. Ease the pastry rounds into patty tins and prick lightly with a fork. Chill while you are making the frangipane.

3 To make the frangipane, measure the butter and sugar into a bowl and beat well together until light and fluffy. Gradually beat in the egg, then stir in the ground almonds and almond extract. Fill the chilled tartlet cases with the frangipane and scatter the flaked almonds on top.

4 Bake in the pre-heated oven for about 15 minutes until the frangipane is golden and firm to the touch. Ease the tartlets out of the tin and on to a wire rack to cool.

5 Sieve the apricot jam into a small pan and warm gently. Brush the tartlets with the apricot glaze and decorate the outside edge with a thin line of ground almonds, then leave the tartlets to cool completely.

French Apple Tart

This delicious tart is an economical choice in the autumn, when you can use your own free apples or get them cheaply from elsewhere. This recipe serves 6.

FOR THE PASTRY
175 g (6 oz) plain flour
75 g (3 oz) diced butter
1 large egg yolk
water, if necessary

FOR THE FILLING
900 g (2 lb) cooking apples
50 g (2 oz) butter
2 tablespoons water
4 tablespoons apricot jam
50 g (2 oz) caster sugar
grated rind of ½ lemon
225 g (8 oz) eating apples
1–2 tablespoons lemon juice
about 1 teaspoon caster
    sugar, for sprinkling

FOR THE GLAZE
4 tablespoons apricot jam

1 To make the pastry, measure the flour into a large bowl, add the butter and rub in with your fingertips until the mixture resembles fine breadcrumbs. Add the egg yolk, stir into the flour mixture with a round-bladed knife, and bring the mixture to a dough, adding a little water if necessary. Knead the pastry very lightly, then wrap and chill in the fridge for about 30 minutes.

2 Pre-heat the oven to 200°C/Fan 180°C/Gas 6. To make the apple filling, cut the cooking apples into quarters, remove the core and chop the apple into chunks (no need to peel). Melt the butter in a large pan and then add the prepared apples and water. Cover and cook very gently for 10–15 minutes until the apples have become soft and mushy. Rub the apple through a sieve into a clean pan, add the apricot jam, sugar and grated lemon rind. Cook over a high heat for about 10–15 minutes, stirring continuously, until all the excess liquid has evaporated and the apple mixture is thick. Set aside to cool.

3 Roll out the pastry thinly on a lightly floured work surface and use to line a deep 20 cm (8 in) deep loose-bottomed fluted flan tin. Cover with baking parchment and fill with baking beans. Bake blind in the pre-heated oven for 10–15 minutes, then remove the paper and beans and bake for a further 5 minutes until the pastry at the base of the flan has dried out. Remove from the oven but do not turn off the oven.

4 Spoon the cooled apple purée into the tart case and level the surface. Peel, quarter and core the eating apples, then slice them very thinly. Arrange in neat overlapping circles over the apple purée, brush with the lemon juice and sprinkle with the caster sugar. Return the tart to the oven and bake for 25 minutes or until the pastry and the edges of the apples are lightly browned.

5 To make the glaze, sieve the apricot jam into a small pan and heat gently until runny. Brush all over the top of the apples and pastry. Serve warm or cold.

Deep Treacle Tart

A familiar option on pub dessert menus, and a popular choice with adults and children alike. Delicious served with cream, ice-cream or custard. This tart serves 6.

FOR THE PASTRY
175 g (6 oz) plain flour
75 g (3 oz) butter
about 2 tablespoons
    cold water

FOR THE FILLING
350 g (12 oz) golden syrup
about 200 g (7 oz) fresh white
    or brown breadcrumbs
grated rind and juice of
    2 large lemons

1 First make the pastry. Measure the flour into a large bowl and rub in the butter with your fingertips until the mixture resembles fine breadcrumbs. Add enough water to mix to a firm dough, wrap in clingfilm and chill in the fridge for about 20 minutes.

2 Pre-heat the oven to 200°C/Fan 180°C/Gas 6 and put a heavy baking tray in the oven to heat up. Roll the pastry out thinly on a lightly floured work surface and use to line a 18 cm (7 in) deep loose-bottomed fluted flan tin.

3 To make the filling, heat the syrup in a large pan and stir in the breadcrumbs and the lemon rind and juice. If the mixture looks runny, add a few more breadcrumbs (it depends whether you use white or brown bread). Pour the syrup mixture into the pastry case and level the surface.

4 Bake in the pre-heated oven, on the hot baking tray, for about 10 minutes and then reduce the oven temperature to 180°C/Fan 160°C/Gas 4 and bake for a further 25–30 minutes until the pastry is golden and the filling set. Leave to cool in the tin. Serve warm or cold.

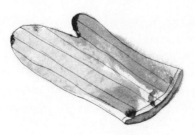

Austrian Apricot and Almond Tart

This tart looks wonderful cooked because the top layer of pastry moulds itself around the apricot halves. I use canned apricots as I have found them more reliable and a readily obtainable alternative than fresh. This recipe serves 8.

FOR THE PASTRY
275 g (10 oz) plain flour
150 g (5 oz) sifted icing sugar
150 g (5 oz) diced chilled butter
1 large egg, beaten

FOR THE FILLING
175 g (6 oz) grated almond paste or marzipan (see page 388 for almond paste recipe)
800 g (1¾ lb) canned apricot halves in natural juice, drained

TIP
You can prepare the tart ahead of time. Cover the uncooked tart in clingfilm and keep in the fridge for up to 24 hours before baking. Remove the tart from the fridge and leave at room temperature for about 20 minutes before baking.

1 First make the pastry. Measure the flour and icing sugar into a large bowl and rub in the butter until the mixture resembles breadcrumbs. Stir in the beaten egg and bring together to form a dough. Form into a smooth ball, put inside a plastic bag and chill in the fridge for 30 minutes.

2 Pre-heat the oven to 180°C/Fan 160°C/Gas 4. Put a heavy baking tray in the oven to heat. You will need a 25 cm (10 in) deep loose-bottomed fluted flan tin.

3 Cut off a little less than half the pastry, wrap it in clingfilm and return it to the fridge. Take the larger piece and roll out to a circle about 5 cm (2 in) bigger than the flan tin.

4 Line the base and sides of the flan tin with the pastry, then trim the excess from the top edge with a knife. Use the trimmings to patch the pastry if necessary. Spread the grated almond paste or marzipan evenly over the base. Dry the apricots on kitchen paper, then evenly space the apricots on top of the almond paste, rounded side up.

5 Roll out any leftover trimmings along with the remaining pastry to a circle large enough to fit the top of the flan tin. Use a little water to dampen the rim of the pastry in the flan tin then, with the aid of the rolling pin, lift the top circle of pastry into position. Trim off any excess pastry then press the edges together so no juices can escape. Again, use the pastry trimmings to patch if necessary.

6 Transfer to the pre-heated oven to bake on the hot baking tray for 30–35 minutes or until pale golden. Watch the pastry carefully: because it is a rich, sweet pastry it browns quickly and mostly around the edge. If it is browning too quickly, protect the edge with crumpled strips of foil.

Chocolate Éclairs

These are sheer luxury and well worth making. Serve for tea or as a dessert. This recipe makes about 12 éclairs.

FOR THE CHOUX PASTRY
50 g (2 oz) diced butter
150 ml (¼ pint) water
65 g (2½ oz) sifted plain flour
2 large eggs, beaten

FOR THE FILLING
300 ml (½ pint) whipping
 cream

FOR THE ICING
50 g (2 oz) plain chocolate
 (39 per cent cocoa solids)
15 g (½ oz) butter
2 tablespoons water
75 g (3 oz) sifted icing sugar

1 Pre-heat the oven to 220°C/Fan 200°C/Gas 7. Lightly grease 2 baking trays.

2 To make the choux pastry, put the butter and water into a small pan and place over a low heat. Allow the butter to melt and then bring slowly to the boil. Remove the pan from the heat, add the flour all at once and beat until the mixture forms a soft ball and leaves the side of the pan. Allow to cool slightly.

3 Add the eggs into the mixture a little at a time, beating really well between each addition to give a smooth, shiny paste. It is easiest to use a hand-held electric mixer for this.

4 Spoon the mixture into a large piping bag fitted with a 1 cm (½ in) plain nozzle. Pipe on to the prepared baking trays into éclair shapes, about 13–15 cm (5–6 in) long, leaving room for them to spread. Bake in the pre-heated oven for 10 minutes, then reduce the heat to 190°C/Fan 170°C/Gas 5 and bake for a further 20 minutes, until well risen and a deep golden brown. (It is important that the éclairs are golden brown all over. Any pale, undercooked parts will become soggy once they have cooled.)

5 Remove the éclairs from the oven and split them down one side to allow the steam to escape. Leave to cool completely on a wire rack.

6 Whip the cream until it is just firm enough to pipe. Fill the cold éclairs with whipped cream, using a piping bag fitted with a plain nozzle.

7 To make the icing, break the chocolate into pieces and put into a bowl set over a pan of hot water, making sure the water does not touch the base of the bowl. Add the butter and water to the chocolate and place the pan over a low heat until the chocolate and butter have melted, stirring occasionally. Remove from the heat and add the sifted icing sugar, beating well until smooth. Spoon the icing over the top of each éclair, then leave to set.

TIP
Do not fill choux pastry items too long before serving, as the pastry tends to go soggy.

Profiteroles

Choux pastry must be well cooked until it is really firm and has turned a good straw colour. The profiteroles look wonderful piled up in a pyramid. This recipe makes 20 profiteroles.

FOR THE CHOUX PASTRY
55 g (2 oz) butter
150 ml (¼ pint) water
65 g (2½ oz) sifted plain flour
2 large eggs, beaten

FOR THE FILLING
300 ml (½ pint) whipping or
    double cream, whipped

FOR THE ICING
50 g (2 oz) plain chocolate
    (39 per cent cocoa solids)
15 g (½ oz) butter
2 tablespoons water
75 g (3 oz) sifted icing sugar

TIP
The pastry can be frozen either before or after baking. To freeze uncooked, pipe shapes on to baking parchment lined with clingfilm and open freeze. When firm, put into freezer bags for up to 3 months. Cook from frozen, allowing a few extra minutes cooking time. For baked choux pastry, split and cool before freezing and pack in rigid plastic containers. Keep in the freezer for 3–6 months. Crisp up in a hot oven for a minute, then cool and fill.

1 Pre-heat the oven to 220°C/Fan 200°C/Gas 7. Lightly grease 2 baking trays.

2 To make the pastry, place the butter and water in a small pan. Heat gently until the butter has melted, then bring slowly to the boil. Remove the pan from the heat, add the flour all at once and beat until the mixture forms a soft ball. Beat over the heat for a further 1 minute.

3 Cool slightly, then add the eggs a little at a time, beating well between each addition. To give a smooth, shiny paste. Spoon the mixture into a piping bag fitted with a 1 cm (½ in) plain nozzle and pipe small mounds on to the prepared baking trays, leaving room for them to spread.

4 Bake in the pre-heated oven for 10 minutes then reduce the oven temperature to 190°C/Fan 170°C/Gas 5. Cook the profiteroles for a further 10 minutes or until well risen and a deep golden brown. Remove from the oven and split open to allow the steam to escape. If you like the centres really dry, after splitting, return to the oven at 180°C/Fan 160°C/Gas 4 for a further 10 minutes. Cool completely on a wire rack.

5 When the profiteroles are cold, use a piping bag fitted with a plain nozzle to fill them with a little of the whipped cream.

6 To make the icing, break the chocolate into pieces and melt in a bowl set over a pan of simmering, not boiling, water along with the butter and water. Remove from the heat and beat in the icing sugar until smooth. Dip each profiterole into the icing to coat the top, then leave to set.

Danish Pastries

It's fiddly and time-consuming to make these pastries in their various traditional shapes, but they'll be better than any you can buy! They are best eaten on the day they are made. The basic recipe filling is almond paste, but do try the alternative fillings too. This recipe makes 16 pastries.

FOR THE PASTRY DOUGH
450 g (1 lb) strong plain flour
½ level teaspoon salt
350 g (12 oz) softened butter
7g sachet fast-action yeast
50 g (2 oz) caster sugar
150 ml (¼ pint) warm milk
2 large eggs, beaten
a little beaten egg, to glaze

**FOR THE FILLING
AND TOPPING**
225 g (8 oz) almond paste or
    marzipan (see page 388
    for almond paste recipe)
1 or 2 large eggs, beaten
100 g (4 oz) icing sugar
1–2 tablespoons warm water
50 g (2 oz) toasted flaked
    almonds
50 g (2 oz) chopped red or
    natural glacé cherries

1 Lightly grease 3 baking trays. Measure the flour and salt into a bowl and rub in 50 g (2 oz) of the butter with your fingertips. Add the yeast and sugar and stir to mix. Make a well in the centre, add the warm milk and beaten eggs, and mix to a soft dough. Knead the dough until smooth, then put it into a clean bowl, cover with clingfilm and leave to rise in a warm place for about 1 hour or until the dough has doubled in bulk.

2 Punch down the dough, knead until smooth and then roll out to an oblong about 35 x 20 cm (14 x 8 in). Cover the top two-thirds of the oblong with half the remaining butter, dotting pieces of butter over the dough.

3 Fold the bottom third of dough up and the top third down to form a parcel. Seal the edges then give the dough a quarter turn so that the folded side is to the left. Roll out to the same sized oblong as before. Dot over the remaining butter in the same way and fold the dough as before. Wrap the dough in clingfilm and leave to rest in the fridge for about 15 minutes.

4 Set the dough so that the fold is on the left again and roll and fold the dough, with no butter, twice more. Wrap the dough in clingfilm and return to the fridge for 15 minutes. The dough can now be divided into 4 equal pieces and shaped, or all the dough can be rolled to make cartwheels (see overleaf):

To make crescents, take one-quarter of the dough and roll out to a 23 cm (9 in) circle. Divide the circle into 4 equal wedges. Place a small sausage of almond paste at the wide end of each wedge and roll up loosely towards the point (see figure 1). Bend them round to form a crescent (see figure 2).

continued overleaf

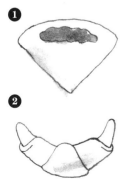

To make **pinwheels**, roll out another quarter of the dough to form a 20 cm (8 in) square. Cut the square into 4. Place a small amount of almond paste in the centre of each square. Make cuts from each corner almost to the centre and fold 4 alternate points to the centre, pressing them down firmly (see figures 3 and 4 below).

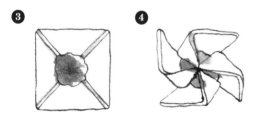

To make **kite shapes**, roll out another quarter of the dough to form a 20 cm (8 in) square. Cut into 4 squares. Place a small piece of almond paste in the centre of each square. Make cuts at opposite corners to create two L shaped strips (see figure 5). Lift the strips, crossing them over the almond paste in the centre (see figure 6).

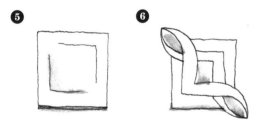

To make **envelopes**, roll out the remaining dough to form a 40 cm (16 in) square. Cut this into 4 squares. In the centre of each square, place a piece of almond paste or some other filling (vanilla cream or apple mixture are especially good here). Fold 2 opposite corners

or all 4 corners into the middle (see figures 8 and 9). Press the edges down lightly.

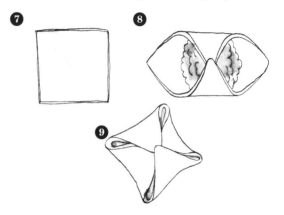

To make **cartwheels**, roll out all the dough thinly, spread with a thin layer of almond filling (see opposite) and sprinkle with a handful of raisins. Roll up the dough like a swiss roll and cut into 5 mm (¼ in) slices.

5 After shaping, arrange the pastries on to the prepared baking trays, cover with oiled clingfilm or put the trays inside oiled polythene bags, and leave to prove for about 20 minutes in a warm place, until they are beginning to look puffy.

6 Pre-heat the oven to 220°C/Fan 200°C/ Gas 7. Brush each pastry with beaten egg and bake in the pre-heated oven for about 15 minutes until golden brown. Lift on to a wire rack to cool.

7 Make up some glacé icing by gradually mixing the warm water into the icing sugar. Spoon a little icing over the pastries while they are still warm. Sprinkle with toasted flaked almonds or small pieces of glacé cherry.

Alternative Danish Pastry Fillings

Almond Filling

This is softer and moister than almond paste. Use it in any of the pastry shapes.

100 g (4 oz) ground almonds
100 g (4 oz) caster sugar
a little beaten egg

Mix the almonds and sugar together and bind with enough egg to form a soft paste.

Vanilla Cream

This is particularly good in the 'envelopes'.

1 tablespoon plain flour
1 teaspoon cornflour
1 large egg yolk
1 tablespoon caster sugar
150 ml (¼ pint) milk
2–3 drops vanilla extract

Mix together the flours, egg yolk and sugar, and blend with a little of the milk. Bring the remaining milk to the boil, pour on to the flour mixture, blend and then return to the pan. Heat gently, stirring, until the mixture comes to the boil. Allow to cool then flavour with a few drops of vanilla extract.

Apple Filling

Use this filling in any of the pastry shapes.

450 g (1 lb) cooking apples
15 g (½ oz) butter
grated rind and juice of ½ lemon
4 tablespoons light muscovado sugar
75 g (3 oz) sultanas (optional)

Wash, dry, quarter and core the apples (no need to peel) and put into a pan with the butter and the lemon rind and juice. Cover and cook until soft. Rub the apples through a sieve, return to the rinsed-out pan and add the sugar. Cook until the sugar has dissolved and the apple mixture is thick. Add the sultanas, if liked. Leave until cold before using.

CHAPTER FOURTEEN

Breads

Nothing can beat the aroma of freshly baked bread, and bread making no longer needs to be a lengthy process. There are now a variety of fast-acting dried yeasts available, which are much quicker and simpler to use than fresh or ordinary dried yeast because they don't need to be reconstituted in liquid first. Simply mix them into the dry flour.

You can also use a food mixer fitted with the dough hook to combine the ingredients and knead the dough, if you don't want to do it by hand. Like with scones, it is always better to have a bread dough on the wet side rather than dry, so if it sticks to your fingers it is a good sign. Where breads are made with yeast, don't be tempted to cut short the proving process – it will affect the bread, causing it to be dense and flat.

Not all bread requires yeast, and **Irish Soda Bread** (page 293) couldn't be simpler to make. It's delicious freshly made for breakfast. I've included some staple recipes, such as a **White Cottage Loaf** (page 285) and **Quick Granary Rolls** (page 284), as well as some more impressive breads like **Focaccia Bread with Onion and Balsamic Topping** (page 294), which is delicious with a dressed salad. Whereas American muffins are raised using self-raising flour and baking powder, the classic **English Muffins** (page 283) is raised with yeast. Fresh muffins are a delicious and generous fare for breakfast or brunch, topped with bacon and a poached egg, or for afternoon tea, spread with jam.

Of course, there are now some good machines to buy that take all the effort out of bread making. Follow the manufacturer's instructions for the best method for your machine. For those who don't have a bread machine and want to make their own bread without one, this chapter shows you how.

English Muffins

These old-fashioned English muffins are traditionally pulled apart through the middle, not cut, and eaten warm with lashings of butter. Any left over will store for 2–3 days in an airtight container and are then best split in half and eaten toasted. This recipe makes about 14 muffins.

675 g (1½ lb) strong
    white flour
2 teaspoons caster sugar
7 g sachet fast-action yeast
1½ level teaspoons salt
450 ml (¾ fl oz) tepid milk
1 level teaspoon fine semolina,
    for dusting

1 Measure the dry ingredients into a bowl or electric mixer then pour in the milk in a continuous stream while mixing the ingredients, to form a dough. Knead the dough with your hands or with a mixer fitted with a dough hook until smooth and elastic.

2 Turn the dough out on to a lightly floured work surface and roll out to a thickness of about 1 cm (½ in) with a floured rolling pin.

3 Cut the dough into rounds using a 7.5 cm (3 in) plain cutter, place on a well-floured baking tray and dust the tops with the semolina. Cover loosely and leave in a warm place until doubled in size (approximately 1 hour).

4 Lightly oil a griddle or heavy-based frying pan and place on the hob to heat. Cook the muffins, in 2–3 batches, for about 7 minutes each side, turning the heat down once the muffins go into the pan. When cooked they should be well risen and brown on both sides. Cool slightly on a wire rack before splitting and buttering to serve.

Quick Granary Rolls

To make a close-textured, more substantial roll you could use all granary flour instead of the mix given here. To glaze the rolls, brush the dough with a little milk and sprinkle with cracked wheat just before baking them. This recipe makes 12 rolls.

350 g (12 oz) strong
    white flour
350 g (12 oz) granary flour
1½ level teaspoons salt
1½ level teaspoons sugar
7 g sachet fast-action yeast
40 g (1½ oz) butter
about 450 ml (¾ pint) each
    of tepid milk and water,
    mixed

1 Lightly grease 2 baking trays. Measure the dry ingredients and the butter into a bowl or electric mixer. If mixing by hand, rub in the butter with your fingertips. If using a mixer, briefly mix in the butter.

2 Add the milk and water mixture in a continuous stream while, mixing the ingredients to a dough. Knead thoroughly until smooth and elastic. Alternatively, use a mixer fitted with a dough hook to knead the dough for a further 2 minutes.

3 Turn the dough out on to a floured work surface and divide into 12 even pieces. Shape the pieces into rounds and place on the prepared baking trays, allowing room for expansion. Cover the rolls with oiled clingfilm and leave in a warm place to prove until doubled in size.

4 Pre-heat the oven to 220°C/Fan 200°C/Gas 7. Uncover the rolls and bake in the pre-heated oven for about 10–15 minutes until they have browned on top and sound hollow when the base is tapped. Lift on to a wire rack to cool.

White Cottage Loaf

This is a good, everyday loaf. You can make it in other shapes if you prefer. Individual rolls will take less time to prove and bake.

450g (1 lb) strong white flour
7 g sachet fast-action yeast
40 g (1½ oz) butter, melted
1 level teaspoon salt
300 ml (½ pint) warm water

TO GLAZE
1 large egg, beaten

1 Measure all the ingredients into a bowl or electric mixer and blend until you have a fairly sticky dough. Knead on a floured work surface, adding a little extra flour if needed. If using a mixer fitted with a dough hook, mix until you have a fairly sticky, soft dough. This will take about 4–5 minutes.

2 Transfer to a large oiled bowl, cover tightly with clingfilm (make sure no air can escape) and leave to rise in a warm place for 1–1½ hours or until the dough has doubled in size.

3 Tip the dough out on to a floured work surface and knock back by hand until smooth. Cut off a quarter of the dough and shape into a round ball. Shape the remaining dough into a large ball and place on a baking tray lined with baking parchment. Sit the small ball on top of the large ball.

4 Flour the handle of a wooden spoon and push the handle through the centre of the two balls until you hit the baking tray, then remove the handle carefully. Slide the baking tray into a large plastic bag so the dough and baking tray are completely covered. Seal the end of the bag completely. Leave to prove in a warm place for 35-45 minutes or until doubled in size.

5 Pre-heat the oven to 220°C/Fan 200°C/Gas 7. Brush with beaten egg and slide into the pre-heated oven for about 20–25 minutes until golden and the bread sounds hollow when tapped on the base. Leave to cool on a wire rack.

Crown Loaf

This loaf is made in a 20 cm (8 in) sandwich tin and breaks off into 12 individual rolls – perfect for a picnic or special meal.

350 g (12oz) strong white flour
2 level teaspoons fast-action
   yeast
1 level teaspoon salt
20 g (¾ oz) butter, melted
225 ml (8 fl oz) warm water
a little milk, to glaze

1 Lightly grease a 20 cm (8 in) sandwich tin. Measure all the ingredients into a bowl and mix together by hand or with an electric mixer fitted with a dough hook until combined to fairly sticky dough.

2 Remove from the bowl and sit on a floured work surface. Knead by hand for about 4–5 minutes, adding a little extra flour if needed.

3 Transfer to a large oiled bowl, cover tightly with clingfilm (make sure no air can escape) and leave to rise in a warm place for 1–1½ hours or until the dough has doubled in size.

4 Tip on to a lightly floured work surface and knock back by hand for about 5 minutes. Divide the dough into 12 evenly sized balls. Arrange the balls into the tin so they are snug and touching. Cover the tin with clingfilm and leave to prove in a warm place for about 30 minutes or until doubled in size.

5 Pre-heat the oven to 220°C/Fan 200°C/Gas 7. Glaze the loaf with a little milk, then bake in the pre-heated oven for about 20–25 minutes until lightly golden on top and well risen. Leave to cool in the tin for a few minutes then remove from the tin and leave to cool on a wire rack.

Cheese and Celery Crown Loaf

This is good with soup or a cheeseboard and best eaten on the day of making. This recipe is quick to make because it has no yeast in it, so the bread does not have to rise before baking.

350 g (12 oz) self-raising flour
40 g (1½ oz) softened butter
freshly ground black pepper
½ level teaspoon salt
3 large sticks celery
175 g (6 oz) mature
    Cheddar
1 peeled garlic clove
1 large egg
6 tablespoons milk
grated Cheddar,
    for sprinkling

1 Pre-heat the oven to 190°C/Fan 170°C/Gas 5. Lightly grease a baking tray or a 20 cm (8 in) deep round cake tin.

2 Measure the flour in to a large mixing bowl and rub in the butter. Add a little freshly ground black pepper along with the salt. Finely chop the celery, grate the Cheddar and crush the garlic. Stir into the dry ingredients. Whisk together the egg and milk and beat into the flour mixture to form a soft dough.

3 Turn out on to a lightly floured surface and either shape quickly into a neat round about 20 cm (8 in) in diameter and place on the prepared baking tray, or divide the dough into 12 evenly sized pieces and place into the prepared cake tin in the shape of a circle, starting from the outside. Sprinkle the dough with a little grated cheese.

4 Bake in the pre-heated oven for about 40–45 minutes or until well risen and golden brown, and the bread sounds hollow when tapped on the base. Cool on a wire rack.

Honey-glazed Walnut Bread

This recipe makes very good bread, very quickly! It needs mixing, shaping and rising only once before baking, which takes about 1¼ hours altogether. Use walnut oil instead of olive oil if you wish. The recipe makes 16 rolls or two 20 cm (8 in) round loaves – and by the way this bread makes the best toast ever!

100 g (4 oz) walnut pieces
350 g (12 oz) granary flour
350 g (12 oz) strong white
    flour
7 g sachet fast-action yeast
2 level teaspoons salt
1 tablespoon black treacle
500 ml (17 fl oz) warm
    milk (1 part boiling to
    2 parts cold)
2 tablespoons good olive oil
100 g (4 oz) sunflower seeds

TO GLAZE
1 tablespoon beaten egg
1 tablespoon clear honey

To freeze the bread, seal in freezer-proof bags, label and freeze for up to 6 months. To defrost, thaw in the plastic bag for 5–6 hours at room temperature. The bread is best served warm, so refresh in a pre-heated oven at 160°C/Fan 140°C/Gas 3 for about 15 minutes or until warmed through.

1 Grease 2 baking trays. Briefly process the walnuts, or coarsely chop by hand, taking care to keep the pieces quite large. Set aside until ready to use.

2 Combine the flours, yeast and salt together in a large bowl. Then add the treacle, milk and olive oil and mix to form a dough, either with your hands or an electric mixer. Add a little more milk, if necessary, to make the dough slightly sticky. Turn the dough out on to a lightly floured work surface and knead for about 10 minutes. Alternatively, use a mixer fitted with a dough hook and leave running for about 5 minutes. When ready, the dough should be smooth and elastic and leave the bowl and your hands clean.

3 Reserve about 2 tablespoons of sunflower seeds, then work the rest of the seeds and the chopped walnuts into the dough. Divide the dough in half, then shape each piece into a smooth round and set in the centre of the prepared baking trays. Enclose each tray inside a large plastic bag, sealing a little air inside so that the plastic is not in contact with the bread. Leave to rise in a warm place for 30–45 minutes or until doubled in size. If your kitchen is cool this may take as long as 1–1½ hours.

4 Pre-heat the oven to 200°C/Fan 180°C/Gas 6. To glaze the loaves, mix together the egg and honey and brush gently over the surface of the dough. Sprinkle with the reserved sunflower seeds, then bake in the pre-heated oven for 20–25 minutes or until the loaves are a good conker brown and sound hollow when tapped on the base. If you are making rolls, remember that they will need less time in the oven. Cool on a wire rack.

Farmhouse Brown Seeded Loaf

This textured loaf is packed with flavour and keeps well.

40 g (1½ oz) linseed
150 g (5 oz) porridge oats
300 ml (½ pint) boiling water
450 g (1 lb) strong white flour
100 g (4 oz) strong wholemeal
 flour
50 g (2 oz) sunflower seeds
1 level teaspoon salt
7 g sachet fast-action yeast
about 350 ml (12 fl oz) warm
 water

TO GLAZE
a little milk, for glazing
a few extra porridge oats,
 to decorate

1 Measure the linseed and porridge oats into a bowl, pour over the boiling water and mix. This can be done by hand or with an electric mixer. Leave to absorb for about 10 minutes and cool slightly.

2 Add the remaining dry ingredients and the warm water and mix to form a soft dough. Knead by hand on a floured work surface for about 5 minutes, or in a mixer fitted with a dough hook. Put into an oiled bowl, cover with clingfilm and leave to rise in a warm place for about 1-1½ hours.

3 Knead for a few minutes and shape into a round, or divide and shape into 2 round loaves. Place on a baking tray lined with baking parchment. Slip the baking tray into a large plastic bag, and leave to prove in a warm place for about 30 minutes or until doubled in size. Pre-heat the oven to 220°C/Fan 200°C/Gas 7. Brush the dough with milk and scatter with oats.

4 Bake in the pre-heated oven for 20–25 minutes or until golden brown and the bread sounds hollow when tapped on the bottom. Cool on a wire rack.

Walnut and Raisin Loaf

This generously fruited savoury loaf with added walnuts is delicious with cheese. This recipe makes 1 large or 2 smaller loaves.

225 g (8 oz) strong white flour
225 g (8 oz) strong wholemeal flour
1 level teaspoon salt
1 level tablespoon light muscovado sugar
1 level teaspoon ground cinnamon
40 g (1½ oz) butter, melted
300 ml (½ pint) warm water
7 g sachet fast-action yeast
100 g (4 oz) chopped walnuts
100 g (4 oz) raisins
extra flour, for dusting

TO GLAZE
1 large egg, beaten, to glaze

1 Measure the flours, salt, sugar, cinnamon, butter, water and yeast into a bowl and mix together by hand or with an electric mixer fitted with a dough hook, until combined to fairly sticky dough.

2 Knead for about 4–5 minutes on a lightly floured work surface or in the mixer, adding a little extra flour if needed.

3 Transfer to a large oiled bowl, cover tightly with clingfilm (make sure no air can escape) and leave to rise in a warm place for 1–1½ hours or until the dough has doubled in size.

4 Tip the dough on to a lightly floured work surface and flatten the ball slightly. Add the chopped walnuts and raisins and knead into the dough, then shape into a long thick sausage shape about 40 x 10 cm (16 x 4 in) or two smaller sausages shapes.

5 Place on a baking tray lined with baking parchment and slide into a large plastic bag, so the dough and baking tray are completely covered. Seal the end of the bag. Leave to prove in a warm place for about 35–45 minutes or until doubled in size.

6 Pre-heat the oven to 220°C/Fan 200°C/Gas 7. Brush the dough with beaten egg and bake in the pre-heated oven for about 20–25 minutes for the large loaf (a little less for two smaller ones) or until golden brown and the bread sounds hollow when tapped on the bottom. Cool on a wire rack.

Irish Soda Bread

Soda bread is quick and easy to make, as it uses no yeast so does not have to rise. Porridge oats can be added to give the bread more texture. Simply replace 50 g (2 oz) of the flour with the same quantity of oats. Soda bread is best eaten on the day of making.

450 g (1 lb) strong white flour
1 level teaspoon bicarbonate
   of soda
1 level teaspoon salt
300 ml (½ pint) buttermilk
   or 150 ml (¼ pint) milk and
   150 ml (¼ pint) natural
   yoghurt, mixed
about 6 tablespoons tepid
   water

1 Pre-heat the oven to 200°C/Fan 180°C/Gas 6. Lightly grease a baking tray.

2 Mix together the dry ingredients in a mixing bowl. Add the buttermilk (or milk and yoghurt mixture) and enough tepid water to form a very soft dough.

3 Turn the dough out on to a lightly floured work surface and shape into a neat round about 18 cm (7 in) in diameter. Place on the baking tray and make a shallow cross in the top with a sharp knife.

4 Bake in the pre-heated oven for 30 minutes, then turn the bread upside-down and continue baking for about 10–15 minutes or until the bread sounds hollow when tapped on the bottom. Cool on a wire rack.

Focaccia Bread with Onion and Balsamic Topping

This is a flat Italian bread with an exciting topping, perfect with soups and pâté.

400 g (14 oz) strong
    white flour
100 g (4 oz) semolina
4 tablespoons olive oil
1 level teaspoon salt
7 g sachet fast-action yeast
300 ml (½ pint) warm water

FOR THE ONION
    BALSAMIC TOPPING
1 tablespoon olive oil
2 large sliced onions
1½ teaspoons balsamic
    vinegar
1 level teaspoon sugar
1 level teaspoon fresh
    thyme leaves
sea salt, to sprinkle

1 Measure all the ingredients for the bread into a bowl and mix by hand or with an electric mixer fitted with a dough hook until you have a fairly sticky, soft dough. Remove from the bowl and sit on a floured work surface. Knead by hand or in a machine for about 4–5 minutes, adding a little extra flour if needed.

2 Transfer to a large oiled bowl, cover tightly with clingfilm (make sure no air can escape) and leave to rise in a warm place for 1–1 ½ hours or until doubled in size.

3 While the dough is rising make the topping. Heat the oil in a frying pan, add the onions and stir over a high heat for a few minutes. Cover with a lid, turn the heat down to low and cook for about 20 minutes until the onions are soft.

4 Remove the lid and turn the heat up to drive off any excess water. Add the vinegar and sugar and fry until golden brown. Add the thyme and season with salt and pepper. Remove from the heat and set aside to cool.

5 Once the dough has risen, tip on to a lightly floured work surface and knock back, using your hands, for about 5 minutes. Roll out into a rectangle about 40cm x 28cm (16 x 11 in) in size. Transfer to a baking tray lined with baking parchment and spread the cold onion mixture over the dough. Slide the baking tray and dough into a large plastic bag and seal the bag so no air can escape. Leave to prove for about 30 minutes or until doubled in size.

6 Pre-heat the oven to 220°C/Fan 200°C/Gas 7. Remove the dough from the bag and bake in the pre-heated oven for about 20–25 minutes or until golden on top and underneath. Cool on a wire rack.

Mushroom and Garlic-stuffed Picnic Loaf

This is an easy bread to make, that does not need any skill in the making or shaping of it. It is baked with a filling of mushrooms, garlic and chopped parsley and so is well flavoured and moist and needs no butter. Jars of wild mushrooms in oil can be found in the larger supermarkets or good delicatessens. Serve with a salad or just home-grown tomatoes seasoned with sea salt. It is also good with grilled meats.

FOR THE DOUGH
350 g (12 oz) strong
    white flour
1 level teaspoon salt
1 level teaspoon fast-action
    yeast
200 ml (7 fl oz) warm water

FOR THE FILLING
290 g jar wild mushrooms
    in oil
a good handful of parsley
    leaves, chopped
3 finely chopped garlic cloves
salt and freshly ground
    black pepper

TO GLAZE
1 large egg
a generous pinch of salt
1 tablespoon sesame seeds

1 Empty the jar of mushrooms for the filling into a sieve placed over a bowl and leave to drain. Save the oil to use in the recipe.

2 To make the dough, combine the dry ingredients in a large bowl or an electric mixer. Pour in the warm water and add 2 tablespoons of the drained mushroom oil. Mix to a sticky dough. You can use a mixer fitted with a dough hook to knead the dough for 5 minutes or do by hand. (The dough will be sticky and hard to work at first, but keep kneading and try not to use any additional flour.) It will take about 10 minutes, but it will develop into soft, smooth dough that leaves the work surface and your hands clean.

3 Dribble a little more of the mushroom oil into the empty mixing bowl. Roll the dough around in it then leave on the work surface covered with the upside-down bowl. Leave for about 2 hours to rise or until doubled in size.

To make 1 large loaf, shape the dough into an oval, then put on to a large baking tray and roll out to an oval about 33 x 23 cm (13 x 9 in). Mix together the drained mushrooms (any remaining mushroom oil to one side), parsley, garlic and some salt and pepper. Spread the mixture over half the dough from one long end to the other and to within 1 cm (½ in) of the edge. Fold the other half of dough almost over the filling, so a narrow border of it is left showing.

To make individual rolls, divide the dough into 8 and roll to 12 cm (4½ in) rounds. Put a heaped dessertspoon of mushroom mixture on each round. Fold as described for the single loaf and put on to a baking tray.

4 To glaze the loaf or rolls, beat the egg with a generous pinch of salt then brush on. Sprinkle with the sesame seeds. Slip the baking tray into a large plastic bag, tuck the ends under the tray and leave in a warm place to prove for 30–45 minutes or until doubled in size. Pre-heat the oven to 200°C/Fan 180°C/Gas 6.

5 Bake the loaf in the pre-heated oven for 15–20 minutes and the rolls for 10–15 minutes or until browned. It is difficult to tell when this bread is cooked because of the filling, so timing is the best indication. Remove from the oven and use a palette knife to transfer the loaf or rolls to a wire rack. Brush the bread liberally with the remaining mushroom oil then leave to cool before eating, if you can resist it!

To freeze the bread, wrap the freshly baked, cooled bread in foil, then seal in a plastic bag. Label and freeze for up to 1 month. Defrost in the bag at room temperature overnight. Sprinkle the loaf with a little water and warm, loosely wrapped in the foil, in a pre-heated oven at 180°C/Fan 160°C/Gas 4 for 10–15 minutes.

CHAPTER FIFTEEN

Fruit Breads

Fruit breads and tea loaves make a delicious addition to the tea table. They are economical and quick to make so they're good cakes to make for fêtes and charity events. You can sell them as whole loaves, or sliced and spread with butter. Present whole loaves in decorative loaf cases, with a pretty label including serving and storing instructions.

There is a good variety of fruit breads to try, from a simple **Banana Loaf** (page 307) and **Crunchy Orange Syrup Loaves** (page 306) to traditional Welsh **Bara Brith** (page 302) and more unusual **Courgette Loaves** (page 313). These fruit breads are best served fresh, sliced and buttered.

Lots of the recipes here call for dried fruit. If you do a lot of baking, buy dried fruits separately – currants, raisins, peel and so on – and mix up your own mixed dried fruit. This can be cheaper, and means you have the individual proportions to your liking.

Making fruit bread is also a delicious way of using up leftover fresh fruit, such as the brown bananas that no-one wants to eat.

Whether you use fresh or dried fruit, make sure you measure the sponge ingredient quantities as accurately as possible, as the wrong fat-to-flour ratio can result in all the fruit or nuts sinking to the bottom of the sponge – it will of course still taste delicious, but won't look as nice!

If you have a surplus of dried fruit, perhaps after Christmas, you can keep it in the freezer in separate freezer bags for up to 1 year.

Sultana Malt Loaves

These can be made in advance as they keep very well and can also be frozen.

225 g (8 oz) plain flour
½ level teaspoon
    bicarbonate of soda
1 level teaspoon baking
    powder
225 g (8 oz) sultanas
50 g (2 oz) demerara sugar
175 g (6 oz) malt extract
1 tablespoon black treacle
2 large eggs, beaten
150 ml (5 fl oz) strained
    cold black tea

1 Pre-heat the oven to 150°C/Fan 130°C/Gas 2. Grease two 450 g (1 lb) loaf tins then line the base of each tin with baking parchment.

2 Measure the flour, bicarbonate of soda and baking powder into a bowl and stir in the sultanas. Gently heat the sugar, malt extract and black treacle together. Pour on to the dry ingredients, along with the beaten eggs and the tea. Beat well until smooth. Pour into the prepared tins.

3 Bake in the pre-heated oven for about 1 hour or until well risen and firm to the touch. Leave to cool in the tins for 10 minutes then turn out, peel off the parchment and finish cooling on a wire rack. These loaves are best kept for 2 days before eating.

TIP
Freeze loaves as soon as they are cold. Some icing loses its sheen in the freezer, so it's usually best to freeze the loaf un-iced. Butter cream icing is an exception.

Bara Brith

There are many versions of this traditional teabread. In Welsh, 'bara brith' means 'speckled bread'. Similar breads are made in different part of Britain, such as Barm Brack in Ireland and Selkirk Bannock in Scotland.

175 g (6 oz) currants
175 g (6 oz) sultanas
225 g (8 oz) light muscovado
   sugar
300 ml (½ pint) strong hot tea
275 g (10 oz) self-raising flour
1 large egg, beaten

1 Measure the fruit and sugar into a bowl, pour over the hot tea, cover and leave overnight.

2 Pre-heat the oven to 150°C/Fan 130°C/Gas 2. Lightly grease a 900 g (2 lb) loaf tin then line the base with baking parchment.

3 Stir the flour and egg into the fruit mixture, mix thoroughly then turn into the prepared tin and level the surface.

4 Bake in the pre-heated oven for about 1½ hours or until well risen and firm to the touch. A skewer inserted into the centre should come out clean. Leave to cool in the tin for 10 minutes then turn out, peel off the parchment and finish cooling on a wire rack. Serve sliced and buttered.

Iced Apricot Fruit Loaf

Like any fruit loaf, this is easy to make. I've found this to be a popular choice at fêtes and charity events, sold in slices or whole.

75 g (3 oz) red or natural
   glacé cherries
3 large eggs
175 g (6 oz) self-raising flour
100 g (4 oz) softened butter
100 g (4 oz) light muscovado
   sugar
100 g (4 oz) chopped ready-to-
   eat dried apricots
150 g (5 oz) sultanas

FOR THE ICING
100 g (4 oz) sifted icing sugar
1 tablespoon apricot jam
1 tablespoon water
2 chopped ready-to-eat
   dried apricots

1 Pre-heat the oven to 160°C/Fan 140°C/Gas 3. Lightly grease a 900 g (2 lb) loaf tin then line the base with baking parchment.

2 Cut the cherries into quarters, put in a sieve and rinse under running water. Drain well then dry thoroughly on kitchen paper.

3 Break the eggs into a large bowl and then measure in the remaining cake ingredients including the cherries. Beat well until the mixture is smooth. Turn into the prepared tin and level the top.

4 Bake in the pre-heated oven for about 1 hour 10 minutes or until the cake is golden brown, firm to the touch and shrinking away from the sides of the tin. A fine skewer inserted into the centre of the loaf should come out clean. Leave to cool in the tin for 10 minutes then turn out, peel off the parchment and finish cooling on a wire rack.

5 To make the icing, measure the sifted icing sugar into a bowl. Heat the apricot jam and water together until the jam melts then pour on to the icing sugar. Mix to a smooth spreading consistency, then spoon over the top of the cold loaf. Decorate the loaf by sprinkling the chopped apricots down the centre.

Banana and Honey Teabread

This teabread has quite a pale colour even when cooked, because of the thick pale honey used. It is a very good way of using up over-ripe bananas.

225 g (8 oz) self-raising flour
¼ level teaspoon freshly
  grated nutmeg
100 g (4 oz) butter
225 g (8 oz) bananas
100 g (4 oz) caster sugar
grated rind of 1 lemon
2 large eggs
6 tablespoons thick pale
  honey

FOR THE TOPPING
2 tablespoons honey
nibbed sugar or crushed sugar
  cubes, for sprinkling

1 Pre-heat the oven to 160°C/Fan 140°C/Gas 3. Lightly grease a 900 g (2 lb) loaf tin then line the base with baking parchment.

2 Measure the flour and nutmeg into a large bowl and rub in the butter using your fingertips until the mixture resembles fine breadcrumbs.

3 Peel and mash the bananas and stir into the flour mixture, along with the sugar, lemon rind, eggs and honey. Beat well until evenly mixed, then turn into the prepared tin and level the surface.

4 Bake in the pre-heated oven for about 1¼ hours or until a fine skewer inserted into the centre comes out clean. Cover the teabread loosely with foil during the end of the cooking time if it is browning too much. Leave to cool in the tin for a few minutes then turn out, peel off the parchment and finish cooling on a wire rack.

5 To make the topping, gently warm the honey in a small pan then brush over the top of the cold teabread. Sprinkle with the nibbed sugar.

Crunchy Orange Syrup Loaves

I've seen loaves similar to these for sale in Wycombe market. They may not look madly exciting, but they are very popular, and delicious.

100 g (4 oz) softened butter
175 g (6 oz) self-raising flour
1 level teaspoon baking
    powder
175 g (6 oz) caster sugar
2 large eggs
4 tablespoons milk
finely grated rind of 1 orange

FOR THE TOPPING
juice of 1 orange
100 g (4 oz) granulated sugar

1 Pre-heat the oven to 180°C/Fan 160°C/Gas 4. Lightly grease two 450 g (1 lb) loaf tins then line the base of each tin with baking parchment.

2 Measure all the cake ingredients into a large bowl and beat well for about 2 minutes. Divide the mixture evenly between the tins and level the surface of each.

3 Bake in the pre-heated oven for about 30 minutes or until the loaves spring back when the surface is lightly pressed.

4 While the cakes are baking, make the crunchy topping. Measure the orange juice and sugar into a small bowl and stir to mix. Spread the mixture over the baked loaves while they are still hot, and then leave to cool completely in the tins. Turn out and remove the parchment once cold.

Banana Loaf

This is a lovely, moist loaf, which really doesn't need to be buttered. It freezes very well. Any bananas left in the fruit bowl are ideal for this cake – the riper they are, the better.

100 g (4 oz) softened butter
175 g (6 oz) caster sugar
2 large eggs
2 ripe bananas, mashed
225 g (8 oz) self-raising flour
1 level teaspoon baking
    powder
2 tablespoons milk

1 Pre-heat the oven to 180°C/Fan 160°C/Gas 4. Lightly grease a 900 g (2 lb) loaf tin then line the base and sides with baking parchment.

2 Measure all the ingredients into a mixing bowl and beat for about 2 minutes, until well blended. Spoon the mixture into the prepared tin and level the surface.

3 Bake in the pre-heated oven for about 1 hour, until well risen and golden brown. A fine skewer inserted in the centre should come out clean. Leave to cool in the tin for a few minutes then turn out, peel off the parchment and finish cooling on a wire rack. Slice thickly to serve.

Carrot and Orange Loaf

This moist loaf needs no buttering. Store it in the fridge if you want to keep it for a length of time.

1 orange
150 g (5 oz) softened butter
150 g (5 oz) light muscovado
   sugar
175 g (6 oz) carrots
2 large eggs, beaten
200 g (7 oz) self-raising flour
1 level teaspoon baking
   powder
½ level teaspoon ground
   mixed spice
about 1 tablespoon milk

TO FINISH
about 2 tablespoons clear
   honey

1 Pre-heat the oven to 180°C/Fan 160°C/Gas 4. Lightly grease a 900 g (2 lb) loaf tin then line the base with baking parchment.

2 Finely grate the orange rind, cut away the pith and slice the orange thinly. Place the rind in a large bowl and add the butter, sugar, carrots, eggs, flour, baking powder and spice and mix well until thoroughly blended. Add the tablespoon of milk if necessary to give a dropping consistency. Spoon into the prepared tin.

3 Bake in the pre-heated oven for about 1 hour or until just firm to the touch. Remove the loaf from the oven and arrange the orange slices over the top. Brush with the honey and return the loaf to the oven for a further 15 minutes or until a skewer inserted into the centre comes out clean. Leave to cool in the tin for a few minutes then turn out, peel off the parchment and finish cooling on a wire rack.

Walnut Teabread

This teabread freezes well. It's delicious spread with good butter, and I like coming across the walnuts in the bread – they give an interesting texture.

100 g (4 oz) granulated sugar
175 g (6 oz) golden syrup
200 ml (7 fl oz) milk
50 g (2 oz) sultanas
225 g (8 oz) self-raising flour
1 level teaspoon baking
   powder
50 g (2 oz) roughly chopped
   walnuts
1 large egg, beaten

1 Pre-heat the oven to 180°C/Fan 160°C/Gas 4. Lightly grease a 900 g (2 lb) loaf tin then line the base with baking parchment.

2 Measure the sugar, syrup, milk and sultanas into a pan and heat gently until the sugar has dissolved. Set aside to cool.

3 Measure the flour and baking powder into a bowl and add the roughly chopped walnuts. Add the cooled syrup mixture to the dry ingredients along with the beaten egg and stir well until the mixture is smooth. Pour into the prepared tin.

4 Bake in the pre-heated oven for 50 minutes – 1 hour or until firm to the touch and a skewer inserted into the centre comes out clean. Cover the top of the teabread loosely with foil towards the end of the cooking time if the cake is becoming too brown. Leave to cool in the tin for 10 minutes then turn out, peel off the parchment and finish cooling on a wire rack. Serve buttered.

TIP
To break up walnuts, or pulverize biscuits or cornflakes, put them in a strong polythene bag and crush with a rolling pin.

Pineapple and Cherry Loaf

This cake would make a lovely present for someone with a sweet tooth. Remember that it is important to keep it in the fridge as it is very moist, and could go mouldy if left in a tin in a warm kitchen.

175 g (6 oz) red or natural glacé cherries

227 g (8 oz) can pineapple rings or chunks in fruit juice

150 g (5 oz) softened butter

100 g (4 oz) light muscovado sugar

2 large eggs, beaten

200 g (7 oz) self-raising flour

225 g (8 oz) sultanas

1 Pre-heat the oven to 160°C/Fan 140°C/Gas 3. Lightly grease a 900 g (2 lb) loaf tin then line the base with baking parchment.

2 Cut the cherries into quarters, put in a sieve and rinse under running water then drain well. Drain the pineapple, reserving 2 tablespoons of juice, and roughly chop, then dry the pineapple and cherries very thoroughly on kitchen paper.

3 Measure the butter, sugar, eggs and flour into a large mixing bowl and beat for about 2 minutes until smooth and well blended. Fold in the sultanas, pineapple and cherries, along with the reserved pineapple juice. Turn into the prepared loaf tin.

4 Bake in the pre-heated oven for 1¼–1½ hours or until the loaf is well risen, golden brown and shrinking slightly from the sides of the tin. Leave to cool in the tin for a few minutes then turn out, peel off the parchment and finish cooling on a wire rack. Store in an airtight container in the fridge.

Cherry Loaf Cake

Always a favourite. Wash and dry the quartered cherries thoroughly to prevent them from sinking to the bottom of the cake.

175 g (6 oz) red or natural glacé cherries
225 g (8 oz) self-raising flour
175 g (6 oz) softened butter
175 g (6 oz) caster sugar
finely grated rind of 1 lemon
50 g (2 oz) ground almonds
3 large eggs

1 Pre-heat the oven to 180°C/Fan 160°C/Gas 4. Grease a 900 g (2 lb) loaf tin then line the base with baking parchment.

2 Cut the cherries into quarters, put in a sieve and rinse under running water. Drain well then dry thoroughly on kitchen paper.

3 Measure all the remaining ingredients into a large bowl and beat well for 1 minute to mix thoroughly. Lightly fold in the cherries. Turn into the prepared tin.

4 Bake in the pre-heated oven for 1–1¼ hours or until well risen, golden brown and a skewer inserted into the centre comes out clean. Leave to cool in the tin for 10 minutes then turn out, peel off the parchment and finish cooling on a wire rack.

Courgette Loaves

Expect this cake to have a sugary top, which is quite normal. Freeze one of the loaves and store the second one in the fridge. Serve sliced and buttered, or spread with low-fat soft cheese.

3 large eggs
250 ml (9½ fl oz) sunflower oil
350 g (12 oz) caster sugar
350 g (12 oz) courgettes (or small marrow), grated
165 g (5½ oz) plain flour
165 g (5½ oz) buckwheat flour
1 level teaspoon baking powder
2 level teaspoons bicarbonate of soda
1 level tablespoon ground cinnamon
175 g (6 oz) raisins
150 g (5 oz) chopped walnuts

1 Pre-heat the oven to 180°C/Fan 160°C/Gas 4. Grease two 900 g (2 lb) loaf tins then line the base of each tin with baking parchment.

2 Measure all the ingredients into a large bowl and mix well to make a thick batter. Pour into the prepared tins.

3 Bake in the pre-heated oven for about 1 hour or until the loaves are firm and a skewer inserted into the centre comes out clean. Leave to cool in the tin for 10 minutes then turn out, peel off the parchment and finish cooling on a wire rack. Store in the fridge and use within 3 weeks.

Orange Wholemeal Victoria Loaf

If you are making this loaf to give to a friend or to sell whole, use loaf tin liners for a simple decorative touch.

100 g (4 oz) softened butter
100 g (4 oz) light muscovado sugar
2 large eggs
50 g (2 oz) wholemeal self-raising flour
50 g (2 oz) self-raising flour
grated rind of 1 orange

FOR THE TOPPING
25 g (1 oz) softened butter
75 g (3 oz) sifted icing sugar
1 tablespoon fine-cut marmalade

1 Pre-heat the oven to 180°C/Fan 160°C/Gas 4. Lightly grease a 900 g (2 lb) loaf tin then line the base with baking parchment, or use a 900 g (2 lb) loaf tin liner.

2 Measure all the cake ingredients into a large bowl and beat well for about 2 minutes until smooth and blended. Turn into the prepared tin and level the surface – don't expect the mixture to fill the tin.

3 Bake in the pre-heated oven for about 40 minutes or until well risen, golden and shrinking slightly from the sides of the tin. Turn out on to a wire rack to cool.

4 To make the topping, measure all the topping ingredients into a bowl and blend together until smooth. Spoon on top of the cold loaf and swirl the top with a small palette knife to decorate.

Borrowdale Teabread

A wonderful moist teabread to serve buttered. The fruit is soaked in tea overnight. You can make two 450 g (1 lb) loaves from this recipe instead of one large loaf, but shorten the cooking time to 30–40 minutes.

100 g (4 oz) sultanas
100 g (4 oz) currants
100 g (4 oz) raisins
475 ml (16 fl oz) strong tea, strained
225 g (8 oz) light muscovado sugar
2 large eggs
450 g (1 lb) wholemeal self-raising flour

1 Put the sultanas, currants and raisins in a bowl along with the tea, cover and leave to soak overnight.

2 Pre-heat the oven to 180°C/Fan 160°C/Gas 4. Grease a 900 g (2 lb) loaf tin then line the base with baking parchment.

3 Mix the sugar and eggs together until light and fluffy. Add the flour along with the soaked fruits and any remaining liquid, and mix thoroughly together. Spoon the mixture into the prepared loaf tin and level the surface.

4 Bake in the pre-heated oven for about 1 hour or until a skewer inserted into the centre comes out clean. Leave to cool in the tin then serve sliced and spread with butter.

CHAPTER SIXTEEN

Buns and Scones

The recipes in this chapter, including **Bath Buns** (opposite), **Hot Cross Buns** (page 336) and Scones (in all their guises – baked in the oven, on top of the stove, or on a griddle) are all classic British bakes at their simplest and finest. They are all quick and easy to cook, too, and rely on inexpensive ingredients that most of us already have in our storecupboards. They are unbeatable eaten fresh and warm, spread with butter and, of course, plain scones generously topped with cream and jam are an essential for a proper afternoon tea.

The recipes here are ideal to have to hand when friends unexpectedly arrive on the doorstep, as they can be made and baked in no time – my **Very Best Scones** (page 320) can be made and cooked in minutes.

Although best served freshly baked, most of the recipes here freeze very well too. Make two batches of **Rock Cakes** (page 332), for example, and freeze the extras so you can pull them out of the freezer and revive in the oven when friends stop by for tea.

To freeze buns and scones, pack into rigid plastic boxes or freezer bags when cold so that you can easily take out the number you require, leaving the remainder in the freezer. Refresh defrosted buns and scones in a moderate oven before serving. Any bakes that aren't eaten fresh are quite delicious toasted.

Bath Buns

The spa town of Bath is famous for its buns, distinguished by the coarse sugar topping. They are said to have been created in the eighteenth century. This recipe makes about 18 buns.

450 g (1 lb) strong white flour
7 g sachet fast-action yeast
1 level teaspoon salt
50 g (2 oz) caster sugar
50 g (2 oz) butter, melted and cooled
2 large eggs, beaten
150 ml (¼ pint) tepid milk
175 g (6 oz) sultanas
50 g (2 oz) chopped candied peel

TO FINISH
1 large egg, to glaze
nibbed sugar or coarsely crushed sugar cubes

1 Measure the flour, yeast, salt and caster sugar into a large bowl and mix well. Make a well in the centre and pour in the melted, cooled butter, eggs and milk, adding the sultanas and chopped peel last. Mix to a smooth, soft dough.

2 Turn the dough out on to a lightly floured work surface and knead for about 5 minutes or until smooth and elastic. Place in an oiled bowl and cover with oiled clingfilm, or put the bowl inside a large polythene bag. Leave to rise until doubled in size, about 1 hour in a warm room.

3 Lightly grease 2 baking trays. Turn the risen dough out of the bowl and knead well until the dough is again smooth and elastic. Divide into 18 equal pieces. Shape each piece of dough into a bun and place on the prepared baking trays. Cover again with oiled clingfilm and leave in a warm place until doubled in size, about 30 minutes.

4 Pre-heat the oven to 190°C/Fan 170°C/Gas 5. Brush the buns with beaten egg and sprinkle with nibbed sugar. Bake in the pre-heated oven for about 15 minutes or until golden brown and sound hollow when the base is tapped. Lift on to a wire rack to cool. Serve buttered.

Very Best Scones

The secret of making good scones is not to handle them too much before baking, and to make the mixture on the sticky side. Either eat the scones fresh or leave them to cool completely then freeze them. Thaw them at room temperature and then refresh in a moderate oven for about 10 minutes. This recipe makes about 20 scones, or 8–10 large scones using a 9 cm (3½ in) cutter, if you prefer.

450 g (1 lb) self-raising flour
2 rounded teaspoons baking powder
75 g (3 oz) softened butter
50 g (2 oz) caster sugar
2 large eggs
about 225 ml (8 fl oz) milk

1 Pre-heat the oven to 220°C/Fan 200°C/Gas 7. Lightly grease 2 baking trays.

2 Measure the flour and baking powder into a large bowl. Add the butter and rub it in with your fingertips until the mixture resembles fine breadcrumbs. Stir in the sugar.

3 Beat the eggs together and make up to a generous 300 ml (½ pint) with the milk, then put about 2 tablespoons of the mixture aside in a cup for glazing the scones later. Gradually add the egg mixture to the dry ingredients, stirring it in until you have a soft dough. The scone mixture should be on the wet side, sticking to your fingers, as the scones will rise better.

4 Turn the dough on to a lightly floured surface and flatten it out with your hand or a rolling pin to a thickness of 1–2 cm (½–¾ in). Use a 5 cm (2 in) fluted cutter to stamp out the scones by pushing the cutter straight down into the dough (as opposed to twisting it), then lifting it straight out. This will ensure that the scones rise evenly and keep their shape. Gently push the remaining dough together, knead lightly then re-roll and cut more scones.

5 Arrange the scones on the prepared baking trays and brush the tops with the reserved beaten egg mixture to glaze. Bake in the pre-heated oven for 10–15 minutes, until well risen and golden. Transfer to a wire rack and leave to cool, covered with a clean tea towel to keep them moist. Serve cut in half and spread generously with strawberry jam. Top with a good spoonful of clotted or whipped cream, if you like.

Make Wholemeal Scones by using 450 g (1 lb) wholemeal self-raising flour instead of white. You may need to add a little more liquid to make the dough.

Special Fruit Scones

Making good scones is so easy if the mixture is not too dry and the dough is not overhandled. Wrap the scones in a clean tea towel after baking to keep them moist. This recipe makes about 14 scones.

225 g (8 oz) self-raising flour
1 level teaspoon baking
   powder
50 g (2 oz) softened butter
25 g (1 oz) caster sugar
50 g (2 oz) mixed dried fruit
1 large egg
a little milk

1 Pre-heat the oven to 220°C/Fan 200°C/Gas 7. Lightly grease 2 baking trays.

2 Measure the flour and baking powder into a large bowl, add the butter and rub in with your fingertips until the mixture resembles fine breadcrumbs. Stir in the sugar and the dried fruit.

3 Break the egg into a measuring jug, then make up to 150 ml (¼ pint) with milk. Stir the egg and milk into the flour and mix to a soft but not sticky dough.

4 Turn out on to a lightly floured work surface, knead lightly and roll out to a 1 cm (½ in) thickness. Cut into rounds with a fluted 5 cm (2 inch) cutter and place them on the prepared baking trays. Brush the tops with a little milk.

5 Bake in the pre-heated oven for about 10 minutes or until pale golden brown. Lift the scones on to a wire rack to cool. Eat as fresh as possible.

Cheese Scone Round

Serve these warm with cold meats, soup or a cheese board – and with butter, of course! This recipe makes 1 large scone round marked into 6 wedges.

225 g (8 oz) self-raising flour
½ level teaspoon salt
½ level teaspoon mustard
    powder
¼ level teaspoon cayenne
    pepper
1 level teaspoon baking
    powder
25 g (1 oz) butter
150 g (5 oz) grated mature
    Cheddar
1 large egg
a little milk

1 Pre-heat the oven to 220°C/Fan 200°C/Gas 7. Lightly grease a baking tray.

2 Measure the flour, salt, mustard powder, cayenne pepper and baking powder into a large bowl. Add the butter and rub in with your fingertips until the mixture resembles fine breadcrumbs. Stir in 100 g (4 oz) of the grated cheese.

3 Break the egg into a measuring jug then make up to 150 ml (¼ pint) with milk. Stir the egg and milk into the dry ingredients and mix to a soft but not sticky dough.

4 Turn out on to a lightly floured work surface and knead lightly. Roll out to a 15 cm (6 in) circle and mark into 6 wedges. Brush with a little milk and sprinkle with the remaining grated cheese.

5 Bake in the pre-heated oven for about 15 minutes or until golden brown and firm to the touch. Slide on to a wire rack to cool. Eat as fresh as possible.

Potato Scones

These scones are particularly moist, excellent if you want to keep them a day or two. They can be made sweet or savoury: for savoury potato scones, omit the sugar and add ½ teaspoon of salt to the flour. This recipe makes about 12 scones.

175 g (6 oz) plain flour
3 level teaspoons baking
　　powder
50 g (2 oz) butter
40 g (1½ oz) caster sugar
100 g (4 oz) fresh mashed
　　potato
about 3 tablespoons milk

1 Pre-heat the oven to 220°C/Fan 200°C/Gas 7. Lightly grease 2 baking trays.

2 Measure the flour and baking powder into a large bowl, add the butter and rub in with your fingertips until the mixture resembles fine breadcrumbs. Stir in the sugar and the mashed potato, mixing with a fork to prevent the potato from forming lumps. Add enough milk to form a soft but not sticky dough.

3 Turn the mixture out on to a lightly floured work surface and knead very lightly. Roll out to a thickness of about 1 cm (½ in) and cut into rounds using a 5 cm (2 in) fluted cutter (use a plain cutter for savoury scones). Transfer to the prepared baking trays.

4 Bake in the pre-heated oven for about 12–15 minutes or until well risen and golden brown. Serve warm and buttered.

Cheese and Olive Scone Bake

Making one large scone is fastest of all, as you don't have to roll and cut out the mixture. If you don't have a traybake or roasting tin, shape the dough into an oblong on a baking tray.

450 g (1 lb) self-raising flour
2 level teaspoons baking
    powder
1 level teaspoon salt
100 g (4 oz) butter
200 g (7 oz) mature Cheddar,
    grated
100 g (4 oz) roughly chopped
    pitted black olives
2 large eggs
a little milk
25 g (1 oz) grated Parmesan

1 Pre-heat the oven to 230°C/Fan 210°C/Gas 8. Lightly grease a 30 x 23 cm (12 x 9 in) traybake or roasting tin.

2 Measure the flour, baking powder and salt into a large bowl. Add the butter and rub in with fingertips until the mixture resembles fine breadcrumbs. Stir in the grated Cheddar and the roughly chopped olives. Break the eggs into a measuring jug and make up to 300 ml (½ pint) with milk. Add to the flour mixture, mixing to form a soft dough.

3 Knead the dough quickly and lightly until smooth, then roll out on to a lightly floured work surface to an oblong to fit the tin. Transfer to the prepared tin and mark into 12 squares, then brush the top with a little milk.

4 Bake in the pre-heated oven for about 15 minutes. Sprinkle the top with the Parmesan and bake for a further 5 minutes or until the scone is well risen and golden. Turn out on to a wire rack to cool.

Drop Scones

These are also known as Scotch Pancakes. In the old days, they were made on a solid metal griddle over an open fire. Now it is more practical to use a large, non-stick frying pan. This recipe makes about 21 pancakes.

175 g (6 oz) self-raising flour
1 level teaspoon baking
   powder
40 g (1½ oz) caster sugar
1 large egg
about 200 ml (7 fl oz) milk

1 Prepare a griddle or heavy-based frying pan (preferably non-stick) by heating and greasing with oil or white vegetable fat.

2 Measure the flour, baking powder and sugar into a large bowl, make a well in the centre and then add the egg and half the milk. Beat to a smooth, thick batter, then beat in enough of the remaining milk to make the batter the consistency of thick cream.

3 Drop the mixture in tablespoonfuls on to the hot griddle, spacing the mixture well apart. When bubbles rise to the surface, turn the scones over with a palette knife and cook on the other side for a further 30 seconds–1 minute, until golden brown. Lift off on to a wire rack and cover them with a clean tea towel to keep them soft.

4 Cook the remaining mixture in the same way. Serve warm, with butter and golden syrup.

Orange Drop Scones

Serve as soon as they are made, with butter and syrup. If you do make them in advance and need to reheat them, arrange them in a single layer on an ovenproof plate, cover tightly with foil and reheat in a moderate oven for about 10 minutes. This recipe makes about 24 scones.

2 oranges
a little milk
175 g (6 oz) self-raising flour
1 level teaspoon baking
  powder
40 g (1½ oz) caster sugar
1 large egg

1 Grate the rind from the oranges and set aside, and then squeeze the juice. Pour the juice into a measuring jug and make it up to 200 ml (7 fl oz) with milk.

2 Measure the flour, baking powder, sugar and orange rind into a mixing bowl. Make a well in the centre and add the egg and half the orange juice and milk mixture. Beat well to make a smooth, thick batter and then beat in enough of the remaining orange juice and milk to give a batter the consistency of thick cream.

3 Heat a large, non-stick frying pan over a medium heat and grease with a little oil or white vegetable fat. Drop the mixture in dessertspoonfuls on to the hot pan, spacing them well apart to allow the mixture to spread.

4 When bubbles appear on the surface, turn the pancakes over with a palette knife and cook on the other side for 30 seconds–1 minute, until golden brown. Transfer to a wire rack and cover with a clean tea towel.

5 Cook the remaining mixture in the same way. Serve warm, with butter and golden or maple syrup, and a little extra grated orange rind, if liked.

Singin' Hinny

This Northumberland griddle cake 'sings' or sizzles as it cooks on the griddle, hence its name. 'Hinny' is Northern slang for honey, a term of endearment applied especially to children and young women. Traditionally the Singin' Hinny is made in one large round, but you can make two or three smaller ones in the same way. This recipe serves 4–6.

350 g (12 oz) plain flour
½ level teaspoon bicarbonate of soda
1 level teaspoon cream of tartar
75 g (3 oz) lard or white vegetable fat (not butter)
100 g (4 oz) currants
about 200 ml (7 fl oz) milk

1 Prepare a griddle or large heavy-based frying pan (preferably non-stick) by heating and lightly greasing it with oil or white vegetable fat.

2 Measure the flour, bicarbonate of soda and cream of tartar into a large bowl, add the lard or white vegetable fat and rub in with your fingertips until the mixture resembles fine breadcrumbs. Stir in the currants. Mix to a soft but not sticky dough with the milk and turn out on to a lightly floured work surface. Knead lightly then roll out to a large round about 5 mm (¼ in) thick.

3 Lift the scone round on to the prepared hot griddle and cook on a gentle heat for about 5 minutes on one side, then carefully turn over and cook on the other side for a further 5 minutes or until both sides are a good brown.

4 Slide the Singin' Hinny on to a wire rack to cool slightly, then split and butter, sandwich back together and serve hot.

Griddle Scones

Make these with white or wholemeal flour and eat them really fresh spread, with butter. If you use wholemeal flour, the mixture will need a little more milk. This recipe makes about 12 scones.

225 g (8 oz) plain flour
1 level teaspoon bicarbonate
   of soda
2 level teaspoons cream
   of tartar
25 g (1 oz) butter
25 g (1 oz) caster sugar
about 150 ml (¼ pint) milk

1 Prepare a griddle or heavy-based frying pan (preferably non-stick) by heating and lightly greasing with oil or white vegetable fat.

2 Measure the flour, bicarbonate of soda and cream of tartar into a large bowl, add the butter and rub with your fingertips until the mixture resembles fine breadcrumbs. Stir in the sugar and gradually add the milk, mixing the dough with a round-bladed knife to a soft but not sticky dough.

3 Divide the dough in half and knead each piece very lightly on a lightly floured work surface. Roll out each piece into a round about 1 cm (½ in) thick, then cut each round into 6 equal wedges. Cook the wedges in batches on the prepared hot griddle for about 5 minutes each side until evenly brown. Lift on to a wire rack to cool. Eat as fresh as possible.

TIP
It is traditional to use bicarbonate of soda and cream of tartar, but you can use self-raising flour and 2 teaspoons of baking powder instead.

Welsh Cakes

For sweet cakes it is traditional to use a fluted cutter, but you may find a plain cutter easier for these as it will cut through the fruit in the dough more easily.

350 g (12 oz) self-raising flour
2 level teaspoons baking
    powder
175 g (6 oz) butter
115 g (4 ½ oz) caster sugar
100 g (4 oz) currants
¾ level teaspoon ground
    mixed spice
1 large egg
about 2 tablespoons milk

TO FINISH
caster sugar, for sprinkling

1 Prepare a griddle or heavy-based frying pan by heating and lightly greasing with oil.

2 Measure the flour and baking powder into a large bowl and rub in the butter with you fingertips until the mixture resembles fine breadcrumbs. Add the sugar, currants and spice.

3 Beat the egg with the milk, then add this to the mixture and mix to form a firm dough, adding a little more milk if necessary.

4 Roll out the dough on to a lightly floured work surface to a thickness of 5mm (¼ in) then cut into rounds with a 7.5 cm (3 in) plain round cutter.

5 Cook the Welsh Cakes on the hot griddle on a low heat for about 3 minutes on each side until golden brown (be careful not to cook them too fast, otherwise the centres will not be fully cooked).

6 Cool on a wire rack then sprinkly with caster sugar. They should be eaten on the day of making, served buttered.

Rock Cakes

These are very traditional English cakes, probably the first things most of us made at school. They're inexpensive, can be large or tiny, and need no special equipment. They are best eaten on the day of making. This recipe makes about 12 cakes.

225 g (8 oz) self-raising flour
2 level teaspoons baking
 powder
100 g (4 oz) softened butter
50 g (2 oz) granulated sugar
100 g (4 oz) mixed dried fruit
50 g (2 oz) currants
1 large egg
about 1 tablespoon milk
a little demerara sugar, for
 sprinkling

1 Pre-heat the oven to 200°C/Fan 180°C/Gas 6. Lightly grease 2 baking trays.

2 Measure the flour and baking powder into a large bowl, add the butter and rub in with your fingertips until the mixture resembles fine breadcrumbs. Stir in the sugar and fruit.

3 Beat the egg and milk together and add to the fruity mixture. If the mixture is too dry, add a little more milk. Using 2 teaspoons, shape the mixture into about 12 rough mounds on the prepared baking trays. Sprinkle generously with demerara sugar.

4 Bake in the pre-heated oven for about 15 minutes or until a pale golden brown at the edges. Cool on a wire rack.

TIP
Use wholemeal self-raising flour if you like, although you may need a little more milk to mix.

Wholemeal Sultana and Apricot Rock Cakes

Wholemeal flours vary a little in the amount of liquid they absorb, so be prepared to add a little more milk if necessary. Wholemeal rock cakes tend to be drier than normal ones, and they are best eaten on the day of making. This recipe makes about 12 cakes.

100 g (4 oz) self-raising flour
100 g (4 oz) wholemeal self-raising flour
2 level teaspoons baking powder
100 g (4 oz) softened butter
50 g (2 oz) light muscovado sugar
50 g (2 oz) sultanas
50 g (2 oz) chopped ready-to-eat dried apricots
1 large egg
about 2 tablespoons milk
a little demerara sugar, for sprinkling

1 Pre-heat the oven to 200°C/Fan 180°C/Gas 6. Lightly grease 2 baking trays.

2 Measure the flours and baking powder into a large bowl, add the butter and rub into the flour with your fingertips until the mixture resembles fine breadcrumbs. Stir in the sugar, sultanas and chopped apricots.

3 Beat the egg and milk together and add to the fruity mixture. If too dry add a little more milk. Using 2 teaspoons, shape the mixture into about 12 rough mounds on the prepared baking trays and sprinkle each mound generously with demerara sugar.

4 Bake in the pre-heated oven for about 15 minutes until beginning to tinge with brown at the edges. Cool on a wire rack.

Coburg Buns

These 'upside-down' buns should be eaten very fresh, on the day of making. You need 12 mini brioche tins to give the buns their pretty shape, but you can make them plain using a 12-hole bun tin, if you like. This recipe makes about 12 buns.

about 50 g (2 oz) flaked
    almonds
150 g (5 oz) self-raising flour
1 level teaspoon baking
    powder
½ level teaspoon ground
    mixed spice
½ level teaspoon ground
    ginger
½ level teaspoon ground
    cinnamon
50 g (2 oz) softened butter
50 g (2 oz) caster sugar
1 large egg
1 tablespoon golden syrup
4 tablespoons milk

1 Pre-heat the oven to 180°C/Fan 160°C/Gas 4. Lightly grease 12 mini brioche tins or use a 12-hole bun tin.

2 Place a few almond flakes in the base of each tin. Measure the flour, baking powder and spices into a large bowl and then add the remaining ingredients. Beat for about 2 minutes until the mixture is well blended and smooth. Divide the mixture between the tins.

3 Bake in the pre-heated oven for about 15 minutes, until well risen, golden and firm to the touch. Leave to cool for a few minutes then turn out so that the almond flakes are on top, and finish cooling on a wire rack.

Hot Cross Buns

This used to be baked as one large bun, but now it is usual to have individual buns. For a more definite cross on the top of the buns, make up 50 g (2 oz) of shortcrust pastry (using 50 g/2 oz plain flour and 25 g/1 oz butter and a little water), cut it into thin strips and lay it over the top of the buns before baking. This recipe makes about 12 buns.

450 g (1 lb) strong white flour
1 level teaspoon salt
1 level teaspoon ground
    mixed spice
1 level teaspoon ground
    cinnamon
½ level teaspoon freshly
    grated nutmeg
7 g sachet fast-action yeast
50 g (2 oz) caster sugar
50 g (2 oz) butter, melted
    and cooled
150 ml (¼ pint) tepid milk
5 tablespoons tepid water
1 large egg, beaten
75 g (3 oz) currants
50 g (2 oz) chopped
    candied peel

TO GLAZE
2 tablespoons granulated
    sugar
2 tablespoons water

1 Lightly grease 2 baking trays. Measure the flour, salt, spices, yeast and sugar into a large bowl and stir to mix. Make a well in the centre and pour in the melted, cooled butter, milk, water and egg, adding the currants and chopped peel to the mixture last.

2 Mix to a soft dough, then turn out on to a lightly floured work surface and knead for about 10 minutes until smooth and elastic. Transfer to an oiled bowl, cover with oiled clingfilm and leave to rise until the dough has doubled in size, about 1½ hours in a warm room. (Because this is an enriched dough, it will take longer to rise than a plain dough.)

3 Turn the risen dough out on to a lightly floured work surface again and knead for 2–3 minutes. Divide the dough into 12 equal pieces and shape each one into a round bun. Make a cross in the top of each bun with a knife, then place on to the prepared baking trays and cover with oiled clingfilm. Leave to rise again in a warm place until doubled in size, about 30 minutes. Pre-heat the oven to 220°C/Fan 200°C/Gas 7.

4 Bake the buns in the pre-heated oven for about 15 minutes until brown and hollow-sounding when the base is tapped. While the buns are baking, dissolve the sugar in the water over a gentle heat. As soon as the buns come out of the oven, brush them with the syrup to give a sticky glaze.

Sultana Streusel Buns

These are fairly plain buns which are best eaten freshly baked. This recipe make 12–18 buns.

225 g (8 oz) self-raising flour
1 level teaspoon baking
   powder
75 g (3 oz) butter
75 g (3 oz) caster sugar
50 g (2 oz) sultanas
1 egg
150 ml (¼ pint) milk

FOR THE STREUSEL TOPPING

25 g (1 oz) self-raising flour
50 g (2 oz) light muscovado
   sugar
25 g (1 oz) butter, melted

TO FINISH
icing sugar, for dusting

1 Pre-heat the oven to 190°C/Fan 170°C/Gas 5. Place fairy cake cases in a 12-hole bun tin. If you want to make slightly smaller buns but don't have two bun tins, cook them in two batches – the recipe can stretch to 18 buns.

2 Measure the flour and baking powder into a large bowl. Add the butter and rub in with your fingertips until the mixture resembles fine breadcrumbs. Stir in the sugar and sultanas.

3 Lightly mix the egg and milk together and add all at once to the dry mixture. Beat well to give a smooth mixture, then spoon into the paper cases.

4 To make the streusel topping, mix together the flour and sugar and add the melted butter. Use a fork to mix until crumbly. Sprinkle this mixture over the tops of the buns.

5 Bake in the pre-heated oven for about 15 minutes until well risen and firm to the touch. Lift the paper cake cases out of the bun tin and leave to cool on a wire rack. Add 6 more fairy cake cases to the tin if you are making 18 buns and bake. Dust the buns with icing sugar to serve.

CHAPTER SEVENTEEN

Hot Puddings and Pies

Hot desserts are exactly what are needed on a cold day – they're filling, comforting and easy to prepare. They suit leisurely weekend dining, and particularly complement a Sunday lunch. Some can even be put in the oven to happily cook with the roast, such as **Sticky Apricot Pudding** (page 345).

There are a number of well known recipes here, including a few of my family's favourites, like **Banoffi Pie** (page 349) and **Classic Apple Pie** (opposite) – I don't think there is anything better than a slice (hot or cold) of well-made apple pie served with custard or clotted cream.

These are reliable recipes that I have turned to on many occasions. Some are inherited, such as **My Mother's Bread and Butter Pudding** (page 342), while others I've picked up over the years and adapted from trips abroad, such as my version of **Pecan Pie** (page 350).

Experiment with different fruit combinations for the fruit puddings, using what's in season or what is best value – fresh or tinned are equally good. Use ready-made pastry made with butter if you feel you don't have time to make pastry from scratch, and good-quality ready-sliced bread to make the recipes even easier to prepare.

Classic Apple Pie

**One of my favourite desserts. I always decorate my sweet pies with
lots of pastry leaves, so that they look more inviting.**

675 g (1½ lb) cooking apples
50–75 g (2–3 oz) caster sugar
4 whole cloves
3 tablespoons cold water

FOR THE PASTRY
175 g (6 oz) plain flour
50 g (1½ oz) diced butter
50 g (1½ oz) diced white
   baking vegetable fat
about 2 tablespoons cold
   water
milk, to glaze
granulated sugar, for
   sprinkling

1 Use an 900 ml (1½ pint) shallow pie dish. Peel, core and cut
the apples into thick slices. Arrange half the slices in the bottom
of the dish, sprinkle with the caster sugar and arrange the cloves
evenly among the apples. Cover with the remaining apple slices
and add the cold water.

2 To make the pastry, measure the flour into a bowl. Add the diced
butter and white vegetable fat and rub in with your fingertips
until the mixture resembles fine breadcrumbs. Add the water and
mix to a firm dough.

3 Roll out the dough onto a lightly floured work surface to a size
that will cover the top of the pie dish. Lift the dough on to the dish
and trim the edges. If you like, cut the trimmings into decorative
shapes and lightly press on to the dough. Chill in the fridge for
30 minutes.

4 Pre-heat the oven to 200°C/Fan 180°C/Gas 6. Brush the pie
with a little milk, then sprinkle the top with sugar. Make a small
slit in the centre of the pie for the steam to escape. Bake in the
pre-heated oven for about 40–45 minutes, until the apples are
tender and the pastry is crisp and pale golden. Cover the pie
loosely with foil towards the end of the cooking time if the
pastry starts to brown before the apples are cooked.

TIP
You can freeze the pie after cooking and when completely cool.
Leave to defrost almost completely before reheating and serving.
Uncooked homemade pastry is an excellent standby for the
freezer. Pack it in separate quantities of 225 g (8 oz) and 450 g
(1 lb), labelling it clearly. Defrost in the fridge or kitchen until
pliable enough to roll and use.

My Mother's Bread and Butter Pudding

A great family favourite as a pudding to follow a weekend lunch. You can use semi-skimmed milk for a healthier pudding, or slices of brioche instead of sliced white bread to make it even richer! Use a rectangular dish as the bread will fit it better. This recipe serves 6–8.

100 g (4 oz) butter, melted

250 g (9 oz) currants and sultanas

75 g (3 oz) caster sugar

grated rind of 1 lemon

½ level teaspoon ground mixed spice

12 thin slices white bread, crusts removed

3 large eggs

600 ml (1 pint) full-fat milk

2 tablespoons demerara sugar, to sprinkle

1 Grease an 18 x 23 cm (7 x 9 in) deep ovenproof dish with a little of the melted butter. Measure the dried fruit, sugar, lemon rind and spice into a bowl and toss to mix well. Cut each bread slice into 3 strips.

2 Take enough breadstrips to cover the base of the dish and dip one side of each strip in melted butter. Lay them in the prepared dish, buttered side down. Sprinkle with half the dried fruit mixture. Repeat the layering, laying the bread strips buttered side up, and sprinkle with the remaining dried fruit mixture. Lay the third and final layer of bread strips on top, buttered side up.

3 Beat together the eggs and milk and pour over the pudding. Sprinkle with demerara sugar, then leave to stand for about 1 hour if time allows. Meanwhile, pre-heat the oven to 180°C/ Fan 160°C/Gas 4.

4 Bake in the pre-heated oven for about 40 minutes or until the top is golden brown and crisp and the pudding slightly puffed up. Serve hot, though there are some who insist that it is just as delicious cold!

TIP
You can prepare the pudding ahead of time and keep it covered in the fridge for up to 6 hours before baking. Don't sprinkle over the demerara sugar topping until 1 hour before you are ready to bake.

Baked Apple Lemon Sponge

Something like the old-fashioned Eve's pudding, but this one makes its own creamy, lemon sauce. If buying lemon curd, check that it contains butter, sugar and lemons. It may be labelled lemon cheese or luxury lemon curd. This recipes serves 6.

FOR THE BASE

300 ml (½ pint) single cream
6 tablespoons lemon curd
2 level tablespoons caster
  sugar
1 heaped teaspoon plain flour
750 g (1¾ lb) cooking apples

FOR THE TOPPING

2 large eggs
175 g (6 oz) self-raising flour
100 g (4 oz) caster sugar
100 g (4 oz) softened butter
1 level teaspoon baking
  powder
2 tablespoons milk
1–1½ tablespoons
  demerara sugar

1 Pre-heat the oven to 160°C/Fan 140°C/Gas 3. Put a heavy baking tray to heat in the oven. You will need a 27 x 18 cm (10½ x 7 in) deep ovenproof dish.

2 To prepare the base, measure the cream, lemon curd, sugar and flour into a bowl and beat until smooth. Peel, core and very thinly slice the apples. (I find it easiest to use a mandolin cutter or the thin slicing disc in the processor.) Mix the sliced apples into the cream mixture, spoon into the baking dish and level with the back of a spoon.

3 To make the topping, measure all the ingredients except the demerara sugar into a mixing bowl. Beat until smooth, then spread gently over the fruit in the baking dish. Sprinkle with demerara sugar.

4 Bake in the pre-heated oven on the hot baking tray for 30 minutes or until perfect golden brown.

5 Cover the pudding with foil then continue to bake for a further 45 minutes or until the sponge springs back when lightly pressed in the centre with a fingertip. Serve warm.

TIP
The unbaked pudding can be kept covered in the fridge for up to 6 hours. Bring up to room temperature before baking in the pre-heated oven on the hot baking tray.

Sticky Apricot Pudding

This is a very adaptable recipe and one of my family's favourites. You can use a variety of different fruits, either fresh or canned. It's a good dessert to serve for Sunday lunch. Just place the pudding on the top shelf, above the roast, and let it cook there. It couldn't be easier. This recipe serves 6–8.

175 g (6 oz) self-raising flour

1 level teaspoon baking powder

50 g (2 oz) caster sugar

50 g (2 oz) softened butter

1 large egg

grated rind of 1 lemon

150 ml (¼ pint) milk

410g cans apricot halves (or other canned fruit), drained

FOR THE TOPPING

50 g (2 oz) butter, melted

175 g (6 oz) demerara sugar

1 Preheat the oven to 230°C/Fan 210°C/Gas 8. Grease a 28 cm (11 in) shallow ovenproof baking dish.

2 Measure the flour, baking powder, sugar, butter, egg, lemon rind and milk in a large bowl. Beat together until the mixture forms a soft, cake-like consistency.

3 Spread the mixture into the prepared baking dish and arrange the apricots, cut side down, over the top. Brush or drizzle the melted butter for the topping over the apricots, then sprinkle with the demerara sugar.

4 Bake in the pre-heated oven for 35 minutes or until the top has caramelized to a deep golden brown. Serve warm, with crème fraîche, whipped cream, ice-cream or even hot custard on a cold winter day.

TIP

You can replace the apricots with whatever fruit you have to hand. Both sliced dessert and cooking apples work well. Arrange the apple slices evenly over the top of the sponge mixture. Other good alternatives are rhubarb and plums. Cut the plums in half and remove the stones, then arrange them cut side down.

Treacle Sponges

A great family favourite for a cold winter's day. This recipe makes 4 individual sponges.

8 tablespoons golden syrup
1 tablespoons lemon juice
grated rind of 1 lemon
100g (4oz) softened butter
100g (4oz) caster sugar
2 large eggs
100g (4oz) self-raising flour
1 level teaspoon baking
   powder
warm golden syrup, to serve

1 Grease four 175ml (6fl oz) pudding basins. Blend the syrup with the lemon juice and divide between the basins.

2 Measure all the remaining ingredients into a mixing bowl and beat well for 2 minutes or until well blended. Divide the mixture between the basins and smooth the tops. Cover each basin with a pleated lid of baking parchment and then foil, to allow for the expanding steam and pudding.

3 Steam in a steamer, or place in a large pan with enough boiling water to come halfway up each basin, for 45 minutes (see Tip). Turn out and serve with extra, warm golden syrup.

TIP
Keep the water boiling in the pan, topping up when needed with more boiling water. Stand the pudding basins on an old, upturned saucer to keep them off the pan bottom.

Crème Brûlée

This baked creamy 'custard' tastes like sheer luxury but is not difficult to make. Choose a shallow dish or individual dishes that will withstand being put under the grill, and be careful not to overcook the mixture, as this will cause it to form bubbles. Use the surplus egg whites to make a meringue dessert from the following chapter. This recipe serves 6–8.

4 large egg yolks

25 g (1 oz) caster sugar and a few drops of vanilla extract, or vanilla sugar (see Tip)

300 ml (½ pint) single cream and 300 ml (½ pint) double cream

about 50 g (2 oz) demerara sugar

TIP
Vanilla sugar adds a wonderful flavour. Simply store two or three vanilla pods in a jar of caster sugar. After about two weeks, the sugar is imbued with the pungency of the vanilla.

1 Pre-heat the oven to 160°C/Fan 140°C/Gas 3. Grease a 900 ml (1½ pint) shallow ovenproof dish or 6–8 small ramekins.

2 Beat the egg yolks with the caster sugar plus a few drops of vanilla extract, or the vanilla sugar. Heat the creams to scalding (just too hot to put your finger in!), leave to cool slightly, then beat into the egg yolks in a steady stream, beating all the time. Pour into the dish or ramekins.

3 Stand the dish in a roasting tin half-filled with hot water. Bake in the pre-heated oven for 45 minutes or until set for the single dish, 25–30 minutes for the ramekins. Remove from the oven and leave to cool. Cover then chill in the fridge overnight. These can be made 2 days ahead.

4 Pre-heat the grill to hot. Sprinkle the top of the custard with demerara sugar to about 5 mm (¼ in) thickness and place under the grill, on a high shelf, until the sugar melts then caramelizes to a golden brown. This takes 3–4 minutes. Keep a careful watch to make sure the sugar does not burn. Alternatively, use a cook's blowtorch to caramelize the sugar, if you have one.

5 Leave to cool, then chill for 2–3 hours before serving. Chilling again after caramelizing the sugar gives time for the hard topping to become slightly less hard, easier to crack and serve. If you leave it considerably longer, the caramel will melt and soften, which is not nearly so attractive and does not taste as good.

Banoffi Pie

The combination of toffee, bananas and cream makes this one of the most popular desserts around. Make sure you use a non-stick pan for the toffee and watch it very closely as you are making it, as it can burn easily.

FOR THE BASE
175 g (6 oz) ginger biscuits
65 g (2½ oz) butter

FOR THE TOFFEE FILLING
100 g (4 oz) butter
100 g (4 oz) light muscovado
  sugar
2 x 397 g (14 oz) cans
  condensed milk

FOR THE TOPPING
300 ml (½ pint) double cream
1 large banana
a little lemon juice
a little grated Belgian milk or
  plain chocolate, for
  sprinkling

1 To make the base, put the ginger biscuits into a polythene bag and crush them to crumbs with a rolling pin. Melt the butter in a small pan, remove from the heat and stir in the crushed biscuits. Mix well, then spread the mixture over the base and sides of a 23 cm (9 in) deep loose-bottomed fluted flan tin. Press the mixture with the back of a metal spoon.

2 To make the toffee filling, measure the butter and sugar into a large non-stick pan. Heat gently until the butter has melted and the sugar has dissolved, then add the condensed milk. Stir continuously and evenly with a flat-ended wooden spoon for about 5 minutes or until the mixture is thick and has turned a golden toffee colour – take care, as it burns easily. Turn it into the prepared crumb crust and leave to cool and set.

3 To make the topping, whip the double cream until it just holds its shape and spread it evenly over the cold toffee mixture. Peel and slice the banana and dip into a little lemon juice to prevent it discolouring. Pile the banana slices on to the middle of the cream and sprinkle the whole pie with grated chocolate. Remove the ring and transfer to a flat plate. Serve well chilled.

TIP
Most condensed milk cans now have ring pulls, so the old method of simmering the can in a pan of water for 4 hours to caramelize the condensed milk is not advised.

Pecan Pie

This is an all-American creation that is delicious served with coffee, or as a dessert served with cream or ice-cream.

FOR THE RICH SHORTCRUST PASTRY
175 g (6 oz) plain flour
15 g (½ oz) icing sugar
75 g (3 oz) diced butter
1 large egg yolk
about 1 tablespoon
    cold water

FOR THE FILLING
25 g (1 oz) softened butter
175 g (6 oz) light muscovado
    sugar
3 large eggs
200 ml (7 fl oz) maple syrup
1 teaspoon vanilla extract
150 g (5 oz) pecan halves

1 To make the pastry, measure the flour and icing sugar into a large bowl and rub in the butter with your fingertips until the mixture resembles fine breadcrumbs.

2 Add the egg yolk and water and mix until it comes together to form a firm dough. Wrap in cling film and leave to rest in the fridge for about 30 minutes. Pre-heat the oven to 200°C/Fan 180°C/Gas 6.

3 Roll out the dough on to a lightly floured work surface and use to line 23 cm (9 in) loose-bottomed fluted flan tin. Prick the pastry all over with a fork, line with baking parchment or foil and fill with baking beans. Bake blind in the pre-heated oven for about 15 minutes. Remove the baking beans and paper and return the pastry case to the oven for 5 minutes or until it is pale golden and dried out. Remove from the oven and reduce the temperature to 180°C/Fan 160°C/Gas 4.

4 To make the filling, beat the butter with the sugar. Add the eggs, maple syrup and vanilla extract and beat well.

5 Put the flan tin on a baking tray, arrange the pecan halves over the pastry flat side down, then pour in the filling. Bake in the pre-heated oven at the reduced temperature for 30–35 minutes until set. The filling will rise up in the oven but will fall back on cooling. Leave to cool, then serve warm with cream or ice-cream.

CHAPTER EIGHTEEN

Soufflés and Meringues

Soufflé and Meringue are both said to be eighteenth-century inventions. Soufflé, meaning 'puffed up', originates from France, while meringue is thought to have been invented by a Swiss pastry cook called Gasparani in a town called Mehrinyghen.

There are three methods to make meringue: meringue Suisse (Swiss meringue), meringue Cuite (cooked meringue) and meringue Italienne (Italian meringue). Meringue Suisse is the most common type used in homebaking and is made by incorporating caster sugar into stiffly whisked egg white. The proportion of sugar to egg white is always 50 g (2 oz) to 1 large egg white. Half the sugar is whisked in gradually and the rest is folded into the mixture. Meringue Cuite is made by whisking egg white and icing sugar over a pan of hot water to create a white, glossy mixture with a very smooth texture that is good for piping. Meringue Italienne (Italian Meringue) is made by whisking a hot sugar syrup into the egg white and requires the use of a sugar thermometer, so it is rarely used in homebaking.

Meringue can be slow-baked so that it becomes very crisp and dry or it can be baked quickly so that the outside is crisp but the inside is soft and marshmallowy, as with the topping of my **Lemon Meringue Pie** (page 361).

Soufflé can be baked, twice-baked, sweet or savoury and some, like my **Hot Lemon Souffle Pudding** (page 368), can be re-heated to serve. I have included only pudding soufflés here.

When making soufflé, grease the sides of the ramekins or soufflé dish well so the soufflé can rise easily. Don't open the oven while they are cooking as they will sink. Time them carefully and when cooked, get them to the table quickly. The **Hot Chocolate Soufflés** (page 366) do sink fairly rapidly so make sure your route to the table is clear of obstacles!

Basic White Meringues

Meringues are easily broken, so store them in a rigid airtight tin or plastic container, with kitchen paper in between them. Meringues should be creamy in colour, not ice-white, or they look as though they were bought in a shop. If you use golden caster sugar, expect darker meringues – they will taste just as good! This recipe makes 18 meringues.

3 large egg whites
175 g (6 oz) caster sugar

FOR THE FILLING
300 ml (½ pint) whipping or
    double cream, whipped
icing sugar, for dusting
    (optional)

1 Pre-heat the oven to 120°C/Fan 100°C/Gas ½. Line 2 baking trays with baking parchment.

2 Put the egg whites in a large bowl and whisk until stiff but not dry. Add the sugar, a teaspoonful at a time, whisking well after each addition until all the sugar has been added. The meringue should be stiff and glossy.

3 Fit a 1 cm (½ in) plain nozzle into a large nylon piping bag and stand, nozzle down, in a large measuring jug. Spoon the meringue into the bag. Squeeze the meringue mixture towards the nozzle and twist the top of the piping bag to seal. Pipe the meringue into 18 'shells' 5 cm (2 in) in diameter on the prepared baking trays. Alternatively, use 2 dessertspoons to shape the mixture into 18 mini meringues.

4 Bake in the pre-heated oven for 1–1½ hours or until they are a creamy colour and can be lifted easily from the baking parchment without sticking. Turn off the oven, leave the door ajar and leave the meringues until cold. Serve them sandwiched with whipped cream.

To make Brown Sugar Meringues, follow the recipe above but instead of 175 g (6 oz) caster sugar use half light muscovado sugar and half caster sugar.

Strawberry Pavlova

A top favourite with all ages. Traditionally the inside of the meringue is soft and marshmallow-like and the outside is crisp. Don't worry if the pavlova cracks on the top – this is all part of its charm.

4 large egg whites
225 g (8 oz) caster sugar
2 level teaspoons cornflour
2 teaspoons white wine
    vinegar

FOR THE FILLING
300 ml (½ pint) whipping or
    double cream, whipped
about 350 g (12 oz)
    strawberries, halved
    or sliced

1 Pre-heat the oven to 160°C/Fan 140°C/Gas 3. Lay a sheet of baking parchment on a baking tray and mark a 23 cm (9 in) circle on it.

2 Put the egg whites into a large bowl and whisk until stiff and cloud-like. Add the sugar a teaspoonful at a time, whisking well after each addition until all the sugar has been added. Blend the cornflour and vinegar together and whisk into the meringue mixture.

3 Spread the meringue out to cover the circle on the baking parchment, building up the sides so they are higher than the middle. Place in the pre-heated oven but immediately reduce the temperature to 150°C/Fan 130°C/Gas 2.

4 Bake for about 1 hour until firm to the touch and a pale beige colour. Turn the oven off and allow the pavlova to become quite cold while still in the oven. If you keep the oven door closed you will encourage a more marshmallowy meringue.

5 Remove the cold pavlova from the baking tray and parchment and slide on to a serving plate. Top with the whipped cream and strawberries, then chill in the fridge for 1 hour before serving.

Strawberry Meringue Nests

Ordinary meringue could be used for these nests, but they won't be quite so firm, nor will they store so well. Meringue Cuite is traditional because it holds its shape so well and is drier. Vary the fruit in these nests depending on the season. This recipe makes 6 nests.

FOR THE MERINGUE CUITE
4 large egg whites
240 g (8½ oz) icing sugar
a few drops of vanilla extract
(optional)

FOR THE FILLING
225 g (8 oz) strawberries
about 2 tablespoons
redcurrant jelly

1 Pre-heat the oven to 140°C/Fan 120°C/Gas 1. Line a baking tray with baking parchment.

2 Put the egg whites into a large bowl and whisk until foaming. Sift the icing sugar through a fine sieve into the egg whites. Set the bowl over a pan of gently simmering water and whisk the whites and sugar together until very thick and holding its shape. Add the vanilla extract, if using, and whisk again to mix. Be careful not to let the bowl get too hot or the meringue mixture will crust around the edges.

3 Spoon the mixture into a piping bag fitted with a large star nozzle. Pipe into 6 basket shapes on to the prepared baking tray, starting at the centre and lastly building up the sides.

4 Bake in the pre-heated oven for about 45 minutes until crisp and dry. Carefully lift off the baking tray and allow to cool on a wire rack.

5 Halve the strawberries, if large, and use to fill the cold 'nests'. Warm the redcurrant jelly in a small pan and gently spoon over the strawberries to glaze.

TIP
To fill a piping bag, stand the bag and nozzle point down in a jug and then fold the top edges of the bag over the top of the jug. That way it is much easier to spoon the meringue (or cream or icing) into the bag without getting it all over yourself!

To make Baby Meringues, follow the ingredients and recipe for Meringue Nests then pipe the mixture into 30 tiny shapes such as baskets, shells, spiral oblongs and fingers. Bake in the pre-heated oven until crisp and dry and then carefully lift off the baking trays on to a wire rack to cool.

To make the fillings, whip 300 ml (½ pint) double cream with 1 tablespoon brandy or liqueur of your choice until it holds its shape. Divide between 2 bowls. Stir 25 g (1 oz) chopped nuts into one bowl, and leave the other cream plain. Sandwich the spiral oblongs and tiny shells together with the nutty cream mixture, pipe a little plain cream into the baskets and use it to sandwich the fingers together. Top the baskets and the sandwiched fingers with a small single piece of fruit, if you like. These are perfect for a party, the different shapes and fillings make a wonderful centrepiece for the dessert table.

Raspberry Meringue Roulade

This is rather an unusual idea, and it makes a generous roulade, an excellent size for a party. It also freezes extremely well. Simply wrap in foil to freeze, then allow about 8 hours to thaw before serving. This recipe serves 8–10.

5 large egg whites
275 g (10 oz) caster sugar
50 g (2 oz) flaked almonds

FOR THE FILLING
300 ml (½ pint) whipping
   or double cream
350 g (12 oz) fresh
   raspberries

1 Pre-heat the oven to 220°C/Fan 200°C/Gas 7. Line a 33 x 23 cm (13 x 9 in) swiss roll tin with baking parchment.

2 Whisk the egg whites until very stiff. Gradually add the sugar, a teaspoonful at a time, whisking well between each addition. Whisk until very, very stiff and all the sugar has been added.

3 Spread the meringue mixture into the prepared tin and sprinkle with the almonds. Place the tin fairly near the top of the pre-heated oven and bake for about 8 minutes until pale golden. Then reduce the oven temperature to 160°C/Fan 140°C/Gas 3 and bake the roulade for a further 15 minutes until firm to the touch.

4 Remove the meringue from the oven and turn it almond side down on to a sheet of baking parchment. Remove the parchment from the base of the cooked meringue and allow to cool for about 10 minutes.

5 While the meringue is cooling, whisk the cream until it stands in stiff peaks, and gently mix in the raspberries. Spread the cream and raspberries evenly over the meringue. Start to roll from the long end fairly tightly until rolled up like a roulade. Wrap in baking parchment and chill before serving.

TIP
Leftover egg yolks should be stored in the fridge in a small container. Pour a tablespoon of cold water over the top, and then cover with clingfilm. Use within a week.

Lemon Meringue Pie

This recipe uses an easy, quick crumb crust rather than the usual pastry base, and the filling does not have to be cooked before pouring into the pie. You have only to stir a few ingredients together and it is ready. Although the filling is made with condensed milk, it is not sickly sweet, but has a fresh, lemony flavour that balances well with the meringue topping.

FOR THE BASE
175 g (6 oz) digestive
    biscuits
75 g (3 oz) butter

FOR THE FILLING
397 g (14 oz) can
    condensed milk
3 large egg yolks
finely grated rind and
    juice of 3 lemons

FOR THE TOPPING
3 large egg whites
175 g (6 oz) caster sugar

1 Pre-heat the oven to 190°C/Fan 170°C/Gas 5. You will need a 20 cm (8 in) deep fluted flan dish.

2 Put the biscuits into a plastic bag and crush with a rolling pin. Melt the butter in a medium-sized pan. Remove the pan from the heat and stir in the biscuit crumbs. Press into the flan dish and leave to set.

3 Pour the condensed milk into a bowl, then beat in the egg yolks, lemon rind and strained lemon juice. The mixture will seem to thicken on standing, then loosen again as soon as it is stirred. This is caused by the combination of condensed milk and lemon juice and is nothing to worry about. Pour the mixture into the biscuit-lined dish.

4 Whisk the egg whites until stiff but not dry. Gradually add the sugar, a teaspoon at a time, whisking well between each addition. Whisk until very stiff and all the sugar has been added.

5 Pile separate spoonfuls of meringue over the surface of the filling, then spread gently to cover the filling to the biscuit edge, lightly swirling the meringue.

6 Bake in the pre-heated oven for 15–20 minutes or until the meringue is light brown. Leave to cool for about 30 minutes before serving warm.

TIP
The flan dish can be lined with the biscuit crumb mix, covered and kept in the fridge for up to 3 days. The filling can be mixed, covered and kept in the fridge for up to 8 hours before baking. Once baked, the pie can be eaten warm or cold, but the meringue shrinks a little on standing.

Hazelnut Meringue Cake

This has become a classic favourite, the raspberries and hazelnuts being a particularly good combination. Fill the meringue about 3 hours before serving; it will then cut into portions without splintering. This recipe serves 6.

140 g (4½ oz) shelled
    hazelnuts
4 large egg whites
250 g (9 oz) caster sugar
a few drops of vanilla extract
½ teaspoon white wine
    vinegar

FOR THE FILLING
300 ml (½ pint) whipping or
    double cream, whipped
225 g (8 oz) raspberries
icing sugar, for dusting

1 Pre-heat the oven to 190°C/Fan 170°C/Gas 5. Lightly brush two 20 cm (8 in) sandwich tins with oil then line the base of each tin with baking parchment.

2 Place the hazelnuts on a baking tray and put in the oven for about 10 minutes, then tip on to a clean tea towel and rub well together to remove the skins. (Some stubborn ones may need to go back into the oven but don't worry about getting every last bit of skin off, it's not necessary.) Grind the nuts in a food processor.

3 Whisk the egg whites until stiff. Add the sugar, a teaspoonful at a time, whisking well between each addition. Whisk until the mixture is very stiff, stands in peaks, and all the sugar has been added. Whisk in the vanilla extract and wine vinegar then fold in the prepared nuts. Divide the mixture between the prepared tins and smooth the top with a palette knife.

4 Bake in the pre-heated oven for 30–40 minutes, but no longer. The top of the meringue will be crisp and the inside soft and marshmallow-like. Turn out of the tins and leave to cool on a wire rack.

5 Whisk the cream until thick and use about two-thirds to sandwich the meringues together along with two-thirds of the raspberries. Spread the remaining cream over the top, scatter on the remaining raspberries and dust with icing sugar. Serve with Raspberry Coulis (see page 391).

TIPS
If you don't have sandwich tins, you can cook the mixture on 2 flat baking trays, spread out into 2 circles. It won't look quite so neat, but it tastes the same! Walnuts can be used in place of the hazelnuts in the meringue. Choose a fruit to complement the walnuts, such as strawberries or ripe peaches in season.

Apricot and Almond Meringue Gâteau

A lovely, delicately flavoured meringue, this is perfect for a very special dinner party. In season, you could use fresh apricots (stone about 350 g/12 oz then cook and purée). Save a few quartered apricots as decoration. This recipe serves 6.

4 large egg whites
225 g (8 oz) caster sugar
75 g (3 oz) ground almonds

**FOR THE FILLING
AND SAUCE**
100 g (4 oz) ready-to-eat
    dried apricots
a strip of lemon rind
300 ml (½ pint) water
100 g (4 oz) granulated sugar
juice of ½ lemon
300 ml (½ pint) double cream

TO FINISH
icing sugar, for dusting
about 150 ml (¼ pint)
    whipping or double cream,
    whipped (optional)

1 Pre-heat the oven to 140°C/Fan 120°C/Gas 1. Line 2 baking trays with baking parchment.

2 Whisk the egg whites until stiff. Add the sugar, a teaspoonful at a time, whisking well between each addition. Whisk until the mixture is very stiff, stands in peaks, and all the sugar has been added. Fold in the ground almonds. Divide the mixture between the prepared baking trays and spread gently into 2 rounds 20 cm (8 in) in diameter.

3 Bake in the pre-heated oven for 1–1¼ hours or until the parchment peels away from the base of the meringue (this meringue mixture is quite sticky so don't worry if it sticks a little in the middle). Leave the meringues to cool on a wire rack.

4 To make the filling, put the apricots in a small pan with the strip of lemon rind and half the water. Heat gently for about 20 minutes until the apricots are very tender. Transfer the apricots to a food processor or blender and process until smooth. In a small pan, heat the granulated sugar in the remaining water, until the sugar has dissolved, then add the lemon juice and boil for 3 minutes to make a sugar syrup.

5 Whip the cream until it holds its shape, and flavour with about one-third of the apricot purée. Use to sandwich the meringues together. Dust the top with icing sugar and decorate with rosettes of whipped cream, if you like. Dilute the remaining apricot purée with the sugar syrup and serve as a sauce.

Coffee and Banana Vacherin

Use half caster sugar and half light muscovado sugar if you prefer a less caramel-flavoured meringue. This recipe serves 6.

4 large egg whites
225 g (8 oz) light muscovado
    sugar

FOR THE FILLING
300 ml (½ pint) double cream
1 level teaspoon instant coffee
    granules, dissolved in a
    little water
2 ripe bananas

TO FINISH
icing sugar, for dusting
150 ml (¼ pint) whipping or
    double cream, whipped

1 Pre-heat the oven to 140°C/Fan 120°C/Gas 1. Line 2 baking trays with baking parchment and mark each with a 20 cm (8 in) circle.

2 Whisk the egg whites until stiff. Add the sugar, a teaspoonful at a time, whisking well between each addition, until the mixture is very stiff, stands in peaks, and all the sugar has been added.

3 Spoon the meringue mixture into a large piping bag fitted with a 1 cm (½ in) plain nozzle, and pipe the meringue out to fill the circles on the baking parchment; pipe in circles in a spiral pattern, starting at the centre.

4 Bake in the pre-heated oven for 1–1¼ hours or until the meringues are crisp and dry and lightly coloured. Allow to cool in the oven and then peel off the parchment.

5 To make the filling, whip the cream until it holds its shape, and flavour with the dissolved coffee granules. Slice the bananas thinly and fold into the cream, making sure they are well coated to prevent discoloration. Spread over one meringue circle, and then place the other circle on top. Dust lightly with sifted icing sugar and decorate with rosettes of whipped cream.

TIP
You can make the meringue circles the day before, but don't keep the filled cake for too long as the bananas will eventually turn brown.

Hot Chocolate Soufflés

Soufflés like this are not difficult to make, but need a bit of care with the timing. This recipe serves 4.

115 g (4 oz) plain chocolate
   (39 per cent cocoa solids)
2 tablespoons water
300 ml (½ pint) milk
40 g (1½ oz) butter
40 g (1½ oz) plain flour
¼ teaspoon vanilla extract
4 large eggs, separated
50 g (2 oz) caster sugar
sifted icing sugar, for dusting
whipped cream, to serve

1 Pre-heat the oven to 190°C/Fan 170°C/Gas 5 and place a baking sheet in it. Grease four 225 ml (8 fl oz) individual soufflé dishes or a 1.2 litre (2 pint) soufflé dish.

2 Break the chocolate into pieces and put in a pan along with the water and 2 tablespoons of the milk. Stir over a low heat until the chocolate has melted, then add the remaining milk and bring to the boil. Remove the pan from the heat.

3 Melt the butter in a small pan, stir in the flour and cook on a low heat for 2 minutes without browning, stirring continuously. Remove from the heat and stir in the hot chocolate milk, return to the heat and bring to the boil, stirring until thickened. Add the vanilla extract and leave to cool.

4 Beat the egg yolks, one at a time, into the cooled chocolate sauce, then sprinkle over the sugar. Whisk the egg whites until they are stiff but not dry. Stir one tablespoon into the mixture, then carefully fold in the remainder.

5 Pour into the individual soufflé dishes or large soufflé dish, run a teaspoon round the edge and bake on the hot baking tray in the preheated oven for 10 minutes for the individual soufflés or about 40 minutes for the large soufflé. Dust with icing sugar and serve at once, with whipped cream.

To make Orange Soufflés, omit the chocolate and the 2 tablespoons of water in step 2, and add the finely grated rind of 2 small oranges and the juice of half an orange to the mixture. Also omit the vanilla extract and increase the caster sugar to 75 g (3 oz).

To make Coffee Soufflés, omit the chocolate and the 2 tablespoons of water in step 2, add 2 tablespoons coffee essence to the milk and omit the vanilla extract.

TIP
If you are serving a soufflé for a supper party, make the sauce base ahead of time, including the addition of the yolks and flavouring then 40 minutes before baking and serving fold in the whisked egg whites, turn into the dish and bake.

Hot Lemon Soufflé Pudding

This is one of my favourite lemon puddings. I have even baked it ahead of time and reheated it very satisfactorily, in a roasting tin of water for 30 minutes in a moderate oven. The top of the pudding is a spongy mousse while underneath is a sharp lemon sauce. This soufflé pudding serves 4–6.

75 g (3 oz) softened butter
250 g (9 oz) caster sugar
3 large eggs, separated
75 g (3 oz) self-raising flour
grated rind and juice of
   2 lemons
450 ml (14 fl oz) milk

1 Pre-heat the oven to 190°C/Fan 170°C/Gas 5. Grease a shallow 1.5 litre (2½ pint) ovenproof dish.

2 Measure the butter and caster sugar in a bowl and beat until smooth. Beat in the egg yolks, then beat in the flour, lemon rind, juice and milk. Do not worry if the mixture looks curdled at this stage – this is quite normal.

3 Whisk the egg whites until they form soft peaks then carefully fold them into the lemon mixture using a large metal spoon.

4 Pour the mixture into the prepared ovenproof dish and place in a traybake or roasting tin. Pour in enough boiling water to come halfway up the dish and bake in the pre-heated oven for 1 hour or until pale golden brown on top.

TIP
Buy thin-skinned lemons that feel heavy for their size. To get maximum juice from them, it helps if the fruit is warm, or at least at room temperature.

Before grating the rind, wash and dry the fruit well. Grate the rind on the small-holed side of the grater, and remember to scrape everything off the back of the grater after grating. A pastry brush is a useful tool to do this.

Baked Alaska

This is impressive to serve but surprisingly easy to make. It makes a good alternative birthday cake, decorated with sparklers.

FOR THE SPONGE BASE
2 large eggs
75 g (3 oz) caster sugar
50 g (2 oz) self-raising flour

FOR THE FILLING
1 tablespoon sherry (optional)
225 g (8 oz) strawberries
1 litre (1¾ pints) strawberry
   ice-cream

FOR THE MERINGUE TOPPING
4 large egg whites
225 g (8 oz) caster sugar
50 g (2 oz) flaked almonds, for
   sprinkling
icing sugar, for dusting

1 Pre-heat the oven to 190°C/Fan 170°C/Gas 5. Lightly grease a 23 cm (9 in) sandwich tin and line the base with baking parchment.

2 To make the sponge, measure the eggs and sugar into a large bowl and beat at full speed with an electric whisk until the mixture is pale in colour and thick enough to just leave a trail when the whisk is lifted. Sift the flour over the surface of the mixture and gently fold in with a metal spoon or spatula. Turn into the prepared tin and tilt the tin to allow the mixture to spread evenly to the sides.

3 Bake in the pre-heated oven for about 20–25 minutes, until springy to the touch and beginning to shrink from the sides of the tin. Turn out and leave to cool on a wire rack.

4 Place the cold sponge on an ovenproof serving dish, sprinkle it with the sherry, if using, then scatter with the strawberries, leaving a small gap around the edge. Slice the ice cream and arrange it in a dome shape over the strawberries. Put into the freezer while you are making the meringue.

5 Pre-heat the oven to 230°C/Fan 210°C/Gas 8. To make the meringue topping, whisk the egg whites at full speed until they are stiff but not dry. Add the sugar, a teaspoonful at a time, whisking at high speed, between each addition. Whisk until all the sugar has been added and the meringue is thick and glossy.

6 Take the cake and ice-cream from the freezer and pile the meringue over the top and sides, making sure that all the ice-cream and sponge have been covered. Sprinkle over the flaked almonds then bake immediately in the pre-heated oven for about 3–4 minutes or until well browned. Dust with icing sugar and serve immediately.

CHAPTER NINETEEN

Cheesecakes

There are two methods of making cheesecake – baking and setting with gelatine. Although this chapter focuses on baked cheesecakes, I have also included some of my favourite gelatine-set cheesecakes for you to try.

Baked cheesecakes originate from Russia and Eastern Europe and have been eaten for well over a century. They traditionally consisted of local soft cheese, some sugar and eggs, baked in a pastry case. I suppose at one time, it was a delicious way of using up eggs and a little bit of cheese.

Gelatine-set cheesecakes are a more recent American creation. They are usually lighter in texture than the European cooked varieties, set with either powdered gelatine or gelatine leaf with a base of pastry, crushed biscuits or sponge. I find powdered gelatine easier to use than leaf gelatine. Don't be tempted to use leaf gelatine if a recipe calls for powdered gelatine, as they are very different quantities and require different treatment.

The gelatine has to be added to the liquid and not the other way around. Sprinkle it over the liquid in a cup or a small bowl, swirl to mix, and then leave it to 'sponge'. The sponged gelatine must then be heated very gently by placing the cup or bowl in a pan of gently simmering water until the gelatine becomes clear (do not allow to boil). Cool the dissolved gelatin before mixing in. If it is too hot, it can form lumps and threads and ruin the texture of your cheesecake.

Make both baked and chilled cheesecakes in a springform tin, as it will be easier to turn out. A loose-bottomed cake tin would work almost as well.

American Chocolate Ripple Cheesecake

This cheesecake easily serves 8–10, as it is quite sweet and rich and so should be served in small portions. Expect the cheesecake to crack on cooling. This recipe serves 8–10.

FOR THE BASE
100 g (4 oz) plain chocolate
    digestive biscuits
50 g (2 oz) butter

FOR THE CHEESECAKE
150 g (5 oz) plain chocolate
    (39 per cent cocoa solids)
700 g (1½ lb) full-fat soft
    cheese
100 g (4 oz) caster sugar
½ teaspoon vanilla extract
1 large eggs

1 Pre-heat the oven to 160°C/Fan 140°C/Gas 3. Lightly grease a 20 cm (8 in) loose-bottomed cake tin or springform tin.

2 Put the biscuits into a plastic bag and crush with a rolling pin. Melt the butter in a medium-sized pan. Remove the pan from the heat and stir in the biscuit crumbs. Press into the prepared tin and leave to set.

3 To make the cheesecake filling, break the chocolate into pieces and melt gently in a bowl set over a pan of hot water, stirring occasionally. Cool slightly. Measure the cheese into a large bowl and beat until soft. Add the sugar and beat again until well mixed. Beat in the vanilla extract and then the eggs, one at a time.

4 Spoon half the cheese mixture on to the biscuit crust, separating the spoonfuls. Add the melted chocolate to the remaining cheese mixture and stir well to mix. Spoon this chocolate mixture in between the plain mixture. Swirl the top with a knife to give a marbled effect.

5 Bake in the pre-heated oven for about 1 hour or until the cheesecake becomes puffy around the edges but is still very soft in the centre. Turn off the oven but leave the cheesecake in the oven to cool. Chill well and then loosen the cheesecake from the sides of the tin using a small palette knife. Serve well chilled.

Chocolate, Brandy and Ginger Cheesecake

A sophisticated cheesecake that serves 8. If you like, you can add a little more brandy to the cheesecake filling. If ginger is a favourite flavour, the quantity used can be increased as well. This recipe serves 8.

FOR THE BASE
100 g (4 oz) ginger biscuits
50 g (2 oz) butter
25 g (1 oz) demerara sugar

FOR THE CHEESECAKE
100 g (4 oz) plain chocolate
    (39 per cent cocoa solids)
15 g (½ oz) sachet powdered
    gelatine
3 tablespoons cold water
2 large eggs, separated
50 g (2 oz) caster sugar
100 g (4 oz) full-fat soft cheese
150 ml (¼ pint) soured cream
4 tablespoons brandy
about 25 g (1 oz) fresh
    ginger, finely chopped

TO DECORATE
150 ml (¼ pint) whipping
    or double cream, whipped
    (optional)
chocolate caraque or curls
    (see page 392)
a few slices of stem ginger

1 Lightly grease a 20 cm (8 in) loose-bottomed cake tin or springform tin.

2 Put the biscuits into a plastic bag and crush with a rolling pin. Melt the butter in a medium-sized pan. Remove the pan from the heat and stir in the biscuit crumbs and sugar. Press into the prepared tin and leave to set.

3 Melt the chocolate gently in a bowl set over a pan of hot water, stirring occasionally. Allow to cool slightly.

4 Sprinkle the gelatine over the measured water in a small bowl and leave for 10 minutes to 'sponge'. Stand the bowl in a pan of gently simmering water until the gelatine has completely dissolved. Leave to cool slightly.

5 Beat together the egg yolks, sugar and cheese in a large bowl. Add the soured cream and cooled chocolate. Stir in the dissolved gelatine. Whisk the egg whites until frothy and fold into the cheese mixture along with the brandy and chopped stem ginger. Pour on to the biscuit base and chill in the fridge to set.

6 When set, carefully remove the cheesecake from the tin before decorating with whipped cream if you like, chocolate caraque or curls, and slices of stem ginger.

Angel Sponge Cheesecake

This is a good cheesecake for a party, as the sponge can be made in advance and frozen. Keep the cheesecake chilled once made, as it contains no gelatine and will soon soften in a warm room. This recipe serves 8.

FOR THE SPONGE
2 large eggs
75 g (3 oz) caster sugar
50 g (2 oz) self-raising flour

FOR THE CHEESECAKE
100 g (4 oz) softened unsalted
     butter
150 g (5 oz) caster sugar
3 large eggs, separated
finely grated rind and juice
     of 2 oranges
200 g (7 oz) low- or medium-
     fat soft cheese
300 ml (½ pint) whipping
     or double cream

FOR DECORATION
icing sugar, for dusting
orange wedges
mint leaves

1 Pre-heat the oven to 180°C/Fan 160°C/Gas 4. Lightly grease a 23 cm (9 in) loose-bottomed cake tin or springform tin and line the base with baking parchment.

2 Measure the eggs and sugar into a large bowl and beat until the mixture is thick and light in colour and the whisk leaves a trail when lifted out of the mixture. Sift the flour on to the beaten mixture and fold in lightly using a large metal spoon or spatula.

3 Turn the mixture into the prepared tin and tilt the tin to allow the mixture to spread evenly to the sides (don't worry that there appears to be little mixture for the size of the tin).

4 Bake in the pre-heated oven for 20–25 minutes or until the cake springs back when lightly pressed with your finger and has shrunk slightly from the sides of the tin. Leave to cool in the tin for a few minutes then turn out, peel off the parchment and finish cooling. Turn out and leave to cool on a wire rack.

5 Wash and dry the cake tin and then line the base and sides with baking parchment. When the cake is completely cold, cut in half horizontally using a serrated knife. Place one layer into the prepared cake tin, cut side up.

6 To make the cheesecake filling, measure the butter into a large bowl and beat it well until thoroughly softened. Add the sugar and beat until light and fluffy. Next add the egg yolks, finely grated orange rind, the strained orange juice and the cheese, and beat well until smooth and thoroughly mixed. Whip the cream until it just holds its shape and fold into the cheese mixture. In a separate bowl, whisk the egg whites until stiff but not dry and fold them into the mixture.

7 Spoon the cheesecake mixture into the tin on top of the sponge and level the surface. Gently place the remaining sponge on top, cut side down, cover with clingfilm and chill in the fridge for about 4 hours or until the cheesecake mixture is firm.

8 To serve, carefully remove the sides of the tin and then gently peel away the paper. Using a palette knife or fish slice, ease the cake on to a serving plate. Dust the top with sifted icing sugar and mark into sections with the back of a knife. Decorate with orange wedges and mint leaves.

Continental Cheesecake

A traditional cooked cheesecake. This recipe makes a good large cake, excellent for a party. Use frozen mixed summer fruits if fresh are unavailable. You don't have to use all the fruits suggested for the topping – choose your own combinations. The centre of the cooked cheesecake dips a little on cooling – perfect to hold the fruit! This recipe serves 12.

FOR THE BASE
100 g (4 oz) digestive biscuits
50 g (2 oz) butter
40 g (1½ oz) demerara sugar

FOR THE CHEESECAKE
65 g (2½ oz) softened butter
225 g (8 oz) caster sugar
550 g (1¼ lb) curd cheese
    or ricotta
40 g (1½ oz) plain flour
finely grated rind and juice
    of 2 lemons
4 large eggs, separated
200 ml (7 fl oz) whipping
    or double cream, lightly
    whipped

FOR THE TOPPING
450 g (1 lb) mixed summer
    fruits (strawberries,
    raspberries, redcurrants,
    blackcurrants and
    blackberries)
caster sugar, to taste
1 level teaspoon arrowroot
150 ml (¼ pint) whipping or
    double cream, whipped

1 Pre-heat the oven to 160°C/Fan 140°C/Gas 3. Lightly grease a 25 cm (10 in) loose-bottomed cake tin or springform tin and line the base with baking parchment.

2 Put the biscuits into a plastic bag and crush with a rolling pin. Melt the butter in a medium-sized pan. Remove the pan from the heat and stir in the biscuit crumbs and sugar. Press into the prepared tin and leave to set.

3 To make the cheesecake filling, measure the butter, sugar, curd cheese or ricotta, flour, lemon rind and juice, and egg yolks into a large bowl. Beat until smooth. Fold in the lightly whipped cream. Whisk the egg whites stiffly then fold into the mixture. Pour on to the biscuit crust.

4 Bake in the pre-heated oven for about 1½ hours or until set. Turn off the oven and leave the cheesecake in the oven for a further 1 hour to cool. Run a knife around the edge of the tin to loosen the cheesecake and push the base up through the cake tin. Remove the side paper.

5 To make the topping, cook the redcurrants, blackcurrants and blackberries (if using) in 2 tablespoons of water in a pan and sweeten to taste. When the fruit has softened and released its juices, remove from the heat.

6 Blend the arrowroot with 2 tablespoons of cold water and add the cooked fruit and liquid from the pan. Return the mixture to the pan, allow to thicken then leave to cool. Stir the raspberries and strawberries (if using) into the other fruits then pile on top of the cheesecake, levelling out evenly. Decorate the edge of the cheesecake with piped or spooned whipped cream.

American Cheesecake

This is a very quick and easy cheesecake to make. It's delicious to eat, too, as the yoghurt gives the filling a wonderfully fresh flavour. This recipe serves 6–8.

FOR THE BASE
175 g (6 oz) digestive biscuits
75 g (3 oz) butter
40 g (1½ oz) demerara sugar

FOR THE CHEESECAKE
225 g (8 oz) full-fat soft cheese
25 g (1 oz) caster sugar
150 ml (¼ pint) double cream
150 ml (¼ pint) Greek yoghurt
juice of 1½ lemons

FOR THE TOPPING
175 g (6 oz) raspberries or
    other soft fruits
about 4 tablespoons
    redcurrant jelly

1 Put the biscuits into a plastic bag and crush with a rolling pin. Melt the butter in a medium-sized pan. Remove the pan from the heat and stir in the biscuit crumbs and sugar. Press over the base and sides of a 20 cm (8 in) loose-bottomed cake tin or a springform tin, then leave to set.

2 Measure the cheese and sugar into a large bowl (or food processor) and mix well to blend thoroughly. Add the cream and yoghurt and mix again. Gradually add the lemon juice, whisking all the time. Turn the mixture into the tin on top of the biscuit crust and chill in the fridge overnight to set.

3 Run a knife round the edge of the biscuit crust to loosen the cheesecake, then push up the base or remove the sides of the tin and slide the cheesecake on to a serving plate.

4 Arrange the fruit on top of the cheesecake. Heat the redcurrant jelly in a small saucepan until it has melted, and then carefully brush over the fruit. Leave to set. Serve chilled.

Austrian Curd Cheesecake

This makes a good deep cheesecake. It is very moist, so there is no need for cream. This recipe serves 10.

150 g (5 oz) softened butter
275 g (10 oz) caster sugar
550 g (1¼ lb) curd cheese
   or ricotta
4 large eggs, separated
100 g (4 oz) ground almonds
100 g (4 oz) sultanas
50 g (2 oz) semolina
grated rind and juice of
   2 lemons
icing sugar, to dust

1 Pre-heat the oven to 190°C/Fan 170°C/Gas 5. Lightly grease a 23 cm (9 in) loose-bottomed cake tin or springform tin and line the base with baking parchment.

2 Soften the butter well in a large bowl and then add the sugar and curd cheese or ricotta. Beat well together until light and creamy. Beat the egg yolks into the mixture one at a time, then stir in the ground almonds, sultanas, semolina and the grated lemon rind and juice.

3 Leave the mixture to stand for about 10 minutes. (This allows the mixture to thicken so that the sultanas don't sink to the bottom of the cake when baking.)

4 In a separate bowl, whisk the egg whites until stiff but not dry and fold lightly into the mixture. Turn the mixture into the prepared tin.

5 Bake in the pre-heated oven for about 1 hour or until firm to the touch. Cover the top of the cheesecake loosely with foil about halfway through the cooking time to prevent the top from becoming too brown.

6 When cooked, turn off the oven but leave the cheesecake inside to cool for about 1 hour. Allow to cool completely, then loosen the sides of the cake with a palette knife and remove the tin. Invert the cheesecake, remove the base of the tin and the parchment and turn back the right way up to serve. Dust with sifted icing sugar before serving.

Buttermilk and Honey Cheesecake

This is a lovely, subtly flavoured cooked cheesecake. You'll find buttermilk with the yoghurts and creams in supermarkets. This recipe serves 8.

FOR THE BASE

1 sponge flan case, about
   20 cm (8 in) in diameter

FOR THE CHEESECAKE

225 g (8 oz) full-fat soft cheese
3 large eggs, separated
75 g (3 oz) caster sugar
2 rounded tablespoons clear
   honey
50 g (2 oz) ground almonds
40 g (1½ oz) plain flour
300 ml (½ pint) buttermilk
a handful of flaked almonds
about 1 tablespoon clear
   honey, to glaze

1 Pre-heat the oven to 160°C/Fan 140°C/Gas 3. Lightly grease a 20 cm (8 in) loose-bottomed cake tin or springform tin. Slip the sponge flan case into the prepared tin, trimming the cake to fit if necessary.

2 Measure the cheese into a large bowl and beat until soft. Beat in the egg yolks along with 25 g (1 oz) of the sugar, the honey, ground almonds, flour and buttermilk. In a separate bowl, whisk the egg whites until stiff, then whisk in the remaining caster sugar. Fold into the cheese mixture. Spoon the mixture on top of the sponge flan case and sprinkle the flaked almonds over the surface.

3 Bake in the pre-heated oven for about 1¼ hours or until firm but still spongy to the touch. Turn off the oven, open the door and leave the cheesecake to cool inside.

4 When cool, take the cheesecake out of the oven, ease it away from the sides of the tin with a small palette knife and slide on to a serving plate. Gently heat the honey in a small pan and brush over the top of the cheesecake to glaze.

Easy Lemon Cheesecake

An excellent, quick cheesecake that's always popular with my family. This recipe serves 8.

FOR THE BASE
10 digestive biscuits
50 g (2 oz) butter
25 g (1 oz) demerara sugar

FOR THE CHEESECAKE
150 ml (¼ pint) single cream
397 g (14 oz) can condensed
    milk
175 g (6 oz) low-fat soft cheese
grated rind and juice of
    3 large lemons

FOR THE TOPPING
150 ml (¼ pint) whipping or
    double cream, whipped
fresh strawberries

1 Put the biscuits into a plastic bag and crush with a rolling pin. Melt the butter in a medium-sized pan. Remove the pan from the heat and stir in the biscuit crumbs and sugar. Press evenly over the base and sides of a 23 cm (9 in) flan dish then leave to set.

2 To make the cheesecake filling, mix together the cream, condensed milk, soft cheese and lemon rind, then add the lemon juice a little at a time, whisking until the mixture thickens.

3 Pour the mixture into the flan case and leave to chill in the fridge for 3–4 hours or overnight. Decorate with swirls of whipped cream and fresh strawberries.

Apricot and Orange Cheesecake

Powdered gelatine is easy to use, provided you soak it in cold water to form a sponge first. This recipe serves 10.

FOR THE BASE
100 g (4 oz) digestive or
   oat biscuits
50 g (2 oz) butter
25 g (1 oz) demerara sugar

FOR THE CHEESECAKE
15 g (½ oz) packet powdered
   gelatine
4 tablespoons water
175 g (6 oz) ready-to-eat
   dried apricots
200 ml (7 fl oz) fresh
   orange juice
3 tablespoons clear honey
225 g (8 oz) full-fat cream
   cheese
150 ml (¼ pint) soured cream
2 large eggs, separated
100 g (4 oz) caster sugar

FOR THE TOPPING
1 tablespoon apricot jam
150 ml (¼ pint) whipping or
   double cream, whipped
10 small ratafia biscuits

1 Put the biscuits into a plastic bag and crush with a rolling pin. Melt the butter in a medium-sized pan. Remove the pan from the heat and stir in the biscuit crumbs and sugar. Press into a 23 cm (9 in) loose-bottomed cake tin and leave to set.

2 In a small bowl, sprinkle the gelatine over the water and leave to 'sponge'. Place the apricots in a pan with the orange juice, bring to the boil then simmer gently for about 5 minutes or until the apricots are tender.

3 Turn the apricots into a food processor and add the honey, cream cheese, soured cream and egg yolks. Process until well mixed and smooth. Alternatively, you can push the apricots through a nylon sieve, then mix with the honey, cream cheese, soured cream and egg yolks with a wooden spoon.

4 Set the bowl of gelatine over a pan of gently simmering water and allow to dissolve. Mix into the apricot mixture. Whisk the egg whites until frothy, add the caster sugar a little at a time, whisking well after each addition. Whisk until all the sugar has been added and the mixture is very stiff. Turn the apricot mixture into the meringue mixture and fold well together.

5 Pour the mixture onto the biscuit crust and chill in the fridge to set. Loosen the edges of the tin using a small palette knife if necessary. Push up the base of the tin and slip the cheesecake on to a serving plate.

6 Heat the apricot jam then push through a sieve. Spread it over the cheesecake, mark into 10 wedges. Spoon a dollop of whipped cream onto each wedge, and place a ratafia biscuit on each section of cheesecake. Serve chilled.

Key Lime Pie

**This is a speciality of Florida, where limes grow on the low coral islands –
the Keys. My adaptation of the original recipe is very quick to make and
delicious! This recipe serves 8.**

FOR THE BASE

150 g (5 oz) digestive biscuits

65 g (2½ oz) butter

25 g (1 oz) demerara sugar

FOR THE FILLING

grated rind of 1 large lime
and juice of 4 large limes

397 g (14 oz) can condensed
milk

450 ml (¾ pint) double cream

1 Put the biscuits into a plastic bag and crush with a rolling pin.
Melt the butter in a medium-sized pan. Remove the pan from the
heat and stir in the biscuit crumbs and sugar. Press over the base
and sides of a 23 cm (9 in) loose-bottomed tin and leave to set.

2 Put the lime juice, condensed milk and 300 ml (½ pint) of
the double cream into a mixing bowl and beat until well blended.
Pour into the prepared crumb crust and gently level the surface.
Chill in the fridge for several hours, until set, then remove from
the tin.

3 Whip the remaining cream until if forms soft peaks and spread
it over the pie, then finish with a scattering of grated lime rind.
Serve well chilled.

Cake Decorations

Almond Paste

You can now buy very good ready-made almond paste, but if you do like to make your own, here is the basic recipe to make 675 g (1½ lb) Almond Paste.

225 g (8 oz) ground almonds
225 g (8 oz) caster sugar
225 g (8 oz) sifted icing sugar
4 large egg yolks or 2 whole large eggs
about 6 drops almond extract

Mix the ground almonds and sugars together in a bowl, then add the yolks or whole eggs and almond extract. Knead together to form a stiff paste. Do not over-knead as this will make the paste oily. Wrap in clingfilm and store in the fridge until required.

To cover a cake with almond paste
There are 2 methods to cover a cake with almond paste; which to employ really depends on the type of icing you are going to use. Fondant or ready-to-roll icing is best put over almond paste with rounded edges, using the first method. For royal icing, it is usually better to use the second method as it gives sharper corners to the cake. For both methods, start by standing the cake on a cake board that is 5 cm (2 in) larger than the size of the cake.

METHOD 1
1 Lightly dust a work surface with sifted icing sugar, then roll out the almond paste to about 5 cm (2 in) larger than the top of the cake. Brush the cake all over with warmed apricot jam that has been pushed through a sieve.

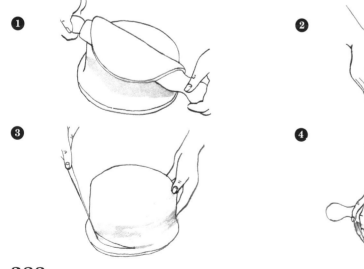

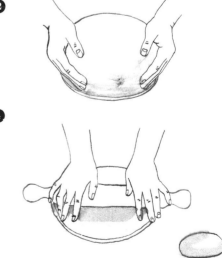

2 Carefully lift the almond paste over the cake with the help of a rolling pin (see figure 1). Gently level and smooth the top of the paste with a rolling pin, then ease the almond paste down the sides of the cake, smoothing it at the same time (see figure 2)

3 Neatly trim excess almond paste off at the base (see figure 3). Use the excess for making holly leaves and berries; keep it wrapped in clingfilm if not shaping immediately.

METHOD 2

1 Lightly dust a work surface with sifted icing sugar, then roll out one third of the almond paste to a circle slightly larger than the top of the cake (see figure 4). Using your cake tin base as a guide, cut the almond paste to the exact size (see figure 5).

2 Brush the cake all over with warmed apricot jam that has been pushed through a sieve. Lift the almond paste on to the cake and smooth over gently with a rolling pin. Neaten the edges (see figure 6).

3 Cut a piece of string the height of the cake including the layer of almond paste, and another to fit around the cake. Roll out the remaining almond paste and, using the string as a guide, cut the almond paste to size (see figure 7).

4 Brush a little more jam along the top edge of the strip as a seal, then roll up the strip loosely, place one end against the side of the cake and unroll to cover the sides of the cake completely (see figure 8). Use a small palette knife to smooth over the sides and the joins in the paste.

The table on page 390 shows you the quantities of almond paste needed to cover the tops and sides of various sizes of cakes.

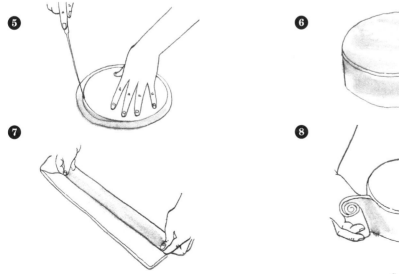

Homemade Fondant Icing

There are some excellent makes of fondant or ready-made icing available. However, if you prefer to make your own, here is the recipe to make 550 g (1¼ lb) of fondant icing.

500 g (1 lb 2 oz) icing sugar
1 generous tablespoon liquid glucose
1 large egg white

1 Sift the icing sugar into a large mixing bowl, make a well in the centre and add the liquid glucose and egg white.

2 Knead together until the mixture forms a soft ball. Turn out on to a work surface lightly dusted with icing sugar, and knead for about 10 minutes until smooth and brilliant white.

3 Add some sifted icing sugar if the mixture is a bit on the sticky side. Wrap in clingfilm and store in the fridge until required.

To cover a cake with Fondant Icing

1 Brush the almond paste with a little sherry, rum or kirsch (this has a sterilizing effect and also helps the icing to stick).

2 Roll out the icing on to a work surface lightly dusted with icing sugar, to about 5 cm (2 in) larger than the top of the cake.

3 Lift the icing on to the cake, using the rolling pin for support. Smooth out evenly over the top of the cake with your hands, easing the icing down the sides of the cake.

4 Trim any excess icing from the base of the cake, then finish smoothing with a plastic cake smoother, or carefully with your hands. Leave to dry out at room temperature for about 1 week before decorating.

The table below shows the quantities needed to cover both the sides and top of various sizes of cakes:

Size of tin	Almond Paste	Fondant Icing
15 cm (6 in) round tin 13 cm (5 in) square tin	350 g (12 oz)	350 g (12 oz)
18 cm (7 in) round tin 15 cm (6 in) square tin	450 g (1 lb)	450 g (1 lb)
20 cm (8 in) round tin 18 cm (7 in) square tin	675 g (1½ lb)	675 g (1½ lb)
23 cm (9 in) round tin 20 cm (8 in) square tin	750 g (1¾ lb)	750 g (1¾ lb)
25 cm (10 in) round tin 23 cm (9 in) square tin	900 g (2 lb)	1 kg (2¼ lb)
28 cm (11 in) round tin 25 cm (10 in) square tin	1 kg (2¼ lb)	1.2 kg (2¾ lb)
30 cm (12 in) round tin 28 cm (11 in) square tin	1.1 kg (2½ lb)	1.5 kg (3 lb)
33 cm (13 in) round tin 30 cm (12 in) square tin	1.5 kg (3 lb)	1.6 kg (3½ lb)

Royal Icing

You can buy 'instant' royal icing, however, if you do like to make your own, the recipe below makes enough to decorate a 20–23 cm (8–9 in) round cake.

2 large egg whites
500 g (1 lb 2 oz) sifted icing sugar
about 4 teaspoons lemon juice

1 Put the egg whites into a large mixing bowl and whisk lightly with a fork until bubbles begin to form on the surface.

2 Add about half the icing sugar and the lemon juice, and beat well with a wooden spoon for about 10 minutes until brilliant white. Gradually stir in the remaining icing sugar until the correct consistency for piping.

3 Once made, keep the icing covered with a damp cloth to prevent it drying out and use as soon as possible.

Raspberry Coulis

Serve this with the American Chocolate Wedding Cake (page 143), with ice-cream or with plain desserts.

1.5 kg (3 lb) raspberries
450 g (1 lb) icing sugar

Put the raspberries in a food processor and blend until they form a purée, then push the purée through a nylon sieve into a bowl to remove the seeds. Gradually whisk in the icing sugar.

Chocolate Decorations

There are many decorations or finishing touches that you can make with chocolate. They're fun to do and look most impressive.

Chocolate Caraque

Pour a thin layer of melted chocolate on to a scratch-proof surface. Using a palette knife, spread the chocolate thinly until it begins to set and go cloudy. Leave until it no longer sticks to your hand when you touch it then, holding a long sharp flexible knife at an angle, shave the chocolate off the surface using a slight sawing action to form scrolls or flakes. White chocolate needs to be more set than plain does before it can be made into caraque.

Chocolate Shapes

These can easily be made by melting the chocolate as with Chocolate Caraque, then cutting it into squares or triangles with a sharp knife or cutter. It helps to heat the knife or cutter first. Use a round plain or fluted cutter to stamp out circles.

Chocolate Leaves

Use a small paintbrush to spread melted chocolate evenly on to the underside of clean, dry leaves. Leave to set and then gently peel the leaf away from the chocolate, not the other way round.

Chocolate Curls

These are very simply made by using a swivel peeler. Make sure the chocolate is at room temperature or it will simply flake rather than curl. Scrape the peeler along the flat side of the chocolate bar. Chocolate-flavoured cake covering is particularly good for this. Hold the chocolate bar in baking parchment if you find it becomes too sticky.

American Frosting

The 'instant' American Frosting works perfectly well, but if you have a sugar thermometer try this 'proper' American Frosting.

450 g (1 lb) caster sugar
135 ml (4½ fl oz) water
2 large egg whites

1 Place the sugar in a large, heavy-based pan along with the water and heat gently until the sugar has dissolved. Bring to the boil and boil to 115°C, as registered on a sugar thermometer.

2 Meanwhile, whisk the egg whites in a large deep bowl until stiff. Allow the bubbles to settle, then slowly pour the hot syrup on to the egg whites, whisking continuously. When all the sugar has been added, continue whisking until the mixture stands in peaks and just starts to become matt around the edges.

3 Use to sandwich and top the Frosted Walnut Layer Cake (page 71) or Devil's Food Cake (page 96). The icing sets rapidly, so work quickly using a palette knife. Leave to set in a cool place, but not in the fridge.

Crystallized Flowers

You may want to decorate a special cake like the Sponge Christening Cake (page 149) with crystallized flowers. They are very simple to prepare but make a lovely finishing touch.

edible flowers (violets, pansies, japonica,
    primroses, little roses and polyanthus)
a little beaten egg white
caster sugar, to dust

Brush the edible flowers with a little beaten egg white. Dust with caster sugar on both sides, then stand them on a wire cake rack in a warm place (over a radiator or in the airing cupboard, for example) and leave until they are crisp and dry, which will take a few hours.

Index

milk 28
millionaires' shortbread 235
mini cakes 244
    mini jammy cakes 245
Mississippi mud pie 97
mixing bowls 13
mokatines 167–8
mousse cake, chocolate 102–3
muesli
    muesli cookies 209
    muesli flapjacks 191
muffins
    blueberry 128, *129*
    chocolate chip American 126
    English 283
    St Clements 127
mushroom and garlic-stuffed
    picnic loaf 296–7

N
New Year tipsy cake 140–1
Nusskuchen 153
nut and fruit cakes 60–77
nuts 62

O
oats
    apricot and walnut sandwich
      bars *236*, 237
    chocolate chip flapjacks 191
    fast flapjacks *190*, 191
    muesli flapjacks 191
    oat rounds 208
    oat and sunflower squares 250
oils 25
onion and balsamic topping,
    focaccia bread with 294, *295*
oranges
    angel sponge cheesecake 376–7
    carrot and orange loaf 308
    crunchy orange syrup loaves
      306
    double orange cake 73
    New Year tipsy cake 140–1
    orange and apricot cheesecake
      384
    orange butterfly cakes 119
    orange drop scones 327
    orange fairy cakes 114
    orange fork biscuits 195
    orange shortbread 231

orange soufflés 366
orange and wholemeal Victoria
    loaf 314
St Clements muffins 127
sticky ginger and orange cake 86
sultana and orange traybake 180

P
Parkin, traditional 81
pastries
    chocolate éclairs 274, *275*
    Danish 277–9
    filo apple strudels 266, *267*
    profiteroles 276
pastry 20, 263, 341
    choux 157-9, 274, *275*m 276
    ready-made 27
    shortcrust 239, 350
pastry brushes 19
pâte sucrée 157–9, 264–5, 269
pavlova, strawberry 356, *357*
pecan pie 350, *351*
petits fours aux amandes 218
pies
    banoffi 349
    classic apple 341
    Key lime 385
    lemon meringue 361
    Mississippi mud 97
    pecan 350, *351*
pineapple and cherry loaf *310*, 311
piping bags 19
poppy seeds, lemon poppy seed
    traybake 181
potato scones 324
pound cake 69
pretzels, sugared 223
profiteroles 276
proving 22

Q
queen cakes 113

R
raising agents 25, 26–7
raisins
    Borrowdale teabread 315
    raisin and walnut loaf 292
raspberries
    American cheesecake 379
    continental cheesecake 378

hazelnut meringue cake *362*, 363
raspberry coulis 391
raspberry meringue roulade 360
raspberry Swiss roll 45
rock cakes 332
    wholemeal sultana and apricot
      333
rolling pins 19
rolls, quick granary 284
roulade, raspberry meringue 360
royal icing 391
rubbing in 22
rum cake, chocolate 101

S
Sachertorte 154
St Clements muffins 127
scales 12
scones
    cheese and olive scone bake 325
    cheese scone round 323
    drop 326
    freezing 318
    griddle 330
    orange drop 327
    potato 324
    special fruit 322
    very best 320, *321*
    wholemeal 320
seed cake, old-fashioned 57
shortbread 228–35
    bishop's fingers 232, *233*
    millionaires' 235
    orange 231
    shortbread cases 268
    special shortbread biscuits 234
    the very best 231
shortcrust pastry 239, 350
Shrewsbury biscuits 202
sieves 18
simnel cake, Easter 146, *147*
singin' hinny *328*, 329
small bakes 110–29
    freezing 112
    see also buns; muffins; scones
soda bread, Irish 293
soufflés
    coffee 366
    hot chocolate 366, *367*
    hot lemon soufflé pudding 368
    orange 366

Acknowledgements

Just under 20 years ago Lucy Young came to assist me and one of her very first challenges was the TV series *Ultimate Cakes* for the BBC. We made umpteen cakes and confections and they were all in the book that went with the series. So now Luc and I have updated the cakes and added many more to make this the *Baking Bible*. Luc is meticulous in the testing and, like my family and me, is passionate about baking. So thank you Luc for your enthusiasm and friendship.

There really is a great team at BBC Books editing and checking our recipes. Muna Reyal and Laura Higginson have worked closely with us with great commitment and dedication – thank you to you both.

Thanks to Smith & Gilmour, Dan Jones and Annie Rigg for making the recipes look so fantastic.

Thank you too to my agents Felicity Bryan and Michele Topham, who after years of working with me still make the grown-up decisions for me!

MARY BERRY